Gathered before God

Gathered before God

Worship-Centered Church Renewal

Jane Rogers Vann

Westminster John Knox Press
LOUISVILLE • LONDON

Book design by Sharon Adams
Cover design by Pam Poll Graphic Design

First edition
Published by Westminster John Knox Press
Louisville, Kentucky

This book is printed on acid-free paper that meets the American National Standards Institute Z39.48 standard. ∞

○

PRINTED IN THE UNITED STATES OF AMERICA

04 05 06 07 08 09 10 11 12 13—10 9 8 7 6 5 4 3 2 1

Library of Congress Cataloging-in-Publication Data
Vann, Jane Rogers, 1945-
    Gathered before God: worship-centered church renewal / Jane Rogers Vann.—1st ed.
        p. cm.
    ISBN 0-664-22630-2 (alk. paper)
    1. Church renewal. 2. Public worship. I. Title.
BV600.3.V36 2004
264—dc22
                                                                    2003055564

Contents

Acknowledgments

This book began as a series of interconnected questions that, at first glance, seemed fairly straightforward. But as any person with even a small helping of curiosity knows, simple questions blossom into multilayered sets of corollaries—additional questions that contribute to our understanding of the larger questions. The insights into congregational life offered here are only partial answers to the original questions. Even this small effort would never have been possible without the interest, collaboration, hospitality, and encouragement of a number of congregations and individuals.

Churches included in this study have been large, small, and in-between. They are located throughout the United States and reflect several streams of ethnic and denominational heritage. Their hospitality has been unfailingly gracious as they have shared their vision and practice of Christian life with me. People have been honest, sometimes painfully so, as they have described their communities of faith and reflected on the meaning and significance of their congregations. I have tried to let participants "speak for themselves," using their own words as much as possible. I am motivated to write this way because many congregations seem to suffer from a failure of imagination. They know their present way of being the church is not healthy, but they cannot envision what another way of being might look like. I have attempted here to describe congregational life, using the voices of lively Christians, so that others can discern their own futures through these stories.

These churches have benefited from strong pastoral and educational leadership over an extended period of time. Trust has been built between leaders and members in a variety of common circumstances so that their relationships provide a reservoir of trustworthiness on which their congregational life rests. They have a "track record" of sticking together through thick and thin. These congregations demonstrate commitment and resilience and have effective strategies for resolving differences. Leaders and members are able to be honest with one another, even (and maybe especially) when they disagree.

Churches included in this study include Old Pine Street (First Scots and Mariners) Presbyterian Church in Philadelphia; Immanuel Presbyterian

Church in Tacoma, Washington; Latrobe Presbyterian Church in Latrobe, Pennsylvania; Palmdale Presbyterian Church in Melbourne, Florida; Covenant Presbyterian Church in Palo Alto, California; Northminster Presbyterian Church in Seattle, Washington; and West Raleigh Presbyterian Church in Raleigh, North Carolina. In addition, members and leaders in the congregations of Westover Hills United Methodist Church in Richmond, Virginia; St. Columba's Roman Catholic Church in Bloomsburg, Pennsylvania; St. Paul's Episcopal Church in Bloomsburg, Pennsylvania; and Wesley United Methodist Church in Bloomsburg, Pennsylvania, provided valuable but less in-depth explorations. These congregations and their leaders have extended to me gracious hospitality as I have entered into congregational research. In their midst I was privileged to witness faithful congregational cultures where God is praised and faith is formed. They have my deepest gratitude and thanksgiving to God for their courage and faithfulness.

This book would never have been written without the generous support of Union-PSCE and its administration. Justin, John, Steph, Jack, Sue, DeVerna, and Rollie have given unfailing encouragement. Daniel, my husband of over thirty years, has devoted many hours of listening, inspiration, advice, and support without which the project would have remained a dream.

Richmond, Virginia
Good Friday, 2003

Introduction

Lorraine Burd, an attractive, middle-aged high school teacher and active member of her church, pauses thoughtfully as she reflects with a friend on the worship and music committee meeting held the night before. Lorraine moderates the committee and led the members in giving abundant time and consideration to the previous month's Easter services. The Maundy Thursday service included the celebration of communion and the stripping of the sanctuary. On Good Friday, when the congregation met at their historic "home," a small chapel out in the country, the service featured the Passion according to St. John, the Solemn Intercession, and the Solemn Reproaches of the Cross. On Saturday evening, again in the countryside chapel, the Easter Vigil was celebrated. This highly participatory and interactive festival included the lighting of new fire, a candlelight procession, extensive readings from Scripture, lavish music, the renewal of the baptismal covenant, the celebration of Communion, and gifts of the delicious bread to take home. Easter Sunday included two services, an early service in the chapel and a later service in the downtown sanctuary.

Committee members and others have given careful attention to planning and participating in the services. At this first meeting since their Easter celebrations, they reviewed in detail each of the services, considering its reception and meaning for members and newcomers, children and adults, and those with special needs. Now, the next day, Lorraine is contemplating the changes in the congregation that have followed the introduction of these new ways of worshiping. "I remember when the only thing the worship and music committee did was iron tablecloths, make sure that the juice and the bread were there for Communion, and set up for teas after worship." Now, says Lorraine, things are different. Each committee meeting starts with some education about worship, usually by the pastor. Then the committee considers carefully the upcoming seasons and celebrations; they study Scripture, review the church's practices from the past, and plan in detail for the congregation's participation in worship. "I think it makes it much more meaningful," she says. "I think that one of the worst things that can happen is when we just kind of go through a rote service, and we do everything because that's the way we've always done it, and we recite things but don't remember why we're doing it or what we're saying even. If there's an awareness of the why's and the basis for what you're saying, it is much more meaningful." Still, Lorraine worries that even with all the ways this congregation tries to include the whole assembly in what they are doing and why, there are many people who don't understand.

Lorraine has reason to be worried. Consider the perspective of Bob Peiffer, Protestant campus minister at a mid-sized state college: "Send me a conservative or fundamentalist Christian undergraduate anytime! At least those kids care about their faith. They are eager to engage in conversation about the questions that face them and are receptive to adults who will stand with them in their struggles." Bob compares these students to young people from the mainline churches who "have been raised on pizza parties and hay rides." They have been exposed to such a mild version of the Christian faith, he says, that they are in effect vaccinated against its claims.

Not all congregations are satisfied with a superficial version of the gospel of Jesus Christ. Many congregations intentionally center their congregational life around the worship of God and give abundant attention to the communal, personal, and social implications of that Divine-human encounter. It is these churches I am eager to describe. In the following chapters I have tried to answer two questions: How do we learn the Christian life from the experience of congregational life? How do renewal in worship and spiritual renewal in congregations complement and support each other?

This book is also written with the conviction that the central purpose for the church is the worship of the triune God made known through the story of the people of Israel and in the life, death, and resurrection of Jesus Christ. It is the calling of the church, in the words of the Presbyterian *Directory for Worship*, to "joyfully [ascribe] all praise and honor, glory and power to the triune God. In worship the people of God acknowledge God present in the world and in their lives. As they respond to God's claim and redemptive action in Jesus Christ, believers are transformed and renewed."[1] Growing out of this central theocentric liturgical purpose is the broader mission of the church, to broaden and deepen the worship of God until all creation sings to the glory of God. Church renewal as understood here, then, attempts to describe the ways the worship of God is deepened among the faithful through participation in worship and reflection on that participation. In addition, renewal comes through prayer and spiritual disciplines, study and instruction, and engagement in ministry and mission. Church renewal also includes the broadening of the worship of God in ways that invite the outsider, the stranger, to join in the church's worship. Church renewal for mainline congregations at the beginning of a new century may not be seen in program expansion or membership numbers but in the living out of a deeper kind of faithfulness, seen most clearly in the deepening and broadening of the worship of God.

Signs of Weakness, Reason for Hope

Not long ago the *New York Times Magazine*[2] featured a lengthy exploration into the life of a fundamentalist family and its strategies for establishing and maintaining itself in the face of contemporary culture. This family of seven children, a stay-at-home mom, and an airline pilot dad focuses on creating a kind of family life that will somehow hold contemporary culture at bay while also teaching traditional family values. Writer Margaret Talbot describes them this way:

> The way they practice their faith puts them so sharply and purposefully at odds with the larger culture that it is hard not to see the Scheibners, conservative and law-abiding though they are, as rebels.
>
> We have arrived, it seems, at a moment in our history when the most vigorous and coherent counterculture around is the one constructed by conservative Christians. That sounds odd to many of us—especially, perhaps, to secular liberals, who cherish our own 60's inflected notions of what an "alternative lifestyle" should look like. . . .
>
> Yet today it is conservative Christians like the Scheibners who, more self-consciously than any other large social group, buck mainstream notions of what constitutes a fulfilled life.[3]

Responding to the article, Miroslav Volf asks, "Why are [mainline churches] seemingly incapable of creating a viable and vibrant alternative?"[4] What is it about congregational life during the latter half of the twentieth century and early years of the twenty-first that has given us this legacy of internal weakness and sometimes pathology in congregations of the Protestant mainline? This question is significantly different from questions of membership decline and loss of cultural influence. While these questions are important for churches and denominations, they reflect the failure of many congregations to offer a commanding vision of the gospel of Jesus Christ. Issues of the aggressive nature of media-driven popular culture; the weakness of other social institutions such as the family, school, and neighborhood; and the erosion of the church's cultural standing in recent decades are also relevant here. But somewhere along the line churches took for granted the compelling vision of the gospel in such a way that it evidently was not adequately communicated to society or even to the next generation of church members.

Sometime during the last century many Christian leaders began to operate on the assumption, often implicit, that a Protestant culture was fairly firmly in place and that it was time for Christians to turn their attention to "character and social problems."[5] As the twentieth century has drawn to a close it has become increasingly apparent that the Protestant culture which provided the foundation for much of the century's mission and social justice agenda has largely eroded. In addition, while the attention of many congregations was focused on these worthy callings, they neglected their own internal culture. Many congregations, suddenly without external reinforcements, find themselves unfamiliar with Christian practices and beliefs and are thus unable to construct a congregational culture that has sufficient depth, conviction, and winsomeness to attract even their own children.

Much has been made of the competition the mainline churches now face from the media and from other religious and nonreligious perspectives with which Protestants one hundred years ago did not have to contend. Rather than a unified worldview, largely Protestant Christian and middle class, we face an increasingly fragmented array of narratives and metanarratives around which Americans are invited to orient themselves. Many of the most aggressively advertised and easily available choices are not simply alternatives to the gospel vision for human flourishing; they are directly and destructively in opposition to it.

Meanwhile many churches continue to display patterns of decorum that have more to do with middle-class manners than with the ordered Christian life. Take Charles and Amanda Baxter, for example. This attractive Christian couple are active in the leadership of their church, hold strong convictions based on their Christian faith, and consistently participate in the Christian education of their children. But they cannot pray together. They love one another deeply and are happy in their marriage, but the boundaries on intimacy within their marriage are such that, as Amanda explained to me, "It would be too embarrassing to pray out loud or talk about my faith in front of Charles. And Charles feels the same way about praying in front of me." This is more than just a symptom of the privatization of religion, though it is that. Here, it seems to me, is an example of Christian faith that has become almost completely dependent on conventional supports, to the neglect of the establishment of a robust communal culture where faith can grow.

In congregations a similar level of reticence exists, indicated by the relative absence of a shared religious or theological vocabulary. I have often noticed that when sharing sad news with fellow church members, while responses are genuinely sympathetic and sincere, people often say, "We'll be thinking about you." They seem unable to say that they will pray for one another. I am sure they *do*, in fact, pray for one another, but a certain social reserve does not permit them to say so. The admonitions of Deuteronomy to "keep these words that I am commanding you today in your heart. Recite them to your children and talk about them when you are at home and when you are away, when you lie down and when you rise" (Deut. 6:6–7) seem largely forgotten. Rather, many members of mainline churches may assume they are living in the time described by Jeremiah, when "no longer shall they teach one another, or say to each other, 'Know the Lord,' for they shall all know me, from the least of them to the greatest. . . ." (Jer. 31:34). We failed to notice that here Jeremiah is describing God's ultimate reign, not our present age or recent past.

Nevertheless religion continues to occupy the consciousness of many Americans. A recent survey of the "religious landscape" in the United States reveals that religion continues to hold significant appeal for most Americans.[6] However, it also reveals that Americans lack basic knowledge of the Bible, foundational Christian doctrines, and the traditional practices of the church. Thus it should come as no surprise that, according to the study, many Americans hold inconsistent or even contradictory beliefs. Many people display a superficial faith characterized by a general belief in God but a lack of trust in God. God exists but makes no difference in the lives of individuals, families, or society at large. People are often unsure of what they believe or why.

The Programmatic Church

For at least the last forty years, the "programmatic church" has served as a model for healthy congregational life. In this model, what the megachurches call a "full service church," there are programs for all ages, interests, and needs. A church with vitality is one where the number and attractiveness of programs makes it possible for most people to find a "niche," a place to fit in, participate, and contribute to the overall programmatic life of the church. "Successful" congregations are ones where programs abound. The dominance of this model has influenced the church in many positive ways, as it helps people become regular participants in congregational life.

But there have also been negative consequences as a result of this model's dominance. Many churches that do not have the capacity for programmatic expansion often suffer from images of failure when they look at their congregations. The dominance of the programmatic model blinds them to the many gifts and graces embodied in their communities of faith. More harmful, however, is the often unspoken assumption implicit in the programmatic model itself. It suggests that when people participate in programs offered by the church, their Christian lives will be faithfully formed. In many of these churches the majority of the congregation's energy is devoted to the creation, administration, and support of programs, while the value of these programs as agents of spiritual formation and transformation is neglected. Yet in order to maintain the image of a lively programmatic church, many congregations continue to offer programs that serve no purpose, especially not the spiritual formation of participants. At the same time the centrality of worship in congregational life has been displaced. As programs have grown in number and popularity, it has been easy for worship to be seen as one among many other programs the church sponsors. In churches like this, if worship does not meet one's needs, if "I don't get anything out of it," worship can be skipped in favor of some other activity. Likewise, worship's integrity is compromised every time it becomes an instrument used to support other programs.

I am not arguing for the disruption or elimination of programs in the church nor for the abandonment of the programmatic model for congregational life. Rather, I want to advocate for a renewal of congregational life with worship at its center. As the church has always proclaimed, worship of the triune God is the central most defining action of the gathered assembly and the paradigmatic action around which all other actions are centered. Education, mission, outreach, advocacy, evangelism, fellowship, and social concerns of all sorts arise from the vision of God's intentions enacted in worship. Likewise, participation in all the activities of the church necessarily orient the faithful toward the worship of God. With this overarching vision in mind, all programs of the church become more and more intentionally oriented around this central practice of the Christian assembly.

All across the landscape there are Christians like Lorraine, Bob, Charles, and Amanda and the churches that nurture them, where the gospel of Jesus Christ is celebrated and preached, meditated on and taught, incarnated and renewed in such a way that deep spiritual formation takes place both communally and individually. In these congregations people gather around Word and sacrament to celebrate God's redeeming claim and purpose for their lives and then live out that purpose in their communities. They are dedicated to learning and teaching Scripture and tradition. Both communally and personally they engage in the formative practices of Christian faith: prayer, stewardship, hospitality, confession, forgiveness, and resisting evil. They open themselves in order to discern a vision of the reign of God and to incarnate that reign in the common life of the church. In these churches there is both a mood of excitement and the serenity and calm that flow from deep trust in God. Even in the midst of continued change and uncertainty, these churches demonstrate a vitality that enlivens the church as the body of Christ and forms the spiritual lives of the members. Thus these churches serve as a sign of the reign of God to the community around them and to the world. They offer a foretaste of God's reign to members and participants, who eat and drink and taste more deeply as they continue to participate. And they are active as instruments for bringing about the reign of God in members' lives and in society.[7]

Worship-Centered Congregational Renewal

Resources for worship-centered congregational renewal abound. More and more mainline Protestants are being reminded, sometimes in not-so-comfortable ways, that this is the church of Jesus Christ. The church does not belong to its members but is held within the very life of God. If Paul's declaration that "whether we live or whether we die, we are the Lord's" (Rom. 14:8b) is true for individual Christians, then it is surely true for the whole church, the body of Christ. So while we have been entrusted to incarnate God's will in the life of the church, we can trust God with the church's ultimate future. This makes Christians acutely aware of the communal and personal discernment required for faithful stewardship in the life of the church in behalf of the gospel of Jesus Christ. The church's thriving ultimately depends on the Spirit of God, attentively discerned and enacted.

The liturgical consensus among mainline Protestant churches, which recovers the centrality of both Word and sacrament, also supports congregational renewal. One has only to read titles of recently published books for pastors to see the increasing emphasis on worship. Even the "worship wars" are symbolic of the renewed appreciation of the centrality of worship for congregational life. While congregations or groups within congregations may disagree as to what constitutes an appropriate worship style, there is an emerging consensus as to the central importance of worship in the life of the church.

Hand-in-hand with congregational liturgical renewal is a renewed sense of the importance of Christian practices for communal and personal spiritual formation. Faithful practices, including the worship of God in the community of faith; study of Scripture; personal and communal prayer; and practices of stewardship, witness, and forgiveness draw congregations together and enable them to discern and respond to the call of God.

Advances in fields such as social systems theory, leadership, and Christian education also contribute to healthy congregational life. Church leaders have gained insight from these fields and have adapted them in creative and faithful ways to the unique dynamics of the church. Knowing how to set a pace for change, for example, and how to identify both support and resistance helps congregational leaders in their faithful exercise of discernment and embodiment of faithfulness. Christian education is presently giving renewed attention to the natural rhythms of action and reflection in congregational life and the ways these rhythms can be deepened and made more pervasive as agents of spiritual formation for the congregation and its members.

Worship and Education: (Unequal) Partners

The natural rhythm of congregational life is that of action and reflection. If you doubt that claim, think back on all the "parking lot conversations" you have observed and participated in. When we participate in an activity, our natural human response is to think back over our experience and consider its importance and implications for us. Learning theorists and adult education theorists claim that this natural rhythm, with its many internal varieties and complexities, forms the basis for all learning. The business section of any bookstore will show that the business and industrial community has been quick to understand and embrace these patterns of adult learning as it adjusts to the global economy.[8] But much of our reflection on worship and other practices of the Christian life goes something like this: "How was church? (Sunday school? Choir practice? Committee meeting? Circle meeting?)" And most of us answer, "Oh, fine." The futility, unease, and/or boredom associated with congregational life often suppresses reflection on worship and on the Christian spiritual life.

The theoretical basis for this book comes primarily from the field of education, but the kind of education envisioned here is not limited to classroom instruction. Rather, what is described here is a pattern of reflective practices, in classroom settings to be sure, but also in committee meetings, pastoral care settings, coffee-hour conversations, circle meetings, parking lots, living rooms, and kitchen tables, where the rhythm of action and reflection becomes a pervasive feature of congregational culture. Such practices include opportunities to recall and savor past experiences and to explore their meaning for oneself and one's community of faith. They also include opportunities to investigate Scripture and the Christian tradition where similar experiences have been encountered and where meaning has been derived. Such reflection prepares Christians creatively to plan and anticipate renewed engagements and encounters with God in worship and elsewhere.

Educators are often excluded from conversations about worship, either because it is assumed they are not interested or because it is feared they will attempt to co-opt worship into another opportunity for programming or instruction. As an educator, my interest in worship has arisen from a deep conviction that learning the Christian life requires all of the resources of the church, beginning with the experience of encounter with God in worship. Surrounding that encounter, the culture of the entire congregation plays a role in the spiritual formation of Christians. My concern is that congregations be supported in orienting their communal life in such a way that deeply formative and transformative Christian spiritual formation can take place. In this book I attempt to describe two defining characteristics that mark such congregations. First, these congregations' cultures are centered in worship. They are clear and unapologetic about their insistence that the most important thing they do is worship together. In fact, worship-centered congregational culture is taken for granted in most of these congregations. When I asked members and leaders whether or not they thought their congregations were worship centered, many looked at me quite quizzically. They had never thought to wonder what the center of their community's life was. They just knew that worship was a never-to-be-missed occasion for encounter with God among those with whom they shared faith. Second, the activities and programs that made up the rest of these congregations' cultures were oriented in such a way that everything moved toward worship and sprang from worship. The cultures had a density or thickness to them, made up of mutually reenforcing practices, language, and relationships that found their center in worship. The strength of these congregations was in the depth of their spiritual commitment, which had its home in worship.

On Easter Sunday morning at Lorraine Burd's church, a family with two young children, boys aged five and seven, sits close to the front of the sanctuary. These boys, I learn later, are surprises born to a couple who thought their parenting days were all but completed. Their older children are away at college and soon will be out on their own. As these parents answered this second call to parenthood, they thought carefully about the ways they had organized their family life the first time around and decided that something different was needed. They had not been active in the church as their older children were growing up, and they were disappointed by the attitudes, behaviors, and values their children espoused as they entered adulthood. In addition, as individuals and as a couple they experienced a spiritual hunger that sent them searching. The family members have found in this church a place where their own search for a deeper life of faith can be nurtured and where their life as a family can be nurtured as well. On Easter Sunday morning the parents and children share obvious joy. They sing and pray, listen and participate with attentive and responsive reverence. Quiet conversations and some "coaching" keep the boys oriented, and the parents find apparent joy in worshiping alongside them. When communion is celebrated and the trays of bread and wine are passed, each person in the congregation serves his or her neighbor with the words "the bread of life" and "the cup of salvation." These words and actions resonate deeply with this family in a way that is vividly communicated to those seated near them. In word and gesture, in serving one another and in eating and drinking together, these Christians are spiritually formed as individuals, as a family, and as a part of the body of Christ.

I believe God is calling the church to be renewed at its life-giving center, worship. But equally important in this renewal is a reorientation of the culture of congregations that will make occasions for reflection on worship (and on other facets of the Christian life) a pervasive feature of congregational life. Resources for this renewal include richly expressive worship that enacts clearly what the church believes about God, itself, and the world. The church needs resources for reflecting on its worship of God and an openness to change that allows for reform and renewal. The church also needs processes whereby leaders and members can uphold one another in ways that allow for discussion, disagreement, and compromise as they discern God's will together. This book is an attempt to offer some of those resources and to describe congregations where worship-centered congregational life and opportunities for communal reflection on that life abound.

Part I

Foundations for Congregational Renewal

Chapter One

Worship at the Center of Congregational Life

West Raleigh Presbyterian Church—A Portrait

As worship begins at West Raleigh Presbyterian Church, the pastor moves to the center of the chancel and invites the congregation to worship God with words from the Presbyterian "Brief Statement of Faith": "Like a mother who will not forsake her nursing child, like a father who runs to welcome the prodigal home, God is faithful still. Let us worship God."[1] There is a relaxed orderliness as the congregation responds with wholehearted participation in song and prayer, Scripture and proclamation, all to the praise and glory of God. Worship is filled with joyful reverence and participation that includes the body, mind, and spirit of the gathered community. The members of the congregation exhibit a kind of attentive expectancy as they sing, hear Scripture, engage in theological reflection during the sermon, and pray with and for one another and for the world during the prayers of the people. Especially during the prayers of the people, a deep meditative calm embraces the congregation, and their own prayers are voiced along with those of the pastors. Time seems to stand still as the celebrations and needs of the world and of the church are named before God. It is clear people find a real spiritual home here, and many are aware that the depth of that spiritual "at-home-ness" is growing.

Elder Ben Mears, chair of the stewardship and finance committee, begins his annual letter to the congregation with these words: "It is amazing to me to sit back and reflect on the changes that have taken place during the last several years and anticipate what God's plan for us might be. . . . None of us fully understands where we are going, but it seems to me more and more of the congregation is preparing for this church journey. This is an exciting time in our church."

West Raleigh Presbyterian Church is located on a small side street off a busy commercial thoroughfare that runs adjacent to a state university. While the modest buildings may not command the attention of passersby, once inside it is clear that there is something distinctive about this community of faith. The congregation of about six hundred members is primarily made up of middle- and upper-middle class professionals—lawyers, educators, doctors, journalists, engineers, and business people. A high level of commitment to the congregation is supported by people's affection for one another and by the spiritually focused life they share. While many nearby churches might seem to convey a certain social status, West Raleigh is not among them. Its identity is grounded in its long-standing commitment to social and economic justice and its outreach to the community. Over the past ten years the church's strong mission outreach has been increasingly matched by liturgical renewal and by an intentional search for a more robust expression of the Christian spiritual life. Particularly in worship, where the people gather with the expectation that they will encounter God, both the Christian spiritual life and involvement in the community are lifted up as necessary responses to God's grace.

As in many churches, programs flourish at West Raleigh and encompass a whole range of worship, fellowship, education, mission, and outreach activities. Everyone agrees, however, that the life of the church is centered in worship. It is in worship where everyone is together, where Scripture is read and proclaimed, where thanksgivings and intersessions are given voice, where spiritual hungers are fed. According to many members the church has a vitality, a vibrancy that is attractive, especially to those who seek to deepen the Christian spiritual life. Everyone gathers on Sunday morning to bless God, to be nurtured with Scripture, to experience life in the community of faith, and to be sent out as Christ's body in the world. They gather in awe and wonder, according to associate pastor Denise Thorpe, to see how God is breaking into their lives. "It is the place where we are called together to be claimed by God's love and presence, and then we want to live that out. There are flashes of [God's love] everywhere, and through that we're called to ministry."

It is the experience of encounter with God that calls the people to worship. It is that same experience that sends them out to live as God's people in the world. "When people come to worship," says pastor Joe Ward, "they have a right to expect an encounter with God somewhere. It might be part of the prayer of confession or the prayers of the people. It might be in the hymns or in the preaching. It might be in the reading of the Word. But you have a right to expect it. We're coming together with the shared expectation that we are going to encounter God. That's been promised to us. We have it on the promise of Jesus: 'When you gather, when you eat this bread and drink this wine in remembrance of me, I will be with you.'" Second, says Joe, worshipers have a right to expect to make what he calls a "depth connection," to go below the surface. "When we pray together there, we are getting down to the 'ground of being.'" At West Raleigh the prayers of the people are inclusive, participatory, and lengthy. All those in need, both in the church and outside it, are mentioned by name by the pastors, with others adding their concerns at several points in the prayers. Deep spiritual participation by the congregation and by worship leaders is apparent.

Third, says Joe, in worship we can also expect to be challenged to live differently as a result of our encounter with God. "It is kind of a three-way rotation, that as we encounter God we encounter one another and we encounter our sense of call to mission." Thus for those at West Raleigh everything flows from an encounter with God in worship and then out into the world. The congregation's call to mission naturally brings the community back into worship. In this congregation worship is marked by joyful reverence, respectful expressiveness, inviting imagery, appeal to the senses, and excellent music and preaching.

People at West Raleigh say that during the last ten years or so, many new and longtime members began looking for a deeper spiritual life. They knew, they said, that if things were going to change, they had to be part of that change, especially as long-time mission projects were discontinued and new mission opportunities were discerned. "When you are more rooted in your spiritual life," says Sarah, a young mother of two, "you can discern more what God wants you to do personally, and that can be the fuel for you to go out into the world." Many contemporary religious and social observers have noted the spiritual hunger that has characterized our time. At West Raleigh, says Sarah, many people seemed to become aware of that hunger at the same time. "I don't think it was anything that our church did. It was just that all of the pieces seemed to come together, and a lot of people were hungry at the same time, and they started listening, and then the transformation started to occur."

An important area of change at West Raleigh began when parents in the congregation became interested in a worship program for their children. No longer satisfied with unstructured child care during worship for children as old as five, they went looking for something worship-centered and age appropriate for young children. As they evaluated available resources, then chose and implemented a new program, parents found that their own lives were changed. They became more aware of the elements of worship, the liturgical seasons and colors, and the various ways of responding in worship. According to Marita Wynands, the adults' awareness of God's presence was heightened as they learned more about worship's structure, flow, and intentions.

The pastors and worship committee are committed to full ritual expression in worship in ways that enable worshipers to discern the presence and activity of God. "Needless to say," says Joe, "we have a lot more kids around because of the paradigm shift that went on here. We expanded the amount of time they are in the sanctuary. We specifically wanted them there for the Lord's Prayer and for the reading of the Word. So now when they go to children's worship they have received the Word with the whole community. We asked ourselves, how do we raise up children as worshipers as opposed to people who, all of a sudden at age fourteen, are plunked into a sanctuary? And they are foreigners to the culture." Through the children's worship program the children and adults of West Raleigh have been changed.

At West Raleigh the spiritual life of the congregation is fed by an active intellectual life. Alec is a young lawyer working in a state office in downtown Raleigh. He is also an accomplished composer, poet, and musician. At West Raleigh he sings in the choir, serves on the church council, and takes part in a spiritual formation group. As chair of the worship committee he became interested in liturgical theology and the history of Presbyterian worship. He wasn't the only one whose interest was awakened by the expanded ritual and liturgical practice of the church. When he was asked to teach a class about worship, Alec was eager to share what he had learned. The first series of presentations on Sunday mornings led to other invitations at circles, retreats, and worship committee meetings. Many like Alec have been nurtured in "habits of mind" that include theological questioning, careful reasoning, compassionate listening, and intellectual integrity. People are intellectually curious and eager to know more about all sorts of things. Most of all they seek to understand why they are doing what they are doing. This means they are eager to study scripture, theology, the history of the church, and the circumstances of the world in which they minister. Christian education for children and adults is taken seriously here with Sunday and week-day programs of all sorts.

One important factor in the spiritual renewal of the congregation has been its search for ways to be in mission in the local community. A "New Ministry Discernment Group" was established to give careful attention to fresh directions the congregation might take. With their leadership and inspiration, the church eventually adopted a ministry group model, adapting the pattern of the Church of the Savior in Washington, D.C., to their own unique circumstances. Staff member Fran Ruggles Albro describes the mission group model this way in a recent newsletter (Oct. 29, 2000):

> The Mission Group model claims that worship, work in the community, and time devoted to prayer, Bible study and other spiritual disciplines are all integral, connected parts of the Christian life. As we weave these elements together, our relationships with God, each other and those on the margins are deepened and strengthened. From these, we are empowered to live out our church's mission.

Members have been led to establish several mission outreach projects, including a program to provide rehabilitated cars at low cost to needy families, one that serves meals not provided in the schedule of regional programs for the homeless, and other ministries of caring to those in need. Many members continue their volunteer involvement in prison and homeless ministries but now see more clearly how those ministries draw them deeper into the Christian spiritual life.

Meetings of the session, the governing board of West Raleigh, reflect the changes in this congregation. Like governing boards in many congregations, these church leaders begin their meeting with prayer, but somehow this seems different. As the room becomes quiet a candle is lighted, and the pastor begins by saying, "The Lord be with you." The gathered elders respond, "And also with you." As they sing psalms, read Scripture, and pray at length for the needs of the congregation, they begin to listen for God's voice among them. Pastor Joe Ward says the first task of church leaders is to "listen for what God is saying to us and to trust that we will hear something." As a result the governing board and other leadership groups are focused on spiritual discernment as much or more than on administrative tasks. The needs and concerns of the congregation are shared and held up in prayer. No one checks the time or seems eager for the group to "get on with it." These elders and pastors seem to "rest in the Lord" as they approach their lengthy agenda, trusting that with God's leading they will be faithful in exercising their call to leadership. The weight of administrative decision-making tasks seems to "float" on a reservoir of trust in each other and in God's leading. According to elder Pam Wilson, "God is a part of everything we are doing here."

There is no question about it; this is a busy congregation. Yet time seems to slow down for them. They seem to savor every moment of their life together, revealing an underlying assumption that their lives are lived, first of all, before God. The experience of encounter with God in worship inspires and guides everything that goes on at West Raleigh. In large and small ways the practices of prayer, study of Scripture, and careful listening inform the entire fabric of the people's life together. Through encounter they discern their call to become aware of the actual circumstances of their community and to be active in mission. Associate pastor Denise Thorpe says the congregation's culture has a "richness" or "thickness" to it. The focus of congregational life is not on particular programs or people but rather on the integrated processes of encounter with God in worship, a communal life of prayer and spiritual discernment, energetic and joyful participation in mission, and a strong commitment to each other and to loving accountability before God. As worship concludes with a charge to be Christ's body in the world and with a blessing in the triune name, people at West Raleigh move to the parlor and cluster in small groups around the coffee pots. The communal spiritual life they share in worship is extended into all parts of congregational life and beyond.

Worship As the Pattern for Congregational Life and for the Christian Spiritual Life

In the story of West Raleigh we see the contours of the life of a worship-centered congregation and how that life shapes engagements with one another and with the world these Christians seek to serve. For members of West Raleigh Presbyterian, as for members of many other congregations, worship is paradigmatic for their life together. It sets the pattern for everything they do. Contemporary congregations give expression to age-old commitments from communities of faith across the centuries and around the globe. Christians throughout history, especially in Reformed churches, have said explicitly that the defining purpose for humankind is to love God and enjoy God forever, and it is in worship that this relationship of love and enjoyment is enacted with clarity, intentionality, and intensity. In fact, when Christian communities fail to gather for worship, their very life is in jeopardy. When the Soviet Union exerted strict controls on religious expression, Christians were told that, of all the possible religious activities they might engage in, only worship in strictly limited times and places would be tolerated. Christian education, witness, and mission were explicitly forbidden. After the collapse of Soviet communism Christians realized that if the situation had been reversed—if they had been prohibited from worshiping but allowed to engage in these other activities—government authorities might have come closer to completely displacing the church. As it happened, communities of faith continued to gather, pray, sing, proclaim the gospel, and celebrate the sacraments, so that when Soviet repression was lifted the church could again flourish. It was worship that set the pattern for Christians' lives and sustained them during those dark years.

Worship sets the pattern for the Christian life and for congregational life in several specific ways. First, worship-centered congregations understand worship as the community's *encounter with God*, and they understand that such encounters do not leave one unchanged. Any substitute for encounter with God in worship is always to be understood as a form of idolatry, and these congregations will not knowingly settle for that. Second, part of worship's paradigmatic quality lies in the fact that it is *ritual*, a kind of patterned communal behavior that naturally brings with it a certain dynamic process that both shapes and expresses the faith of the community that enacts and participates in it. These congregations know that ritual processes require a kind of holistic participation on their part—participation that includes cognitive, affective, physical, social, and relational levels of interaction—and they revel in it. Worship is evocative, unhurried, richly sensory, and fulsome in its ritual enactments. A mood of relaxed, joyful reverence permeates these celebrations.

The ritual of worship does not take place in isolation, however. Worship exists in a communal setting where a unique congregational culture surrounds the practice of worship. In a complex interchange worship both influences and is influenced by the culture of the congregation. In worship-centered congregations *worship shapes the overall culture of the congregation*. This shaping follows the patterns established in worship and is directed toward the spiritual formation of members and participants. Thus worship-centered congregations show a priority for deepening maturity in the Christian spiritual life and an active concern for God's activity in and for the world. Worship-centered congregations turn out to be profoundly committed to and active in mission.

Worship is also paradigmatic in that it is at its most basic level a human *experience*. People have no way to participate in worship other than experientially. In worship-centered congregations, even while the presence of God is the focal point for worship, the experience of worshipers is taken seriously. While attention to the content of worshipers' experience may not take place within worship itself, the fact that worship is understood as a concrete experience on which people can reflect makes worship paradigmatic for reflection in all other aspects of congregational life. Worship stands at the center of congregational life (1) when there is an expectation of encounter with God in worship, (2) when preparation for worship is taken seriously by worship leaders and worshipers, (3) when the programmatic life of the congregation supports worship participation for people in all circumstances of life, and (4) when reflection on the worship is pervasive throughout congregational life.

Educators since the Greeks have understood that humans learn from experience, but that learning is far from guaranteed. Without reflection on our experiences, they point out, the possibility of learning from them is greatly diminished. The congregations described in these pages thrive on their experience of encounter with God in worship, in congregational life, and in their lives in the world. They have developed and nurtured a variety of ways to reflect on experience so that learning is enhanced and deepened. Thus their congregational renewal is deeply spiritual as they learn to live in the presence of God. Liturgical renewal for these congregations has borne fruit in spiritual renewal.

Worship as Encounter With God

Worship stands as the central act around which all other actions and reflections of the congregation are configured. To say it another way, all actions and theological reflections of communities of faith are subject to the principal action of the assembly gathered to "joyfully [ascribe] all praise and honor, glory and power to the triune God."[2] Or as Marva Dawn has said, worship invites us to royally waste our time in the presence of God.[3] Thus worship fulfills its paradigmatic function when all actions and theological reflections of the congregation seek to be in continuity with what is said and done, sung and prayed, proclaimed and promised in worship. The congregations described here understand that all of life is lived before God.

Liturgical theologians have named the rhythm of action and reflection centered on the Christian assembly "primary" and "secondary" liturgical theology. *Primary* liturgical theology is an enacted theology, embodied by real people as they participate in liturgical words, actions, and relationships. The meaning of worship—its theology—is an enacted theology that is known first of all in participation. *Secondary* liturgical theology includes the reflections, written and spoken, that occur as a result of or in response to participation in the enactment of the liturgy. Gordon Lathrop writes, "Primary liturgical theology is the communal meaning of the liturgy exercised by the gathering itself. The assembly uses combinations of words and signs to speak of God. . . . Secondary liturgical theology, then, is written and spoken discourse that attempts to find words for the experience of the liturgy and to illuminate its structures, intending to enable a more profound participation in those structures by the members of the assembly."[4] Educators have long valued action and participation as essential components in education. Likewise, participation in an activity naturally leads to some sort of reflection on that activity. Otherwise it is not usually "educative." With worship understood as the principal activity of the faith community through the disciplined rhythm of action and reflection on the liturgy, congregations become communities of Christian integrity where all parts are knit together into a coherent whole. Here members support and challenge one another into the future because a vision for that future is clearly discernable among them and is enacted as they gather for worship.

Of course, Christians encounter God in innumerable times, places, and circumstances, and their covenant with God can be enacted in an equally unlimited array of possibilities. But, as Thomas Groome says, "By symbolically mediating the presence of the Risen Christ in the community, the liturgy is an intensified experience of the encounter between God and humankind in their covenant relationship."[5] The "real presence" of Jesus Christ made known in Word and sacrament comes to the Christian community as they gather to hear Scripture proclaimed and to share the holy meal, to share their lives with one another, and to share the gospel with the world. In worship the commonplace actions of everyday life are represented and encountered in ways that intensify their meaning and invest them with both the promises of God and the hopes and needs of humankind. Congregations do not just "go through the motions" of accustomed Christian worship. By the grace of the Holy Spirit, the presence of God is mediated through their words and actions and communal participation. "Worship is offered as a common prayer action by the whole church, and the church can do so because of the presence of the Risen Christ through the indwelling Spirit to the community. In Christian faith, then, fitting worship is by the grace of God's Spirit in Jesus Christ; it is human participation in a divine initiative."[6]

We have heard Joe Ward say that as a pastor he understands people's expectations for an encounter with God in worship. Members of the youth group at Sleepy Hollow Presbyterian Church in San Anselmo, California, call such encounters "God sightings."[7] Worship is the primary arena for "God sightings" and sensitizes Christians to see God at work in other times and places. James Empereur says it this way: "The reality of the resurrection forms the background of our human vision, experience, and action, and through this resurrection the Spirit of Christ permeates our lives. . . . The Christian meaning the liturgy is to convey is the experience that Jesus Christ is alive and is our redeemer. It must create an *experienced* background for our vision, experience, and action. Out of this transformed vision, experience, and activity we can see Christ in and through the transformed possibilities of our own lives."[8]

At Old Pine Presbyterian Church in Philadelphia, encounter with God is an eagerly anticipated part of Sunday worship. As member Bill Van Orten describes it, "it is like spiritual bungee jumping!" Such descriptions may seem out of place in this historic church, but the reality is attested to by many members. The historic building is located in one of Philadelphia's oldest neighborhoods, and the elaborately decorated pastel sanctuary has been described as looking like "the inside of a Ukrainian Easter egg." Worship is truly the center of this congregation's life, with the ratio of members to worship attendance significantly higher than average for mainline churches. Members gather every Lord's Day for Scripture and preaching, sacrament and song, and to lift their joys and concerns before God in prayer. Many members say they encounter God in expressive and evocative liturgy and in the love of Scripture and excellent preaching. But for most everyone in this congregation, the opportunity to share joys and concerns and to pray for and with one another is the living heartbeat of worship at Old Pine. Relationships with God, with the church, and with one another are incarnated as people rise to share their joys and concerns and ask for prayers. There is a healthy balance between appropriate self-disclosure and true vulnerability in the ways people say what is on their minds. It is not unusual for tears to be shed or for appropriate applause to rise. People truly care for one another and are faithful in their prayers for one another within Sunday worship and in their personal spiritual disciplines.

In worship the encounter with God includes seeing ourselves and the world from God's perspective. Worship is paradigmatic for congregational life and for the Christian life because worship articulates and enacts "the way things really are." In worship we put on a pair of glasses through which to see the world, according to Frank Senn. At first we must adjust our sight because of the difference between the worldview of worship and the secular vision imposed on us by the surrounding culture. The more we participate in and reflect on encounter with God in worship, the more we begin to see the world as the arena of God's redemptive activity and also to see our role in that redemption. Part of a Christian's continuing conversion is seeing the world more and more from God's perspective.[9]

Worship: Patterned Communal Action

Some have said that to be human is to engage in ritual. The pervasive presence of ritual, including religious ritual, across global cultures is unmistakable. When Christians participate in the rituals of worship, their loving response to God's action is given communal physical expression. The shared experience of worship binds communities together and helps form their identity as Christians. Worship celebrates the presence of God and gives expression to the community's response to God's presence among them. While Christian worship has taken many forms across the globe and throughout history, recent theological and historical study has given the church a pattern for worship that includes gathering in God's name, reading and proclaiming Scripture, celebrating the Eucharist, and sending into the world. This fourfold pattern can be witnessed in mainline Protestant, Roman Catholic, and Orthodox churches throughout North America and across the world.[10] Some expressions of this pattern may be more complete than others and/or more elaborate than others. Nevertheless, the repeated fourfold pattern forms the ritual framework for Christian worship and serves at least two purposes. First of all, it directs the attention of worshipers toward God by giving primary attention to the telling and enactment of the story of God's way with humankind in Scripture and in their common life. Second, it serves the memory of worshipers by calling these very experiences to mind through Word and sacrament.

Latrobe Presbyterian Church in Latrobe, Pennsylvania, in addition to its downtown buildings, is blessed with a beautiful historic chapel and cemetery located on a green hilltop several miles from town. There worshipers gather at dusk on Holy Saturday to celebrate the Great Vigil of Easter. They light new fire and read lengthy passages of Scripture, beginning with the story of creation and concluding with the resurrection of Jesus. Each reading is accompanied by a sung response and prayer. The readings take over an hour, but even the smallest children revel in the storytelling and the rhythm of prayer and song. Many of the readers and cantors are children and youth. When they reflect on their participation in worship leadership, the shaping effects of worship's story resonate powerfully in their experience. "Our church uses every age group," says David Mills, a high school student with several younger brothers and sisters. "Pretty much every age group is involved. Even the youngest ones participate in the service. At the vigil they read the story of Ezekiel and the 'Valley of the Dry Bones,' and the littlest ones got to rattle the bones. They participated that way to demonstrate the story better." Cynthia Campbell gets it right when she says, "We need to hear the whole story . . . because to be a Christian is to give oneself over to being shaped by that story until we become remade after the image of Christ so that he lives in us. Worship is a place where we hear and learn and internalize the story."[11]

In worship we are shaped by the story of God's way with humankind throughout the ages and especially in Jesus Christ. It is this story, rehearsed and retold in worship, that becomes our Christian story. "In worship we locate our memories in the story of God and begin to discover thanksgiving and healing there," says Gregory Jones.[12] The paradigmatic quality of worship, then, lies in part in its ability to enable us to hear and participate in the story of God's ongoing redemption of the world. In worship our participation is contained in our very enactments of prayer and praise, lament and thanksgiving. According to Shirley Guthrie,

> the story we Christians have to tell is not only about how God has been present and at work in our individual lives; it is to set our little stories in the context of the story of all God's people. To tell this story is to tell the long story about a just and loving Creator who created all human beings in God's own image, and who from the very beginning and throughout the history of the world has been at work for the good of all human beings, every one of whom God loves. It is to tell the story of a living Christ who by the Holy Spirit continues his healing, reconciling, liberating work not only in the lives of Christians but also in the lives of people of other religions and no religion at all.[13]

Throughout human societies particular stories are told at particular times. The day that I am writing this, for example, is the thirtieth anniversary of one of my favorite National Public Radio news shows, and so throughout the day one can hear reflections on the origins of that program, its early development, and the events that have shaped its thirty years of programming. Time, the passing of days and years, shapes the stories that are told, when they are told, and how they are told. The same is true for Christian worship. The patterns of time that structure Christian worship are inextricably linked to the stories of God's redemption in the past and promises concerning what is to come. "There is a new appreciation," says Harold Daniels, "of the evangelical dimensions of the [liturgical] calendar and the ability its use has in building people up in the faith."[14] When congregations live out patterns of time shaped by the stories of God's redemption, it is not only particular stories that shape them. The larger pattern of the stories becomes apparent and people are drawn into their orienting orbit. Time serves to shape scriptural stories into narrative wholes that carry the community from hope and anticipation into promises fulfilled. The stories of Advent, Christmas, and Epiphany move the church from anticipation and preparation through incarnation and recognition of Jesus as God's anointed. Lenten, Easter, and Pentecost narratives invite the church to repentance; into the betrayal, denial, and death of Jesus; into the celebration of his resurrection; and into the Holy Spirit's continuing presence in the church. It is the pattern of these central stories that has shaped the church's time and thus its worship.

Pastor David Batchelder says, "The first question we ask is, 'What time is it?'" And it is important to know the answer. In Latrobe the church building occupies an especially visible site in the downtown area with its graceful Romanesque arches giving Main Street an unmistakable focal point. The spacious building houses a robust schedule of liturgical and programmatic activities. The congregation celebrates Eucharist frequently and is moving towards weekly communion, and they use several different styles of serving the sacrament. Sometimes the people remain seated in the pews and are served by passing trays of broken bread and small cups of unfermented wine. At other times they are served by intinction as they walk forward, receive a piece of broken bread, and dip it into the wine. At the Easter vigil people walk forward and are served by intinction with both fermented and unfermented wine or, for those who want it, there is a common cup of fermented wine. The moods of Eucharistic celebrations vary according to the liturgical season and the mode of serving. During Advent and Lent, celebrations of the sacrament take on a somewhat meditative tone as the celebrations of Christmas and Easter are awaited. Then during the seasons of Christmas, Epiphany, Easter, and Pentecost the celebrations are lively and festive.

Here, as in many Protestant churches, many members have experienced only somber, meditative celebrations of communion—what some have called "a funeral for Jesus"—and are troubled when festive celebrations break this pattern. Lively music, for example, seems out of place to them. To quote one Latrobe member, "I'm trying to meditate and reflect on Jesus' dying on the cross for me. This music got in the way." In light of "always knowing what time it is," David acknowledges that "we planned it that way. In Easter we're especially conscious of the fact that the *risen* Christ is in our midst. There is an accent on the joy of his presence throughout Eastertide. It is a rich celebration that calls us into a new awareness that the One who was crucified and risen calls us into a community of the resurrection. So the music is intended to help accent that aspect of the Eucharist's meaning. At other times of the year—Ash Wednesday, for example, or especially Maundy Thursday and certainly during Lent—other music is appropriate. The fullness of what this meal means for us can't be emphasized all at once. The seasons hold up certain aspects for us to savor. Over the course of the year there is a balance." It is in this larger sense that worship's unique mode of keeping time gives shape to the yearly cycle of our lives.

In celebrating according to liturgical time we are not engaged in a reenactment of past events, as significant as those are. Rather, we are participating in a here-and-now proclamation of God's redeeming actions in Christ. We ourselves become participants in the stories. In this way the communal activity of liturgical celebration becomes an encounter with the saving work of Christ. This is true not only for the yearly patterns of celebration, as seen above, but for the weekly patterns of Lord's Day celebration as well. Following the disciples' pattern of gathering on the first day of the week to celebrate the resurrection of the Lord, we acknowledge that Sunday is the first day of the new creation. In confession, forgiveness, and celebration of the holy meal, we participate in newness of life on every Lord's Day. The patterns of prayer, Scripture, and thanksgiving established there in turn shape spiritual disciplines for all days and seasons. The study of Scripture, personal and family prayers, thanksgiving at meals, and participation in ministries of justice and mercy are all set in place according to the patterns of Lord's Day worship in the community of faith. According to Gordon Lathrop, "The Sunday meeting, juxtaposed to our experience of all things in time, is constitutive of Christian faith."[15]

Ritual by its very nature enacts familiar patterns and predictable juxtapositions that welcome regular worshipers into God's presence. These patterns provide a framework of order and familiarity. Worshipers are able to focus on God's presence discerned in worship rather than on the details of what might come next. In enabling us to be open to God in this way, rituals become one of the means by which God's transformative work can be accomplished in us. Worship may be a source of comfort and reassurance to us in times of difficulty. At the same time the trust engendered through worship's comforting aspects is precisely the entryway God can use to call us into the deepening and challenging transformation into the likeness of Christ.

Religious ritual, like religion in general, deals in a patterned way with matters of ultimate consequence for humankind—matters of life and death; of identity, meaning, and purpose. In taking up these matters, ritual takes the data of everyday experience and sets it into a larger context of meaning.[16] Through ritual the stuff of ordinary human encounter and becoming is understood in a context of ultimate significance. Christian rituals, made up of multiple symbols, words, actions, and objects, and woven together into multiple patterns, gives expression to the community's commitments and, through enactment and participation, promotes and shapes these commitments.

Ritual communication takes place in two distinct but interrelated ways: through verbal symbols (words) and presentational symbols (gestures, actions, and objects). These two modes of ritual communication blossom into a variety of further categories, such as rhythm, tone, and silence in music and in the color, design, and texture of vestments, decorations, and ritual objects. Architectural design and liturgical space also contribute to the ability of ritual enacted within that space to communicate adequately. In carrying out its rituals, the community both says and does what it believes.

A source of fruitful reflection in the congregations described here centers around questions of continuity and discontinuity in the worship and life of the congregation. These congregations are always asking themselves whether or not their worship practices adequately reflect what they know and believe about God, themselves, and the world. At the Latrobe church such reflections are the constant concern of the worship and music committee. The committee keeps careful notes on various liturgies, especially festival services such as the Easter Vigil, and carefully considers their aesthetic, procedural, theological, and relational content. Worship, they know, tells the community's sacred story, and they want to tell it faithfully, beautifully, and expressively. Rituals in general embody a particular pattern for the shaping of time, space, and identity through the use of ritual action, objects, speech, and sound.[17]

In Christian worship the many aspects of ritual are shaped first of all by and for the sake of memory. Worship begins with the remembrance of who God is and who we are before God. The patterns of time, space, ritual identity, and the use of ritual words, actions, and songs serve to recall for the community the mighty acts of God throughout Scripture and history and to enable the people's participation in the worship of this same God. Thus ritual provides the means by which worshipers can overcome the distances of time and space. Past and present and future become part of our contemporary experience of the presence of God in the community of faith. Philip Pfatteicher describes the ritual experience this way: "We do not simply review what God has done in the past. As the ritual erases the separation of time and space, what is described in the readings becomes contemporary and a personal experience. Bondage is broken, slavery is ended. We hear this in our own experience as a declaration that our intolerable self-enclosure is breached, the walls of self-centeredness are shattered, our prison is torn down. We are redirected to live no longer for ourselves but 'in Christ.'"[18] Ritual serves this transformative intention in the ways it employs prayer and story, gesture and song, embodied presence and communal participation in the service of God.

Whenever human commitments are communally enacted in ritual, those enactments serve to communicate and intensify the commitments they embody. At the same time communally enacted rituals form and transform the identity of those who participate in them. Rituals shape our understanding of the world and our place in it by the ways they mark time, confer persons with particular roles, and mark communal transitions. Gwen Neville and John Westerhoff put it this way: "Ritual is a social drama which embodies the memories and visions of a community. It is through the repetition of these symbolic actions that we evoke the feeling of the primordial event which initially called the community into being, with such power that it effects a present presence at that event. In other words, through the intuitional mode of consciousness, ritual re-presents revelation."[19] Elsewhere Westerhoff describes rituals as rites of intensification or rites of transition. In rites of intensification the identity of the community and members is strengthened as they "follow the calendar, binding a people into community, establishing meaning and purpose for the lives of its members, and both sustaining and transmitting to the next generation its world view and value system. Transition rites of passage and initiation aid in understanding and accepting change during life-cycle movements."[20] In the communal enactment of ritual the community of faith learns in one way or another, to a greater or lesser degree, how the community understands itself and its place in the world. A particular worldview is enacted wherein the nature of life before God can be understood. Encounter with God in the communally enacted rituals of the congregation, along with other practices, serves to form spiritually the community and its members.

The congregations described here intuitively know that what they are doing is largely out of the ordinary. The ways they engage in ritual and the meanings their rituals communicate stand in stark contrast to the larger culture and to the practices of some other congregations. Many members and leaders in these congregations lead demanding, influential, and sometimes high-profile lives in the communities where they live. Yet many of them say their ultimate identity does not rest in their public roles. Rather, they say the Christian identity established in worship shapes all the other aspects of their lives. This means that their decisions and actions are sometimes at odds with the expectations of the surrounding culture. But part of the importance of the congregation is its enduring "culture of resistance" in the face of competing claims and values. Worship is the center of a "culture of resistance" or a counterculture. These people echo what Gregory Jones says when he points out the difference between cultural time and time shaped around the celebrations of the Christian story. We don't need more time, he says. "We need time of a different quality . . . that renews, refreshes and redeems."[21] In worship, where time is different, people share in renewal and redemption in such a way that makes other options in timekeeping increasingly less attractive. It is the experience of encounter with God that renews and redeems. Explicit critique of cultural patterns that distort and destroy can be taken up in other settings. Thus the culture of resistance in worship is implicit. In worship the community's attention is focused on God in expectation of encounter.

Worship-Centered Congregational Culture

Not long ago I saw a book whose title proclaimed that the purpose of the church was to serve the world. While I would not entirely disagree with this viewpoint, it is more complicated than that. The purpose of the church, in response to the saving love of God known in Jesus Christ, is to give glory and praise to God and to join God in the redemption of the world to the end that all creation will join in giving praise and glory to God. Such fulsome praise of and cooperation with God requires that each and all of us be formed, transformed, and conformed into the likeness of Christ.

The process for our ongoing conversion is continual spiritual formation, whereby we are nurtured, challenged, broken, and renewed, until we are filled with the very fullness of God (Eph. 3:14–19). It is this orientation toward giving praise and glory to God and the resulting spiritual formation that informs all the church is and does. "Growth in one's spiritual life," says Marjorie Thompson, "invites a process of transformation in the life of a believer. It is a process of growing in gratitude, trust, obedience, humility, compassion, service, and joy."[22] Such transformation is not individualistic but implies a community of faith where support and challenge are a way of life. It also implies that the community will always be attentive to the needs of the world.

We all chuckle when we hear the suggestion that the seven last words of the church might be "We've never done it that way before." Yet even these words are revealing in that they show the church to be a coherent social system, embodying a culture or subculture that is unique to each congregation. Congregations have particular histories and sets of practices that are identifiable as "the way we do it here." Each congregation's history and shared memory are held communally as a set of shared practices that have endured over time. Worship-centered congregations orient the culture of their church around the central activity of worship. Sometimes these orientations are intentional. At West Raleigh, for example, people began to see the contradictions between their eagerness to worship God and the distractions of committee business. A long-standing pattern had been for the pastors, worship leaders, and governing board members to meet for prayer before worship. But over the years more and more business was tacked onto the gathering. A quorum of only three session members was required to conduct business, so often prayer before worship was displaced by deliberations and decision making. Here's how Joe Ward described it:

> There was a mythology that parking is bad here, and that people are [only] here on Sundays. So we had a one-day-a-week church. The rest of the week the place was pretty much a children's center. The process of getting session and deacon's meetings off of Sundays was a lengthy process of prayer and study, prayer and study. We went through a long process of looking at the size of our boards and when we meet and how we meet. We had to refocus the way we understood the work of the committees, away from seeing them as the assets of the church. Now we see them as the infrastructure that enables the essence of congregational life to go on in worship, study groups, mission groups, prayer meetings, and fellowship gatherings.

At other times a reorientation of congregational culture around the centrality of worship happens less formally and more organically as worship continues to shape the worldview and consciousness of the worshiping community. At Old Pine Presbyterian the changes came gradually as deepening practices of faith sharing and prayer during worship began to permeate all parts of congregational life.

Whether reorientation of congregational life around the centrality of worship is intentional or naturally emerges, in the congregations described here worship has become the defining activity and experience for the life of the whole congregation. Worship has become paradigmatic for congregational life in that what is said and done in worship sets the pattern for all other aspects of congregational life. Thomas Groome says that

> as an expression of communal faith, [worship] can inform, form, and transform participants in renewed Christian faith as well. Like lovemaking in marriage, liturgy in the life of Christians should be both an *expression* and a *source* of faith, hope and love. From this perspective, we recognize the "educational" power of liturgy. To nurture people and communities in Christian identity and living is the learning outcome for Christian religious education. . . . Though the primary intent of liturgy is to worship God, it always has existential impact on the lives of participants that is profoundly educational.[23]

To say it another way, all actions and theological reflections of communities of faith are subject to the principal action of the assembly, gathered to "joyfully [ascribe] all praise and honor, glory and power to the triune God."[24] Thus all actions and theological reflections of the congregation seek to be in continuity with what is said and done, sung and prayed, proclaimed and promised in worship.

The distinctive identity of a congregation has both internal and external manifestations. Congregational identity is made up of the worshiping community's history, environment, and its particular religious tradition or heritage.[25] Established over time, the identity of most congregations is apparent to those both outside and within the church and functions in a public way like the identity of other social institutions and organizations. On a deeper level, the identity of the worshiping assembly is established in the community's encounter with God. "The church begins to know itself not by contemplating its own identity," writes Gordon Lathrop, "but by beholding the face of Christ in that word, bath, and table that manifest God's identity. In these things the church is filled with the power of that Spirit to bear witness in the world to the truth about God. The meeting for worship is itself the ground and beginning of such witness. The meeting for worship is the church becoming church."[26] In that encounter the church is called ever more deeply into its life in God, the God of Word and sacrament, the Creator of heaven and earth made known in Jesus Christ.

Since identity establishes both who we are and who we are not, in worship the limits of that identity are clarified in the ways we are called to say "yes" to God and say "no" to all that distorts or detracts from the face of Christ encountered in worship. The effect of this identity is unexpected in that it calls the community to a new perspective of responsiveness to the stranger. The God whose presence is the focal point for the church's communal identity is "one unknown," a reality beyond our knowing. Thus our capacity to embrace the stranger is enlarged through encounter with God. As Darrell Fasching puts it, "a holy community has its center outside itself, in a transcendence whose social analogue is the stranger. Thus a holy community defines the human in terms of an otherness that gives birth to an ethic of hospitality. . . . Compassion binds the individual within the holy community to the individuals in the society beyond its borders."[27] All the churches described here participate in extending such hospitality as they care for the hungry, the homeless, the mentally ill, the imprisoned, and the poor.

Experience of Encounter With God

Thus far I have argued that worship sets the pattern for the Christian life and for congregational life in its orientation toward praising, thanking, and beseeching God. It requires communal ritual participation, thus forming a community of encounter and commitment. At the same time participation in such a community is made up of events and is experienced personally by each of its members. Thus participation in worship is also the paradigmatic *experience of encounter with God* that shapes the life of every Christian. While it is never to be denied that God can be encountered in an unlimited array of circumstances, the communal experience of encounter with God in worship shapes all other encounters. As we have seen, it is in beholding Christ that the community is given its identity, so it is with caution that we turn to examine worship as experience, even paradigmatic experience, in the Christian life. When one makes such a turn the temptation is to displace encounter with God as the focal point for worship and to give priority to the experiencing person or persons. It is true that the ability of worship to enable our encounter with God cannot be avoided. It is for the sake of such encounters that worship exists at all. However, when I hear people describe worship as a "worship experience," the phrase is a signal that the experiencing person has become more important than the God encountered in worship.

For much of the remainder of this book we shall shift the focus of our exploration away from worship's theocentric requirements and direct our attention to the inseparable dimension of human experience that is integral to all encounters with God. In doing so, however, we must never put the cart before the horse. The intentions of worship are not for the sake of human experience in worship. In fact, such an approach undercuts its own intentions. Once we have shifted our attention from God and are more concerned for our own or others' experience, the possibility of significant encounter with God is diminished. It is in sustained contemplation and adoration of God that truly formative and transformative experience in worship can occur. Any approach that focuses on "worship experience" rather than the worship of God is more likely to deform rather than faithfully form or transform.

How, then, can we reap the abundant fruits of worship as the paradigmatic experience for the Christian life and for congregational life if a focus on "worship experience" undercuts the divine encounters around which Christian life is centered? First of all, we must take care to make a clear distinction between *experience* and *reflection on experience*. A necessary step in learning from experience is reflection on experience. Reflection can take many forms and can occur in a variety of contexts, but the distinction is clear. Experience—one's actual participation in ongoing life in the world—cannot be replaced by reflection. It is often the case that experience is interrupted by reflection in the very act of participation. One often sees this kind of experiential interruption when worship is "explained" as it goes along. We must resist the temptation to mentally move away from experience and allow reflections to eclipse the present, here-and-now reality of lived experience. Second, it is of utmost importance that reflection in all its varieties be valued for what it is, the occasions through which we construct meaning out of the "raw material" of experience. Both experience and reflection are indispensable in the Christian life and in congregational life. Each has a particular place in the unique culture of congregations. We must never forget, even in our explorations here, that reflection serves experience and not the other way around.

Thomas Groome reminds us that the effectiveness of worship in faithfully shaping congregational life and the lives of Christians is to be found in "how effectively [worship's] symbols draw people into an intensified experience [so] that God's life is mediated to them in love" in such a way that they express their own lives to God, and that they are empowered for God's reign in the world.[28]

Like newborn children who arrive on the scene in the midst of an already established pattern of family relationships and practices, we enter into Christian worship patterns that long precede our arrival. They have the historic capacity to disclose before us God's presence and to give expression to our deepest thanksgiving and longing for the divine presence. At the same time these patterns of liturgical practice are never the same from one occasion to another. Christian worship, claims Gordon Lathrop, is a lively combination of "myth and rite, story and enactment, so that combinations of words and signs are its natural means."[29] Thus Christian ritual makes use of a mode of meaning making that is dialectical. Neither words nor signs can hold or communicate the fullness of what Christian ritual is meant to express. It is the endlessly variable possibilities of "juxtaposition" that combine, interact, break open, and recombine to form the patterns of meaning enacted in worship. This being the case, paradox and ambiguity become the most profound means of encountering truth in the Christian community.

The congregations described in this study are all seeking to encounter God and faithfully to discern and respond to God's leading. All the while they are asking, How might we learn the Christian life from the experience of congregational life? Pastor Joe Ward in Raleigh asked parents and educational leaders precisely this question as the congregation began their children's worship program: "What do we want to give a young person the opportunity to experience between the ages of three and eleven? How do we raise up children as worshipers of God?" The remainder of our explorations will be in response to these and similar questions.

Chapter Two

Experiential Learning in Congregational Life

B ruce and I talk in a small conference room while his sons finish liturgical dance practice and confirmation class. Bruce is a shy man whose
family have been members of West Raleigh Presbyterian Church for
about twelve years. He plays the guitar, he tells me, for the fourth-grade
Sunday school class as part of a small ensemble that includes a banjo and
piano. He felt called to this ministry, he says, after three or four years in
the children's worship ministry. "I felt called, so I thought about it, read
about it, prayed about it. When someone says they need you, then if you
say yes, you give it all you've got." Bruce likes the fact that he's had the
opportunity to take up different ministries, to rotate and not get burned
out.

Bruce agrees that West Raleigh is a worship-centered congregation.
The Sunday service brings everyone together, kind of like a "high mass."
Not that it is overly formal, but it is, says Bruce, "sanctified, set apart
time. People of all ages and beliefs sing out loud together. It is a time to
further your walk with Christ and get in touch with the deeper values of
life. Most people here are fairly committed to the journey, both the inward journey and the outward journey." Bruce likes the structure and the
order for worship within which the community can join in praising God.

As I thank Bruce for our conversation and he prepares to collect the
boys and head for home, he turns and thanks me for the opportunity to
talk about his life of faith. "It's been, well, sort of therapeutic," he says.
There is not time to ask him what he means by that, but I have a sense of
its importance to him. In the course of our conversation he has had the
opportunity to think about and describe several aspects of his Christian

life, both within the church and outside it. In the process he has told me and told himself the gospel of his own life.[1] In reflecting on his "inward journey and outward journey" Bruce has learned something of what it means to worship the triune God and to respond to God's call in his life. It is "therapeutic," to use Bruce's term, because the experiences he has described have not been allowed to become absorbed into the daily routines of his busy life but have been remembered, cherished, analyzed, and understood in ways that deepen Bruce's spiritual life.

Learning from Experience: Pervasive Patterns

Specialists in experiential learning theory claim that "learning, change, and growth are seen to be facilitated best by an integrated process that begins with here-and-now experience followed by collection of data and observations about that experience. The data are then analyzed and the conclusions of this analysis are fed back to the actors in the experience for their use in the modification of their behavior and choice of new experiences."[2] Learning theorists identify a four-part cycle of action and reflection that is the natural progression for adult learning: *concrete experience*, *reflective observation*, *abstract conceptualization*, and *active experimentation*, as shown in figure 1.

1. Concrete experience: Learning begins with personal engagement with and participation in *concrete experience*. It is named "concrete" experience here to highlight the often overlooked fact that experiences are not merely conveyed by the senses to become present in the mind but are actual events that involve us in the real world. We are physically present and participate in real events even when we position ourselves as a distant observer. Experience, then, has a concreteness to it made up of the "material conditions of our existence."[3] We participate in concrete experience in the way we perceive and respond to events around us. Concrete experience is the defining moment for experiential learning. While remembering, probing, and assessing the meaning of our experience involve three of the four processes of experiential learning, we do well to remember that the experience itself remains central.[4] In the cycle of experiential learning, actual participation in an event or events makes up one quarter of the cycle while specific styles of reflection on that experience make up the other three quarters. All four elements of the cycle (experience and the three modes of reflection) are essential for intentional and fruitful adult learning.

Figure 1

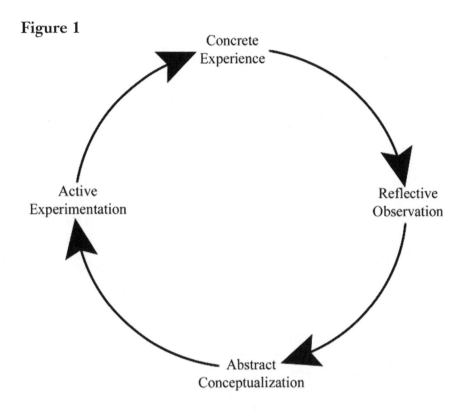

Notice the one-to-three ratio. It might seem that reflection on experience overshadows the experience itself and that experience is of less importance than reflection, but this is surely not the case. Nothing can take the place of actual participation in concrete experience in its power to shape human consciousness and conduct. It must also be said, however, that for purposes of intentional learning in adulthood, reflection on experience cannot be left to chance. In the congregations described here, reflection on experience, especially reflection on the paradigmatic experience of the worship of God, is a pervasive feature of each congregation's culture. The one-to-three ratio represents not a devaluing of experience in favor of reflection but a careful valuing of experience as the ground of all our knowledge by reflecting on experience in a variety of ways and for a variety of purposes.

Thus the cycle of experiential learning begins with actual participation in an activity. We are constantly surrounded by objects, persons, and activities that make up our environment and come to us as experience. David Kolb writes, "What you see, hear, and feel around you are those sensations, colors, textures, and sounds that are so basic and reliable that we call them reality."[5] Because experience is made up of both objective and subjective elements, it naturally includes our own thoughts, emotions, and responses to situations in which we find ourselves. Experience, then, is made up of cognitive, affective, physical, social, interpersonal, and imaginative dimensions of human consciousness. We are having experiences all the time and, following that old maxim, we learn from our experience. But as John Dewey has pointed out, we do not learn equally from every experience. What is required, learning theorists say, is reflection on experience, reflection that is the concern of the other three movements of the learning cycle.

2. Reflective observation: The second movement in the cycle of experiential learning is *reflective observation*, wherein a particular experience or set of experiences is remembered and described in some detail and reviewed from various points of view. Many of the details of an experience are called to mind and various aspects of the experience are named. Rather than fading into forgetfulness, the detailed attributes of our experiences are intentionally recalled, savored, and pondered in order that we might learn what they have to teach us. Like the experience itself, however, our reflections at this stage tend to be unsystematic, with particular attention given to our emotional and affective responses to experience. Reflective observation is tentative in its mood, focused more on detailed recall and pondering than on analysis, assessment, or deep understanding. At this stage matters of meaning making come to us as questions for consideration (Could our experience mean *this*? Or *that*? Or *both*?) rather than matters of settled intention. Conversation centers around memory, exploration, and questioning.

3. Abstract conceptualization: The third movement in experiential learning is called *abstract conceptualization*. Here order is introduced into our experience through the use of abstract concepts that help us make sense out of the experience and our responses to it. Abstract concepts have several sources. Sometimes they are introduced by the experience itself and our reflections on it as we invent appropriate categories to clarify our understanding. On Ash Wednesday evening at Palmdale Presbyterian Church in Melbourne, Florida, my husband and I happened to sit in front of a group of gray-haired women as we prepared for the service of ashes. Conversations were subdued as these long-time members greeted one another and looked over the order of service for the evening. "We never had Ash Wednesday service before Bill Anderson became our pastor," says one woman. "I know," replies her friend. "When I was growing up we thought it was too *Catholic.*" "That's the way I grew up, too," says the first woman. "But, you know, it does make it more *meaningful.*" In just this brief exchange these women engaged in serious reflection on their previous experience of Ash Wednesday and their anticipation of the service to come. They remembered what happened before, at Palmdale Presbyterian and elsewhere, and constructed the conceptual category of "meaningfulness" to name what they knew. While "meaningful" may be an imprecise term, it is, nevertheless, a conceptual construction that contains both the experience and the meaning they made during their reflection.

At other times we draw on concepts from other sources in order to "sort out" our experiences. In the church these abstract concepts come primarily from Scripture and Christian tradition. We continually and systematically study Scripture, the writings of the church, and the wisdom of that great cloud of witnesses in order to put our own experiences into perspective. Scripture and the Christian tradition shed radiant light on our lives and assist us in understanding our present callings. Theological concepts contained in words such as grace, faith, incarnation, redemption, sin, forgiveness, and reconciliation make up the vocabulary of the church. We might, like Bruce, speak about the inward journey and outward journey of the Christian life. The church also borrows selectively from other fields of inquiry, such as psychology, human development, history, and economics, for example, but these other disciplines are always in the service of the gospel of Jesus Christ. Over time congregations develop specialized vocabularies to name their common experience, and members learn to conceptualize experience and to refine their understanding through comparison and contrast with the experience of others, both those sitting beside them and those presented in Scripture and tradition. The meaning of experience becomes clearer as people find ways to name that experience and integrate it into their ongoing lives of faith.

4. Active experimentation: The fourth movement in the cycle of experiential learning is *active experimentation.* Here we embrace a deeper appreciation for previous experience and anticipate a future encounter with similar circumstances. We plan for participation in worship, prayer, and spiritual disciplines. We prepare for engagement in instruction, ministry, mission, and leadership within the church and in the world. We imaginatively project ourselves into the future, set goals, anticipate future circumstances, and plan how we shall respond. We are proactive in preparing for fruitful engagements in future experiences. Breaking bread at the Lord's Table calls many Christians to consider the needs of the hungry. Members of Old Pine joyfully participate in feeding the hungry in their "Saturday for Seniors" program. They enact in their neighborhood a kind of table fellowship that heightens their anticipation for gathering to celebrate communion in the community of faith.

Let's return to Bruce and his description of his life of faith nurtured at West Raleigh. Bruce has had many experiences over the past twelve years but when asked about the most important, without hesitation he names worship, that sanctified, set-apart time when people of all ages and beliefs sing out loud together, as the most important to him and to the church. In his descriptions one can almost reenter the sanctuary on Sunday morning with him. His eyes focus on some indistinct middle distance as his imagination carries him back to the many worship occasions he has experienced. The concrete experience of worship with the whole community of faith has made an indelible mark on his consciousness. As we talk, Bruce has the opportunity to recall, reflect, and begin to discern the meaning of these experiences. He explains their significance using such abstract concepts as "call" and "inward journey and outward journey," which have been learned in the community as a part of their everyday vocabulary of faith. He anticipates his continued participation by promising to give it all he's got. Bruce has "learned" his Christian life through the experience of active participation in the life of the community of faith and through a three-fold pattern of reflection on that experience that allows him to "know" something about himself and his church that he may not have known otherwise. The cycle of experience followed by careful reflection on that experience is one defining characteristic of the culture of West Raleigh Presbyterian Church. This cycle of action and reflection is not a mechanical or programmatic lock-step imposition but is a part of the culture of the congregation. It is natural here for members to ask one another questions that help them focus on the meaning of their experience and to prompt their reflections.

While common worship sets the pattern for all of congregational life, it is not the only concrete experience within the life of a congregation. As in any community, the experience of life together takes many forms and includes multiple times, places, persons, and circumstances. In this study, prayer and spiritual disciplines, study and instruction, ministry and mission, and congregational leadership provide the structure for our exploration of experiential learning in the congregation. In the following chapters we examine these dimensions of congregational life in the light of experiential learning theory. We want to see how renewing congregations engage in the activities of their common life so that the Christian life is learned through the experience of congregational life and renewal in worship goes hand in hand with spiritual renewal within the congregation.

The underlying motivation for reflection on experience in all of its manifestations is the desire to learn from experience. Within the Christian life this desire takes on added importance as congregations and individuals seek to discern the call of God for their lives. Experience and reflection on experience form explicit strategies for spiritual discernment, but more than that, they are practices which, along with other Christian practices, contribute to the spiritual formation of congregations and the persons who inhabit them. The priority for spiritual formation within experiential learning deserves explicit attention, and it is the practice of asking questions that shapes the processes of spiritual formation. Within the pattern of experiential learning, the practice of asking questions initiates, deepens, and propels the cycle, and particular questions are appropriate to each movement in the cycle. When we engage in the practice of asking ourselves and others questions about the Christian life and congregational life, we have the opportunity to break through the "taken-for-granted" nature of our practices and to discern God's presence anew. We shall explore such questions as we go along, but here it is important to say that the inclusion of spiritual formation questions in every phase of the experiential learning cycle is essential. Woven into every dimension, activity, and phase of the church's life is the question "Where is God in this?"

The Concrete Experience of Congregational Life

Concrete experience always exists in the present tense. Human experience begins with the act of being involved in immediate human situations in a personal way. From our earliest moments of life we are immersed in a world of sensation and social interaction, making all experience both personal and communal. Because experience is necessarily restricted to the here-and-now, we "apprehend" experience in an intuitive, artistic way. We perceive experiences as complex wholes, only partially organized and understood, where the interrelationships among the discrete elements of an experience are as important as the elements themselves. We are concerned with the uniqueness and complexity of present reality so that as we proceed through the experience we appreciate its intricacies without necessarily understanding all of them.

It has been said that if one cannot be human alone, neither can one be Christian alone. All human experience is entered into both personally and interpersonally or communally. Our introduction to this interconnected world of experience begins at birth and deepens as we mature. The writers of *Common Fire: Leading Lives of Commitment in a Complex World* put it this way: "Indeed, as our consciousness begins to absorb the daily experience of living in a more complex social world, the dynamic, relational, and interdependent character of all of life becomes increasingly evident, and the ancient debate between nature and nurture reforms itself yet again."[6] In congregations the way social and interpersonal relationships contribute to spiritual formation (or malformation) is particularly discernible. The depth, commitment, intimacy, trust, and endurance of relationships in the congregation contribute substantively to the ability of congregations to engage in intentional spiritual formation. People in the congregations in this study seem comfortable, often eager, to talk together about the Christian spiritual life. They have abandoned a kind of privatized, individual practice of Christian spirituality in favor of shared life in Christ.

The stories, activities, and material objects, as well as the values and commitments that lie behind them, make up the unique culture of each congregation's life. The elements of congregational culture come to expression in the *practices* of the congregation, the particular ways of acting, speaking, and relating that are taken as "natural" for that community. Participation in congregational life is the *concrete experience* through which we learn the Christian life. "The process of coming to faith and growing in the life of faith is fundamentally a process of participation," says Craig Dykstra. "We come to recognize and live in the Spirit as we participate more and more broadly and deeply in communities that know God's love, acknowledge it, express it, and live their lives in light of it. . . . In words that capture an older language, God uses the community of faith as 'means of grace.'"[7]

All of the congregations in this study understand themselves to be "worship centered." Each congregation means something slightly different by that term, but all share the belief that what they do in worship sets the pattern for all of the other practices, activities, programs, and relationships they engage in, both personally and communally. Worship is, says Robert Martin, "an epiphany of the Reign of God."[8] As such it constitutes the experience in congregational life on which all other experiences depend for their form, content, and meaning. Worship provides a paradigmatic pattern of the Christian life but, more than that, worship provides a formative *experience* of that life. We attend to worship the way we attend to all experiences—impressionistically, sensually, personally, and interpersonally—so that we are immersed in its sensibilities without necessarily understanding or analyzing all that is happening. We can revel in the sounds, smells, tastes, touches, and images of worship, delighting in their variety and complexity, absorbing worship's many moods, celebrations, laments, and reconciliations. Later, of course, we shall ponder and seek to understand and learn from our experience. But for now the experience of worship itself invites our full attention.

In the life of a congregation, worship is surrounded by an astonishing array of relationships, encounters, activities, and programs that make up congregational life. The people next to us in worship are often the same people who are next to us in Bible study or in the soup kitchen or in a decision-making body. Congregational life is multidimensional, as many educators and congregational studies specialists have pointed out.[9] As a result of their history, social and cultural context, and their religious heritage, each congregation's culture is unique. The impact of this unique culture is twofold. First, congregational culture takes on a particular shape and content as it gives expression to a congregation's character, values, and worldview. "We've always done it this way," members say. Shared practices, patterns of interaction, stories, and objects used in particular ways give expression to each congregation's culture. At the same time the members of a congregation are themselves shaped by church culture. They receive experiences of congregational life through particular frames of reference that are themselves shaped by the culture of the congregation. Members' expectations, patterns of interaction, belief systems, and ways of understanding are shaped by the culture of the congregation.[10] Thus persons in a particular congregation are spiritually formed in unique ways through participation in that congregation's life.

Remembering and Valuing: Reflective Observation in Congregational Life

Recent years have seen a rising interest in "spirituality" of all sorts. During this same period of time the complexity and pace of most people's lives have increased. The hunger for practices and communities that support spiritual nurture may be in part a response to the very real human need to reflect on and make sense of life's many and varied circumstances. In experiential learning, opportunities for *reflective observation* of concrete experience are essential. During times of reflection we focus on understanding the meaning of situations and ideas by carefully recalling and describing them. Concerns for "practical results" are set aside as we ask, "How did things happen?" "What sights, sounds, smells, actions, and interactions made up the experience?" "What memories, feelings, and emotions were evoked in me and in us during the experience?" "What assumptions are called into question?" "What do we/I wonder about? What are we/I curious about?" "Where is God in this?" This is the time to look at things from fresh perspectives and perhaps relive experiences in order to observe them and describe the possible meanings they contain. The interrelationships among elements within an experience are recalled and described. Descriptions of experiences and the tentative meaning ascribed to those experiences are often quite personal. At this stage of the learning cycle the important activities of description and questioning are given priority. Critique and evaluation are not introduced into reflection at this point. Rather, attention is given to detailed and honest description of events and the emotions and responses they evoke. In the Christian life such moments of reflective observation often come in times of prayer, meditation, and contemplation. Thus nurturing these spiritual disciplines makes up an important element of Christian practice in the congregations described here.

At West Raleigh, where the outreach and mission of the church are under serious consideration and revision, reflection on the life of the congregation has taken on a particularly high-profile position in the consciousness and practice of the community. There are prayer groups, a mission discernment task force, and ongoing practices of personal reflection and discernment, all of which keep the mission of the church in the forefront of their concern. These groups and individuals reflect on the past mission involvements of the church, especially on its commitment to the poor, and cultivate an attitude of open discernment concerning the future missions to which the church is being called. The Mission Formation Group serves as a clearinghouse for emerging mission endeavors, offering support, critique, and when appropriate, funding for projects to which church members feel called. At a recent meeting people gathered for Scripture study and prayer. They were then led in a review and further exploration of a model of mission discernment that has served as a conceptual framework for their work. Then Mary Lee Hall, an elder who lives near the church, began to describe the tension in the neighborhood as a result of differing cultural patterns exhibited by new immigrant neighbors. As Mary Lee and others investigated complaints about trash in the yards, they discovered a number of gaps in the support systems intended to assist these families. Mary Lee had reflected on her experience of friendship with these new neighbors and was happy to have the Mission Formation Group's support in discerning the shape of a possible

mission. She and others used open-ended questions, particularly questions directed toward discerning God's presence in the situation, to understand the experience and set the stage for more learning.

In all of the congregations considered in this study, personal and communal dimensions of the reflective process are distinguishable but not
separable. Individuals nurtured in congregational cultures where reflection on experience was a well-established practice of faith are encouraged
to develop capacities for remembering, describing, and reflecting on
their experiences, particularly experiences of worship. At West Raleigh
many members keep prayer journals and practice contemplative prayer
and *lectio divina*, a pattern of reading and praying with Scripture. (More
will be said about this practice in chapter 4). Wednesday midday prayer
brings members together to pray for people and circumstances that they
also pray for individually. During Sunday worship the prayers of the people are given abundant time (in spite of some low-level grumbling) as
persons and situations are named and prayed for by the assembly. Pastors
Joe and Denise say they consider carefully how to keep the tone of these
prayers from deteriorating into gossip. Rather, they strive to invite the assembly into the presence of God and into one another's lives for the sake
of the working of the Holy Spirit in places of pain and distress, celebration and thanksgiving. In these and many other ways *reflective observation*
of previous experience is nurtured as a spiritual practice.

*Discovering Frames of Understanding: Abstract Conceptualization in
Congregational Life*

The fruit of reflective observation is the construction of abstract concepts—
tentative hypotheses or theories concerning the truth of our experience.
Even children, maybe especially children, construct elaborate theories to
explain what happens to them. At West Raleigh a monthly Sunday evening
"Faith Fest" includes a shared meal, an intergenerational program, and
evening prayer with communion. Alec Peters, the father of a very active little boy, says that when John Walker was two years old he received communion for the first time. Alec and Sarah had been nurturing John Walker
toward the Table since he was born, on Sunday mornings and at Faith Fest
celebrations, but whenever they asked if he wanted to receive communion
John Walker said, "No." On this particular evening John Walker was especially restless and distracted, but when time came to go forward to receive
communion, he said he wanted to go. As they stood in line Alec whispered
some questions to John Walker in order to remind him of their previous

conversations about communion. "John Walker, do you remember that we've talked about communion before? Do you remember what we've said?" The little boy seemed intent on taking in all that was going on around him and paid no attention to Alec's questions. Finally, after his dad had repeated the questions a couple of times, John Walker answered impatiently, "Yes, Daddy! I know! It's Jesus' bread and he wants me to have some!" John Walker's experience and the teachings of the church came together in a conceptual understanding of communion just right for a two-year-old.

Reflection on experience gives rise to a kind of careful analysis and a somewhat more systematic assessment of the meaning of experience. From our earliest encounters in the community of faith, we have been heirs of the fruit of such conceptualizations and have often been nurtured in the process of formulating concepts for ourselves.

A diagram of the process of reflection at West Raleigh might look something like figure 2.[11]

Figure 2

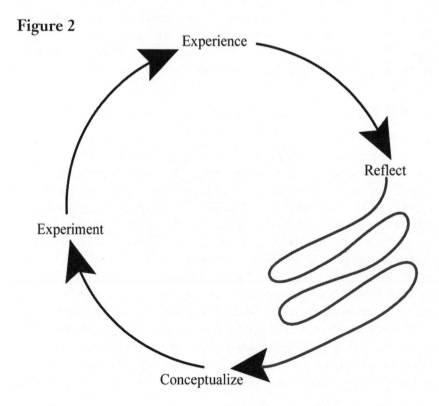

As aspects of experience are recalled, described, and reflected on and as meanings are ascribed to the experience, there is a movement from experience to reflection to conceptualization and back again. The process is complex and multilayered as the surplus of meaning within experience is unfolded and carefully considered. No one reflective insight is given privilege over another, as the priorities of hospitable participation for all and theological focus inform the whole process. Within this process implicit assumptions are made explicit and are available for examination, validation, and/or critique.

In instructional settings the process of learning may *begin* with abstract conceptualization. Teachers often present sets of abstract concepts and introduce learners to ways of conceptualizing that are new to them. In order for these unfamiliar ways of conceptualizing to become incorporated into learners' ways of understanding, a process of comparison, contrast, and integration with previous experience is necessary. At West Raleigh, for example, when the model of discernment was introduced by staff person Fran Albro, members of the Mission Formation Group were encouraged to compare their own experience of discernment with the model and to note the ways it reflected or did not reflect their own experience. Conversations then included consideration of the group's understanding of previous experience and of the model itself. Fran encouraged a kind of questioning and exploration that allowed group members to understand the model of discernment, critique their own experience, and embrace a flexible meeting of the two.

The process of abstract conceptualization is both personal and communal. Our hypotheses about the meaning of our experiences must necessarily be compared with the experiences and reflections of others and evaluated according to theological and other criteria. One function of the community of faith is participation in the collaborative process of articulating as clearly as possible what the community believes, what it is called to be, and what it is called to do. Each member of a congregation is called, by virtue of baptism, to participate in the articulation of the community's beliefs and callings.

Of course congregations are not left on their own to figure out Christian faith from scratch. The church of Jesus Christ exists within a mighty stream of theological reflection contained in Scripture, creeds, art, poetry, music, architecture, and other resources that serve as wellsprings for our own articulation of Christian faith. These resources are at our disposal to inform, support, and correct our personal and communal reflections. Likewise, the unique circumstances of our own lives call forth new insights that become our gifts to the ongoing conversation of Christian faith. We all have insights and points of view that are important to the shape of the whole community. At the same time no one set of ideas or formulation of theological concepts is sufficient to articulate the fullness of Christian faith. Scripture and other writings interact and inform our experience in such a way that our participation in conversations which aim to discern the "big picture" of Christian faith is always personal and communal. We need the collaborative and disciplining conversations of the Christian community in order to conform congregational faith and practice to the mind of Christ.

Abstraction, the statement of ideas in symbols, gives us the ability to take a step back and critically evaluate the "truth" of the ideas, the symbols used to express them, and their relative completeness in light of the experiences that gave rise to them. The precision and coherence of theological proposals become central criteria for both modifying and embracing the ideas contained in them. At West Raleigh the Mission Formation Group has been studying Scripture together and has sought out other ancient and contemporary resources on the subject of discernment. All of these resources have been used in light of the congregation's experiences of being in mission in the city of Raleigh and elsewhere. In this way their insights into their experiences have been shaped by conceptual frameworks drawn from Scripture and other sources.

The process of abstract conceptualization is initiated and energized by asking questions of our experience and our reflections on experience. These questions include "How might we 'explain' our experience?" "What does Scripture have to say about such experiences?" "What can we learn from the church through the ages and around the globe?" "Whose voices have we not heard?" "What would those who disagree with us say?" and "What might psychology, sociology, education, economics, or some other theory have to say?" Always the church must ask, "Where is God in this?"

Putting Learning to the Test: Active Experimentation in Congregational Life

Christian faith is not a contemplative faith only, though Presbyterians have sometimes been described as worshiping from the neck up. Soon enough we must ask ourselves the questions "If we understand God to be doing this . . . how shall we respond? How can we join in what God is doing?" Active experimentation includes all of the necessary planning and preparation for renewed participation in worship, congregational life, and mission where our biblical, theological, spiritual, and practical hypotheses will be tested in the real world. Here the community relies on problem solving and decision making as they work out the practical application of their renewed understandings of the gospel. Questions that help to guide movement from abstract conceptualization to active experimentation include "What difference do the insights gained from reflection and conceptualization make? If we take these insights seriously, what will need to change?" "Where do we discern God's call to renewed engagement in prayer, instruction, mission, leadership, etc.?" "What will prepare us spiritually for renewed engagement?" "How should we plan and prepare for renewed engagement?" "What resources and expertise do we need?" "What resources and expertise do we have?" "How should we organize, train, rehearse, prepare?" "Where is God in this?"

Learning here is action oriented as the circumstances of the present situation are considered and energy is directed toward preparation for active engagement in action on a new level. The community is not the same as it was when it last gathered for worship or prayer or instruction or mission. It has been changed by its experience and reflection and by its fresh conceptualization of the gospel in light of its experience and reflection. The preparation we undertake is necessarily experimental. Those who say, "We've never done it this way before" are right! We have changed and the way we see the world has changed. Our preparation is active because it has the real world of congregational life, family life, and community life in view. We continue to live in a real world even as we are converted, increasingly conformed to the likeness of Christ.

At Northminster Presbyterian Church in Seattle, Washington, most of the members of this congregation of under two hundred are involved in feeding and housing six to eight homeless, mentally ill adults. Four nights a week, every week, members of Northminster and other nearby churches provide transportation to the church for their guests, prepare and share a meal with them, listen, talk, play games, and offer companionship, and then provide transportation to another nearby church where the guests will sleep. In rotating teams they set up, prepare food, offer hospitality, drive, and stay overnight with their guests in ways that inspire the guests to say they are "at home" in Northminster church. Almost everyone in this congregation participates in some aspect of the ministry. Homebound members do telephone scheduling. The youth group, says associate pastor Karen Breckenridge, is enthusiastic about its relationships with the guests and is disappointed when their turn to prepare the meal and extend hospitality has to be rescheduled for some reason. These members plan, prepare, and reflect on their ministry as they continue to grapple with questions of how God is calling them. The God whom they worship together calls them, they know, and so they reach out to those in need, knowing that in the process they will be changed. Thus they continue to worship, practice spiritual disciplines, and study Scripture in order to discern more clearly the presence of God in their relationships with their guests.

Constructing Mental Models

According to learning theorist David Kolb, "Learning is *the* major process of human adaptation. This concept of learning is considerably broader than that commonly associated with the school classroom. It occurs in all human settings, from schools to the workplace, from the research laboratory to the management board room, in personal relationships and the aisles of the local grocery. It encompasses all life stages, from childhood to adolescence, to middle and old age."[12] Kolb goes on to claim that experiential learning is so pervasive that it brings together such concepts as creativity, problem solving, decision making, and attitude change, each of which tends to focus on only one aspect of adaptation.

What is actually going on in experiential learning? Learning theorists have answered this question in various ways, but most point to the evidence for learning as a process of constructing "mental models."[13] As a result of innumerable experiential learning experiments starting in infancy, humans establish particular patterns for understanding and responding to the world. The process is a continuous one where each experience builds on and elaborates what has been learned from previous experiences. John Dewey maintains that "the principle of continuity of experience means that every experience both takes up something from those which have gone before and modifies in some way the quality of those which come after."[14] In this way particular mental models, what learning theorists call "cognitive structures," are constructed around particular categories of meaning.

Learning is a holistic process of adaptation to the world. Thus learning is not confined to the acquisition of information or accumulation of knowledge but includes all aspects of human engagement with the world. As Kolb puts it, "to learn is not the special province of a single specialized realm of human functioning such as cognition or perception. It involves the integrated functioning of the total organism—thinking, feeling, perceiving, and behaving."[15] It is impossible to separate our thinking from our perceptions or our emotions from our decisions to act. While we may, in particular settings and for specified reasons, take on an "objectivist" viewpoint, humans necessarily function as integrated organisms. We have learned from physicists, for example, that even the most careful scientific experiments have embedded within them the heartfelt commitments of the scientists who design them. In becoming Christian persons, then, our approaches must include a holistic understanding of human learning and appropriately call on all our human faculties for adaptation to the world.

In experiential learning we begin with concrete experience, but as many have pointed out, we never encounter the world "raw" or uninterpreted. All our sensory experiences and perceptions are filtered and shaped by the meaning we have constructed from previous experience. Our mental models take the form of "meaning perspectives"[16] and give us an already-established point of view through which we perceive and interpret each new experience. These meaning perspectives influence the way our attention is focused, what we concentrate on, and what we ignore, thus shaping the way we perceive and understand what happens around us. In order to make sense of the world, we use a "meaning that we have already made to guide the way we think, act, or feel about what we are currently experiencing."[17] Recall how we overheard Ash Wednesday worshipers at the Palmdale church describe their experience as "meaningful." The practice of receiving ashes on Ash Wednesday had once seemed "too Catholic" to these women, but through the experience of the rite and reflection on that experience, Ash Wednesday has become "meaningful" to them. Even though this term relays no specific content, we understand that the experience means something memorable or important. It is clear that the process of meaning making is inseparable from experience itself and that it involves the whole person.

Meaning perspectives have a variety of characteristics and come from several sources. Some mental models are focused on particular experiences, ideas, or activities and include specific interpretations of these things. Other meaning perspectives are more inclusive and are made up of several related domains of meaning. The unique shape of each person's cognitive structures comes from a complex set of interactions among his or her way of learning, the surrounding culture, and the individual's psychological makeup. Thus each person exhibits a unique point of view and style of interacting with the world. Nevertheless, people with a lot in common, say the same family or hometown or culture, share many commonalities in their cognitive structures. The full array of our meaning perspectives, both perspectives that are shared and perspectives that are unique to the individual, come together to form a "worldview."

Most of the time cognitive structures function at a preconscious level so that we are largely unaware of the ways they shape our ongoing experience of the world, our "collective absolute presuppositions."[18] Unless some perplexing encounter forces the question, we operate in a more or less common-sense mode, wherein our interpretations of the world go unnoticed. Cognitive structures can be few or many. They can be intricately interconnected into a cohesive worldview or loosely related, even compartmentalized, into several distinctive worldviews. Cognitive structures can be flexible and open to the integration of new learning, or they can be rigid and resistant to any adaptation or reconstruction.[19] In congregational life, where many worldviews interact, one of the tasks of Christian conversion is the progressive, continued reorientation of the congregation's worldview toward a theocentric worldview. The congregations described here strive faithfully to be oriented toward God in such a way that members can discern God's presence and action in the world.

At Immanuel church in Tacoma, Washington, pastor Paul Galbreath admits that he says the same thing every Sunday. "There are a few things I say every week one way or another. One is that God's grace extends to all people." Paul also centers his preaching on Scripture and the sacraments as significant focal points for encounter with God, whether or not the sacraments are being celebrated on a particular Lord's Day. "The more people absorb the fact that this isn't *our* Table, it's not *our* liturgy, it's not *our* blessing that we extend to people, even when there are disagreements; the more people live into that, we create an environment where everyone can be included." The experience of worship and the categories of meaning that are pervasively present there create within the congregation a shared worldview of grace and inclusion through the presence of Christ in Word and sacrament. The cognitive structures constructed through experience and reflection on that experience make up sets of shared expectations and perceptions through which these Christians see the world.

There are those who seem unaware that the taken-for-granted meaning perspectives by which they organize their lives are available for reflection. When this is the case, it has been said that rather than *having* beliefs, people *are* their beliefs. When we are unaccustomed to reflecting on the patterns and beliefs that shape our experience, the process can seem threatening. Reflection as called for in experiential learning serves to help us gain some distance from our experiences so we can examine them somewhat critically. It is not surprising that some people should find this difficult or threatening. According to Jack Mezirow, all reflection involves a critique.[20] Reflection involves an intentional reassessment of prior learning in light of new experience in order to identify and correct distortions in our understanding. In this way we are able either to reestablish the validity of what we know to be important, just, relevant, truthful, and authentic, or to come to some new understanding.

In order for reflection to be effective in this way, the implicit assumptions that help to shape our meaning perspectives and mental models must be made explicit and examined. Before this process can be undertaken by most people, they must feel safe. They must be assured that both their beliefs and their selfhood will be respected and treated with care in order to engage those beliefs in an even mildly critical manner. This is especially true when one's identity is closely linked with particular beliefs and practices. For some these conversations can be somewhat academic and take on the character of temporary "thought experiments." For others they seem to be matters of life and death, being and nonbeing. (If I question and perhaps give up this belief within which I have understood my most basic identity, who will I be? Or will I "be" at all?)

Psychologists call such a trustworthy setting a "holding environment," a place where persons can be supported, where their needs are met, and where their concerns are given consistent respect. At the same time a "good enough" holding environment provides appropriate challenge and critique so that new circumstances are faced with energy and courage.[21] The tasks of the holding environment, according to Robert Kegan, are to provide adequate support suitable to our need, to release us to explore new circumstances and ways of being, and to remain "in place" as a home to which we can return in a new state of maturity.[22] As with children, there is a time to hold and a time to let go, a time to support, and a time to challenge. Church leaders must develop this sensitivity as they help persons and congregations confront existing meaning perspectives and the assumptions that inform them.

As we have said, the process of reflection is critical, full of questioning and reconsideration of accustomed patterns of perceiving, thinking, and acting. But rather than being negative, it is essentially a constructive process with an eye always toward faithfulness to the gospel and human flourishing. Christians have called this process by various names— conversion, sanctification, growing into the likeness of Christ. While educators may provide helpful terminology and procedural details for the process, the congregations described here enter into these natural learning processes with spiritual nurture and Christian faithfulness clearly in view. They also understand their faith to be in God who created heaven and earth, not in their naturally limited ways of articulating that faith. Many beginning seminarians, in anticipation of just such a critical process of examining faith, have been warned not to let seminary "destroy your faith." In a similar way, if the critical reflection necessary for learning from experience serves only to dismantle existing meaning perspectives, it is an unfaithful approach and should be abandoned. Reflection that gives emphasis to critique without a complementary move toward constructing meaning perspectives that are faithful to the gospel would be a most inadequate implementation of experiential learning. Rather, through shared reflection, critique, study, and renewed participation in congregational life, congregations can work together to build one another up in faith and love.

The Culture of Experiential Learning in Congregational Life

For the sake of clarity I have described the four-part experiential learning cycle sequentially, showing how experience naturally leads to reflective observation, conceptualization, and preparation for renewed action. But as any member of a congregation knows, congregational life does not follow such a prescribed pattern. Congregational life is complex, multidimensional, interactive, and multilayered. No learning theory (or any other theory) can tidy up its natural "messiness," and this is probably a good thing. Nevertheless, the basic patterns and practices of learning through experience and reflection can serve to help congregations orient themselves around the defining *practices* of Christian faith. Communities throughout the ages have centered their lives on encounter with God in worship, prayer and spiritual disciplines, study and instruction, and participation in mission and ministry. In addition there are those called out to exercise leadership in the congregation, an experiential practice that also calls for reflection. These practices happen to reflect the movements of the experiential learning cycle.

I have argued from the beginning that the experience of encounter with God in worship sets the pattern for all other aspects of congregational life. In worship-centered congregations, opportunities for *reflection* on encounter with God come most often in practices of prayer and spiritual disciplines. Study and instruction provide opportunities for *forming concepts*, striving for more systematic clarity concerning the Christian life.

Ministry and mission involvement are places where Christians naturally *experiment*. They put into practice what they know about God, themselves, and the world. Congregational leaders have an awareness of the congregation as a whole, a kind of *metacognition* that enables them to discern the contours of the congregation's experience of encounter with God and the various kinds of reflection the congregation undertakes.

Worship is not the only experience within congregational life, and it is certainly not the only experience that calls for serious reflection in all of its forms. Practices of prayer and spiritual discipline in which we recall and reflect on encounter with God, themselves become *experiences* on which we are called to *reflect, form concepts*, and *experiment*, moving ever more deeply into relationship with God. Study and instruction draw us into experiences of learning that then require us to reflect, form concepts, and experiment with new ways of learning and understanding. Participation in mission is an experience of many congregations that may most often call for reflection, concept formation, and further experimentation. On the other hand, leadership may be one of the practices of congregational life where learning from experience is often least valued (unless, of course, you include the parking-lot "meeting after the meeting" as reflection on the experience of leadership). Congregations in this study recognize leadership in many of its degrees and manifestations, and invite serious reflection, concept formation, and experimentation among teachers, committee members, trustees, worship planners and leaders, choir members, kitchen helpers, circle leaders, and many more. The "messiness" of experiential learning in congregational life is represented by the diagram in figure 3.

I have tried to clarify how experiential learning seems to work in worship-centered congregations. But let me be clear about what I am *not* suggesting. I am not suggesting that rigid cycles of experiential learning need to be established in all aspects of congregational life. Rather, this study attempts to describe ways in which these patterns and practices are naturally present in the culture of thriving, worship-centered congregations. These congregations naturally engage in practices that demonstrate their belief that experience has value and that communal reflection on experience is a natural part of the Christian life. To say it another way, it is *not* the patterns of experiential learning that form the structure of these congregations' worship-centered life. Rather, it is the congregational culture that centers its life on worship, prays and reflects on its common life, values intellectual curiosity and questioning, and risks its life in ministry and mission that demonstrates its understanding of learning through participation. Learning to live

Figure 3

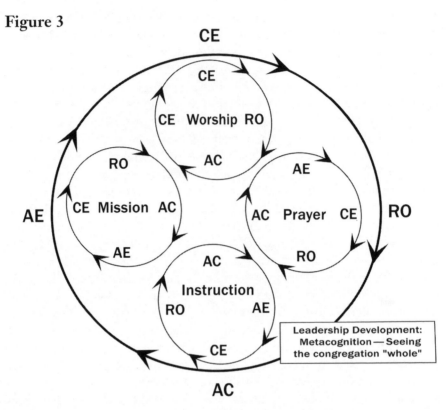

The worship of God is the Concrete Experience (CE) that sets the pattern for the Christian life and is the focal point of congregational life. Reflective Observation (RO) often takes place in prayer and spiritual disciplines. Abstract Conceptualization (AC) often takes place during study and instruction. Active Experimentation (AE) often takes place during participation in ministry and mission activities. Reflection on the *concrete experience* of congregational leadership can lead to a kind of metacognition, seeing the congregation "whole."

Christianly in the world is a participatory, experiential process, and congregations are the locus of that learning.

In addition to requiring opportunities for worship, prayer and spiritual disciplines, study and instruction, ministry and mission, and leadership, experiential learning in the congregation requires three further ingredients: enduring relationships, a climate of questioning, and a vocabulary for naming the many dimensions of the Christian spiritual life. The congregations described here all exhibit levels of intimacy in relationships that go beyond everyday social expectations. With Christian spiritual maturity in mind and committed relationships as the norm, members are not shy about calling on one another in order to discern God's presence and leading. They often ask one another, "Where do you see God in this situation?" These congregations are places of lively "wonder," posing frequent questions to one another as they seek to discern God's leading. And these congregations have developed over time a rich "native language" based on their experience and reflection. A vocabulary of faith permeates their conversations and enables them to name their experience and to reflect critically on it.

Immanuel Presbyterian Church in Tacoma has an excellent music program, and Bob Arpke has sung in the church's choir for sixty-five years, beginning when he was in his teens. "I'm not sure how good a church person I would have been without the choir," he says. "It's been the key to coming back week after week." The church is full of loving, caring people, according to Bob. Even when the church has gone through difficult times, "we stick together, through fat and lean, thick and thin." For Bob, when times of unbelief came, as they come to everyone, those relationships provided the necessary support for him to raise difficult questions and search for new understanding. Relationships of depth, commitment, trust, endurance, and intimacy are a prerequisite for asking probing questions and exposing long-held assumptions. In congregations where individuals come to know one another through common worship and ministry, engaging together in experience and reflection, relationships emerge that can provide an environment for courageously facing difficulties and for celebrating deeply. Within the culture of the congregation is a level of intimacy that welcomes a communal spiritual life. The manner of conversation and interpersonal engagement in these congregations moves well beyond the superficial or well-mannered. In these congregations a climate of spiritual expectation and intellectual curiosity is pervasive. There are frequent occasions where it is natural to ask questions and share one's doubts and discernments. These congregations are the "holding environment" where critical reflection on one's most deeply held beliefs can be undertaken and where faith can be renewed through the support and challenge of the community.

The process of shared exploration into all aspects of the Christian life gives rise to a robust vocabulary of faith, a rich "native language" of terms that name various aspects of the Christian spiritual life. As this vocabulary emerges within a congregation, it enriches the congregation's power to spiritually form its members. We have already noted how at West Raleigh terms like "call," "discernment," and "spiritual journey" have been used by members to name their experience of God's presence in their lives and have shaped the communal response of the congregation to those in need. As one element of the reflection and conceptualization process, words like these serve to shape cognitive structures and frameworks for perception and understanding. Many have noted the recent erosion of biblical literacy and with it the nuanced language of Christian faith. Such a language seems necessary in order for Christians symbolically to envision their life in God. Joe Ward, pastor at West Raleigh, says his introduction of such a vocabulary was intentional. "I wasn't willing for the fundamentalists to have all the good words," he says. As a result some words in the West Raleigh vocabulary are new, arising out of shared experience and study. Other elements in their vocabulary represent a "rehabilitation" of classic Christian expressions that have been subject to uncritical distortion in recent decades.

These three elements—relationships, question asking, and a vocabulary of faith—along with worship of God, prayer and spiritual disciplines, study and instruction, and mission and ministry, make up a set of practices that distinguish the congregations described here. The cultures of these congregations, distinctively marked by these practices, contribute to the lively, energetic, serious, and faithful Christian witness incarnated in their communities.

Part II

Congregational Practices

Chapter Three

How Congregations Worship

Shortly before his retirement from Eleanore Presbyterian Church in Eleanore, West Virginia, pastor Frank McCraven, his face glowing with gratitude, told me this story. When he first came to Eleanore some eight years before, he introduced participatory prayers into the service—prayers said by everyone or prayers said by a leader with responses from the whole congregation. Before the introduction of this new pattern, the pastor's voice had been the only voice of prayer for the congregation. Frank encouraged the congregation to try the pattern of shared prayer for three months, after which time the congregation's leaders would evaluate its use in worship. At the end of the three months, Frank waited anxiously to hear what the church's "patriarch" would have to say, knowing that the congregation would follow his lead. "Now I can pray, too," said this patient saint. "Now I can participate." Like faithful pastors everywhere, Frank took the experience of worship for his congregation seriously, and he knew that experience in worship that is formative begins with "full, conscious, active participation."[1]

Humans are pattern-seeking, storytelling, meaning making beings who hunger for communities and practices that support this natural impulse to reflect on and make sense of life's many and varied circumstances. Anthropologists tell us that among all the levels of meaning—which they name as information, metaphor, and participation—the highest level is participation.[2] So it should not surprise us that from the smallest churches to the largest, participation in worship is a natural practice. Liturgy naturally carries out two functions simultaneously. It both shapes *and* expresses a worshiping community's deepest beliefs and affections toward God, toward one another, and toward the world. In this chapter we shall explore the many dimensions of the practice of worship as it gives expression to the faith of congregations and, at the same time, forms them, we hope more faithfully, into the body of Christ. This dual effect of expression and shaping constitutes the experience of congregational life that is the concern of this book.

As we noted in the previous chapter, liturgical theologians refer to this participatory, embodied communal activity of the believing assembly as *primary liturgical theology*. According to Gordon Lathrop,

> The meaning of the liturgy resides first of all in the liturgy itself. If the gathering has a meaning for us, if it says an authentic thing about God and our world—indeed, if it brings us face to face with God—then that becomes known while we are participating in the gathering. The liturgical vision engages us while the order of actions flows over us and while we ourselves perform the patterns and crises of this public work. The liturgy itself is primary theology. . . . Primary liturgical theology is the communal meaning of the liturgy exercised by the gathering itself.[3]

Take, for example, the Latrobe congregation as it celebrates Pentecost. It is obvious that the day is a special day. There is an air of festive excitement throughout the church, and all—children, youth, and adults—are wearing red. A procession of banners, red balloons, choir members, ministers, and the whole congregation forms in the sanctuary's gathering space. Music—sometimes celebratory, sometimes mysterious—leads the people into worship and supports their worship of the God who dwells with us through the Holy Spirit, given on this day. After worship the celebration continues with birthday cake, conversation, and lots of laughter in the fellowship hall.

As these Christians enact the stories of their faith, in this case the story of the coming of the Holy Spirit at Pentecost, they express their awareness of the Spirit's presence in their own lives and their gratitude to God. At the same time that their discernment of and orientation toward God's presence is deepened, their capacity for gratitude is expanded. Thus the communally enacted celebration of Pentecost both shapes and expresses their faith. It is *primary liturgical theology*, to use Lathrop's term, because it flows over participants in enacted patterns and proclaimed vision.

Worshipers often ask *what* liturgy means, a necessary and important question that we will take up later. Fred Holper reorients the question when he suggests that an equally important approach is to ask *how* liturgy means. Worship, he says,

> invite[s] the whole person and the whole community to participate in a symbolic journey of discovery. Thus, the rites for Baptism and Renewal of the Baptismal Covenant bid us to "grow into our baptism," to explore how baptism means to a child, how baptism means to a couple who will follow Christ in the particular relationship of marriage, how baptism means to those whose life has been changed by disease, divorce or disability, how baptism means for those facing death.[4]

As thickly symbolic communal enactments—complex juxtapositions of words and gestures to the assembly's own presence and participation—the worship of the church has meaning that can never be exhausted. *How does worship mean?* Worship means in a multilayered, complex, communally enacted and symbolic way that can be known first of all through participation and then supported by reflection on that participation.

The Experience of Worship

Worship-centered congregations take experience, especially the experience of worship, seriously. These congregations know that when they are formed in the likeness of Christ, the people of God are responding to "a totally embodied religious experience and religious vision."[5] Their attentiveness to all the aspects of worship is intended to invite the gathered community into such an experience, an invitation that arises out of their own deep and heartfelt response to the presence of God among them. Worship engages people as whole beings—body, mind, and affections. Worship engages their natural social and relational nature. Worship invites people into the ancient and ongoing story of the people of God. But most of all, worship enlivens the imagination in ways that make the presence of God vividly discernable. In the following pages we shall examine each of these experiential domains: *physical/sensory, affective, narrative, cognitive, social, relational,* and *imaginative.*

Worship is not only given depth and detail by its many inherent juxtapositions; it is also experienced simultaneously on many levels of human receptivity and understanding. You will recall from the previous chapter how the pattern of experience and reflection, when represented in diagram form, contains many U-turns, detours of thought wherein a single experience is considered and reconsidered from many different perspectives. The dimensions of experience listed above represent some of the opportunities for reflective detours as the people of God continue to learn the Christian life from the experience of congregational life, beginning with the experience of worship.

The Physical/Sensory Dimension

A famous Norman Rockwell painting features a family walking to church, dressed in prim finery, through a rough and tumble neighborhood where the remnants of Saturday night stand in sharp contrast to Sunday morning. This painting always reminds me of the sheer physical nature of "going to church." This family has engaged in a lot of physical activity in order to prepare themselves for worship. They are scrubbed and starched and polished, and their act of walking together toward the church is full of physical energy. The embodiment of worship begins with our preparations for gathering as the worshiping assembly, but it surely does not end there. My colleague Ron Byars says that "the exercise of our 'royal priesthood' (I Peter 2:9) does not take place only within the mind, but also requires engagement of the whole self, body as well as soul."[6] Every congregation has a particular way of enacting its worship of God. According to Don Saliers, "Each element of a service of worship is 'performed' in a specific manner. . . . Congregations have tacit understandings of what constitutes integrity and authenticity in the 'realization' of the texts."[7]

Our physical and sensory participation is complex. There is, of course, the visible bodily activity involved in participation, some of which is conscious and volitional while other elements are unconscious or spontaneous. In addition, and maybe more important, is the simultaneous inner sensation of physical activity, inseparable from bodily activity but at the same time distinct from it. Harold Daniels describes these aspects of human personhood well.

> The human person is a soul, a spirit, a body, a mind, a wonderful complex of physical and spiritual realities. There is an inseparable relationship between gesture and our inner feelings and attitudes. In gesture, posture, and action we express our deepest feelings. We clasp another's hand in expressing warmth in greeting. We embrace another in showing affection. Furthermore, we know that the body often communicates more truthfully than one's lips. Since gesture,

posture, and action involve our whole being, they reinforce and intensify our attitudes and can even evoke feelings within us.[8]

The consequences for liturgy are, of course, significant, given that worship is an enacted, communal affair where all aspects of human participation presume physical presence and participation. "We pray with the
body as well as with our lips and minds," says Daniels.[9] The combination
of external and internal, conscious and unconscious components of physical activity requires sustained reflection in order to discern the deeper
meanings they may contain. In addition, they combine with other elements of participation and add to the complexity of human experience.
Thus reflection on worship becomes all the more important.

The sacraments of baptism and Eucharist are occasions for a congregation's thorough physical and sensory participation whereby they can be
continually formed in the likeness of Christ. Ellen Charry writes of meeting a woman who said she "became a Christian because she needed a God
she could eat, take into herself and be continuously transformed by."[10]
Charry reminds us that "sacraments are concrete actions by which Christians may be marked, fed and touched by the Holy Spirit so that the reality of God and the work of Christ become embedded in the body and
psyche."[11] Thus the embodied practices of the congregation have formative as well as expressive significance for worshipers.

During the Reformation, when much of the ceremonial gesture of
worshipers and leaders was abandoned, the criteria for whether or not
such practices ought to be included in worship was, according to John
Calvin, whether or not they led people to Christ. "Ceremonies, to be exercises of piety, ought to lead us straight to Christ."[12] The congregations
in this study are careful in their use of bodily gesture and other physical
elements of participation. Many say that the inclusion of new practices
has stretched them to understand their faith in new ways. At Immanuel
church in Tacoma during mid-week Lenten communion, participants
form a circle around the Lord's Table and offer the elements to one another with the words "The bread of life; the cup of salvation." This act of
taking and offering, eating and drinking together has marked this community with the reality of God's presence among them. Eucharistic generosity shapes their life together and their care for the community in
which they live. They and those to whom they minister are "led to
Christ" by their sacramentally formed lives. At a recent session meeting,
during the worship committee report, personal responses to these weekly
communion services make their way into the conversation. "It wasn't too

long ago we only had communion once every three months," comments one elder. "This is quite a welcome change." "I like saying the words 'The bread of life; the cup of salvation,'" says another. "When we use the bread that is broken [rather than pre-cut] you can't miss the meaning," comments someone else. "There is a deeper level of participation when we come forward, when we exchange the words and the bread and the cup. That is a really important part of sharing communion." These elders, the most vocal of whom are middle-aged and older men, are aware of how all of their senses and their physical presence are involved in the way they give and receive communion. They participate physically but also spiritually in ways that are new and exciting to them.

The Affective Dimension

Though it is not always apparent in the practice of some mainline Protestant churches, human experience always brings with it an affective dimension. Brain researchers tell us that all our thoughts and physical sensations are routed first through a part of the brain that governs the emotions.[13] According to Fred Edie,

> emotion is increasingly understood as both integral and essential to human knowing and acting, and by extension, to human social interaction and moral life. Further, the role of emotion in memory is increasingly well-understood; especially the ways in which the affective tonality of recalled experience shapes the ways persons lean into the future. Finally, emotion is also increasingly framed within the context of relationality; that is, not as a discrete self-contained experience of the individual but as a response which resonates with (and elicits responses from) others in the environment.[14]

Liturgy "moves" people. "Liturgy elicits from God's people a broad sweep of emotion, from ecstasies of praise to the sorrows of lamentation. Its power is a visceral 'felt' power in the hearts and bodies of those who practice it."[15] But attention to liturgy's natural affective component is not manipulative. Rather it is, as Don Saliers points out, a natural schooling of the affections toward love of God and neighbor. "There is no religious life without our being profoundly affected: doctrine without experience is empty; religious experience without doctrine is blind."[16]

Worship-centered congregations recognize the importance of the affective dimension of worship and give particular attention to it in their enactment of worship. And because worship both shapes and expresses religious commitments, these congregations are wise to attend carefully to the affective tone of their gatherings for worship. At Covenant Presbyterian in Palo Alto, California, pastor Isaiah Jones is leading the congregation into patterns of worship that include a broader range of emotional expression, and he is doing it in a way that helps worshipers find their own levels of comfort. "I look for things that are familiar and take them to a new level," he says.

When we speak of religious affections and their necessary inclusion in the practice of worship, we are not speaking of shallow sentiments nor expressions of emotionalism. Rather, we have in mind the deeper dispositions and contours of character that are made apparent through a person's actions, perceptions, and feelings over time. "The principal point," says Saliers, "is that in the moral and religious life, we are more accountable for what we *are* than for what we immediately feel. . . . What we *are* in our intentions and actions, is more adequately revealed by referring to the dispositions which constitute a 'sense' of the heart than by referring to what we feel or what ideas we have at the time."[17] Thus it is that participation in worship "schools the affections," the deepest commitments of heart and life, through encounter with God in the midst of the community. Sometimes gradually, sometimes suddenly, our character is shaped through repeated encounters with God in worship.

In order for this to be the case, however, our coming before God must include a kind of spiritual honesty that surpasses the polite decorum of many kinds of public gatherings. Joining in worship is a gathering of an altogether different sort, where nothing but the truth of our lives will do. Walter Brueggemann observes that "very many people have the impression that it is 'meet, right and our bounded duty' to pretend that life does not hurt. That is correlated to a false notion of God who does not traffic in grief, rage, and pain. . . . In a society of cover-up and denial, the liturgic practice of honesty can permit new vitality in the community and in communion with God."[18]

Denise Thorpe says that in worship at West Raleigh there is an emerging honesty, discernable in the prayers of the people. Whereas in the past various groups in the church came together to form a loosely knit "confederacy" of particular interests, the congregation is beginning to see itself as one congregation. "There were these groups within the church that got along well but had very different interests and commitments. The reason everybody got along is they didn't get close enough to disagree. Everybody knew that if you got too close you would disagree. That was a fear." As the church has become more spiritually centered and has sought to integrate all parts of its life around the centrality of worship, there has emerged a greater willingness to discuss areas of disagreement and, at times, agree to disagree. "I find myself continuing to say it is okay to talk about these things and to disagree about them because of what holds us together. It isn't our politeness. What binds us together is the love of God made known to us in Jesus Christ, and that's really what the church is all about. That is our foundation and we can trust that. We can trust it so much that we can be honest." The centrality of worship and a communal life of prayer shape all that the congregation is and does. "Our orientation in everything that we do comes from the life of the Spirit, from our understanding of who we are, a people claimed by God. It begins with our worship together. Our ministry and mission are shaped first of all there. Then our ministry actions and other decisions come back in and shape our life of worship and prayer. A lot of this has been forged in our struggle, in the places where conflict and struggle emerged, and were then surrounded by worship and prayer."

The Narrative Dimension

Many have noted that in the Jewish tradition, when children ask questions, their questions are often answered with a story. During the Passover Seder meal when the child asks, "Why is this night different from all other nights?" the answer comes in the form of the narrative recounting of slavery in Egypt, God's triumphant leading out and the forming of the people of Israel in the deserts of Sinai, and their arrival in the promised homeland. Likewise, Christians are a story-formed people,[19] formed after the likeness of Jesus Christ through the continual remembrance of his life, death, and resurrection. Week by week the story of God's way with humankind in Scripture and history is woven together with the congregational, family, and personal stories of a community of faith. In this way the lives of worshipers become part of a larger narrative, especially the narrative of Scripture. Community and identity are established by means of shared stories, common memories of who we are and to whom we belong. Thus we are called into the "communal memory of those gathered about the font, the book, and the table."[20]

As any good storyteller knows, stories have a way of imaginatively involving hearers in the plot and action of the story. Listeners enter into the world of the story in ways that allow them to share the experience of the characters. Especially with God's people, their stories, told and retold in the church, become "our story" as we become God's people, too. "We experience salvation for our time by remembering and reencountering the Story of God's saving deeds," says Thomas Groome. "When we remind God and ourselves of the Story, it is as if even God cannot but be moved by the memory, and for us it becomes a saving 'event' once more."[21] The biblical story becomes our story as we experience the saving acts of God and take our place alongside others who have gone before us.

Storytelling of any kind has a remarkable way of weaving together the past, the present, and the future. Through the stories of faith, Christians can remember a shared and treasured past, can orient themselves toward God's saving action in the present, and can envision a future that is in the care of this selfsame God. While participation in worship always takes place in the present tense, the story of the past and a vision for God's future are pervasively present. Past, present, and future become united as they mutually inform and influence one another. As Christians we live in both the "already" and the "not yet" of the reign of God. Especially in worship we are invited into this eternal vision as the past, present, and future of God's reign are enacted in story, sacrament, prayer, and song. The narrative qualities of worship insure that we who gather in God's presence will become part of the story of God's redemption. Pam Wilson, who sings in the choir at West Raleigh Presbyterian, says that it is more than just listening to Scripture. "You really must *participate* in worship and in Scripture. First of all you have *read* the Word. Now that sounds pretty simple, but in point of fact, to go about that in a disciplined and sustained way is not that easy, at least for me. I have to keep doing it over and over, reminding myself how to read Scripture. Second, you have to be open to being shaped by what God reveals to us (and to me personally) in the Word. Scripture is not just a collection of stories or histories. While it is all of these things, it is so much more than that as the inspired Word of God. It's really one way that God speaks to me and to us simultaneously. So it means to study, whether alone or with other people, and then to be open to what the Word says we should do."

The Cognitive Dimension

If, as Saliers says, religious experience without doctrine is blind, then we can be especially thankful for the many theologians across the centuries who have given to the church the gift of sound doctrine. Worship's cognitive dimension is related, at least in part, to the ways liturgy enacts the principal doctrines of Christian faith. At Madison Avenue Presbyterian

Church in New York City, changes in architecture, furnishings, and their arrangement signal new insight into primary Christian beliefs. "A historic church," writes James White, "the church of Henry Sloane Cofffin, George Buttrick, and David Read, Madison Avenue Presbyterian now focuses on a pulpit, a large communion table, and, in the central aisle, a font large enough to immerse an infant. At Madison Avenue prayer is offered from the communion table; the Scriptures are read where they are preached. The ambiguity of having both a pulpit and a lectern—which all too often reflected an era of topical preaching when Scripture and sermon were isolated entities in the order of worship—is avoided."[22] The arrangement of worship space and the enactment of the liturgy give physical and spatial concreteness to the beliefs of the worshiping assembly.

A list of cognitive functions typically includes knowledge, comprehension, application, analysis, synthesis, and evaluation.[23] Various levels of cognitive functioning are called on in the course of participation in worship as worshipers relate previous knowledge to present experience, encounter new knowledge, and seek to comprehend the relationships between previous knowledge and that which is new. Worship also invites participants to compare and contrast aspects of worship with one another and with previous worship occasions. And worship calls participants to evaluate the importance of worship's claims about God and the world, thus leading us to a critical engagement with the world and a deeper commitment to God. An important element in this process is a biblical, theological, and spiritual vocabulary that offers verbal symbols used to convey abstract concepts. Such a vocabulary both shapes and illuminates the experience of encounter with God.

Insights about the cognitive domain of human experience from the field of education can help us here. Teaching can be arranged in two broad categories: teaching *that* and teaching *to*.[24] Teaching *that* includes all of the ways we convey information about a particular subject matter. Teaching *to*, on the other hand, is what we might call "coaching." It includes all the ways we demonstrate an activity, encourage practice, give constructive and corrective feedback, and initiate novices into details of a skill. The cognitive domain in worship consists much more in *teaching to* or "showing how" than in "telling that." There is always information to be given and insights to be shared, but when learning the Christian life, especially in worship, *teaching that* is always in service of *teaching to* or "showing how." Learning how the community worships God comes primarily through *participation* in the enactment of worship. Whatever information is necessary to enable, broaden, and deepen that participation is in service of "learning how."

At Covenant Presbyterian Church in Palo Alto, Isaiah Jones is leading the way, showing how worship can be energetic and lively, even while it upholds the long-standing traditions of the congregation. Diane Jones, a member of Covenant, says that an eagerness to learn has always been a prominent characteristic of the congregation. Pastors over the years, including the current pastor, have included the work of prominent biblical scholars and theologians in their preaching and teaching. "That kind of intellectual curiosity has encouraged me to look at other aspects of the Christian life. I have gotten interested in the practice of Christian spirituality. We have an adult class now where we read Scripture, study together, and practice *lectio divina.*" Deeper knowledge of the Christian tradition has inspired people like Diane to take up practices of Christian spirituality that they might never have discovered. Knowing about the Christian spiritual life has led them into learning how to practice it with heartfelt dedication.

Part of the meaning-making inclination of the human mind is to bring some sort of systematic order to the buzz of activity that pervades our senses. The cognitive domain is fruitfully engaged in worship when worship itself demonstrates *how* the assembly's praise enacts consistent patterns of faithfulness to its own theocentric intentions. The words, symbols, gestures, and actions of the community, repeated week by week, cohere in a way that corresponds with what the community is and does. There is logical consistency in the claims made by worship on the lives of members of the assembly so that the intellect is stretched even as its need for systematic order is satisfied. As Gordon Lathrop reminds us,

> a community doing its liturgy will be remembering the series of rituals that the participants have known and will be reorganizing, reinterpreting, and reforming—criticizing—those memories by means of the on-going ritual enactment. The current ritual performs and reforms what is remembered and known "by heart." A book and a discussion may help us to sort out the local memories, in relationship to the patterned communal memories from the history of the church, giving us specific tools for doing the next liturgy. So the perceived juxtapositions of the *ordo* or the discussion of strong signs and strong critique of the signs have yielded concrete proposals for the continual reshaping of our local assemblies. But the actual critical force of the *ordo*, like the primary meaning of liturgical theology, will be found in the next liturgy we do.[25]

Throughout his work Lathrop uses the structure of the *ordo* (the four-fold pattern of gathering, service of the Word, Eucharist, and sending) and its inherent "juxtapositions" to note the dependable patterns of Christian worship and the expansive and surprising possibilities within that *ordo*. In the practice of liturgy, the texts, actions, objects, songs, gestures, and assembly itself are "juxtaposed" to one another in ways that proclaim God's surprising grace. Seasons, stories, actions, objects, sound, and silence all interact in unpredictable ways, giving our cognitive faculties both familiarity and novelty through which to discern the patterns of God's presence. Our cognitive faculties naturally search for patterns in the juxtapositions that are both familiar and yet ever new.

Most Protestants have grown accustomed to the ways the sermon dominates the assembly's worship and has generally appealed to a strongly cognitive dimension of human nature. Congregations like these are finding that when they take into consideration additional important aspects of human experience in worship, their knowledge of God and of their world is strengthened. Thus there is a kind of reciprocal complementary relationship between the cognitive dimension of worship and all its other dimensions.

The Social and Relational Dimensions

The social structures and relational dynamics of a congregation are manifested in many areas of the community's life. In worship-centered congregations significant attention is given to how these social and relational aspects of congregational life are enacted in worship. In the social domain various roles, responsibilities, and levels of communal authority are enacted. Acolytes, ushers, eucharistic ministers, pastors, readers, and members of the assembly all have specific roles to play in the enactment of the community's praise. Thus it is important to ask, What patterns of social order are projected by the enactment of our liturgies? What are the implicit manifestations of assumptions about such things as diversity in gender, race, ability, and age? What does our worship say about the social standing and power of lay and clergy members of the assembly? What kinds of imagery predominate, and to whose experience does it refer? What patterns of authority are demonstrated by passive and/or active participation? How does leadership reflect service to the assembly alone? Or does leadership reflect authority accrued in some other social order? Congregations keep these and similar questions in mind as they participate in worship and anticipate future participation.

At St. Paul's Episcopal Church in Bloomsburg, Pennsylvania, planning for the Easter Vigil begins early in Lent and includes a wide variety of members of the church. Leadership for this most important service demonstrates that service to the assembly is primarily focused on the ability of the leader to support and enliven the people's prayer. Matters of social status within and outside the congregation are of little concern here. Rather, worship leaders are chosen for their gifts for leadership and for their maturity in faith. And so when the vigil is celebrated, leaders include people of many ages, backgrounds, and abilities. All are well prepared for their roles in the service and demonstrate a kind of spiritual leadership that invites the full participation of the community.

We have said that one quality that distinguishes worship-centered, spiritually lively congregations is the nature of their relationships. In these congregations there are frequent demonstrations of genuine affection and intimacy among members and leaders. The importance of the Christian spiritual life is apparent in the ways individuals relate to one another. The kind of caring intimacy the community expects is enacted Sunday by Sunday at St. Paul's between rector Marjorie Menaul and the acolytes who serve with her. Acolytes carry the cross, candles, and gospel book in the entrance procession, when the gospel is read in the midst of the assembly, and again in the final procession. They also assist her in the preparation and serving of the Eucharist. In this congregation of about three hundred there are more than twenty-five teenagers who are eager to serve as acolytes. This enthusiastic participation by young people has both advantages and disadvantages, however. Marjorie says that the school and activity schedules of the young people, coupled with the liturgical schedule of the church, mean that acolytes serve only once every six weeks.

Marjorie makes sure the young people have thorough training in their roles as acolytes, both in the local parish and at regional and national acolyte camps. Nevertheless, without frequent enactment of their roles, these young people are apt to need some coaching as they serve the worshiping assembly alongside the priest. Watching the relational enactment of liturgical service between Marjorie and the acolytes is heartwarming in a way that draws worshipers into a kind of communal intimacy, while at the same time contributing to the joyful reverence that is natural to worship. As Marjorie, in quiet words and gestures, reminds and coaches the acolytes through their responsibilities, it is as though they are truly preparing a meal together, not going through the ritual motions of preparing bread and wine. Anxiety about "getting it right" seems completely absent here, as

Marjorie presides in ways that support and direct the central actions but do not dominate or control. Congregations like these also demonstrate a kind of honesty before God and one another that makes it possible for them to weather the ups and downs present in any community. Based on the relationships established in the celebration of the worship of God, these people are able to ask one another, "How goes it with you and God? Where is God in this?" Their relationships are lived out before God, and so their ability to share the truth of their lives is grounded in their knowledge of the steadfast faithfulness of God.

The Imaginative Dimension

At worship recently one of the texts was Hebrews 11–12, where the writer names and describes the faithful lives of the people of God through the centuries and then calls the attention of readers to the "great cloud of witnesses" that surrounds the community of faith. As the preacher creatively called the attention of the congregation to the many witnesses of the faith that had gone before us in First Presbyterian Church of Bloomsburg, my eyes were drawn to the brilliantly colored windows that surrounded us. The Gothic shapes of the windows reminded me of head-and-shoulder silhouettes of our forebears, surrounding us as we joined them in the worship of God. I imagined the many men and women of faith, some of whom I knew and some I had heard about in Scripture, song, and congregational story. I knew their presence nearby and gave thanks for their witness. The designers of those windows did not intend that they be seen as silhouettes of the cloud of witnesses. I imagined their presence. Or, to put it more accurately, I discerned their presence through the experience of the biblical witness "juxtaposed" to the artistic design of the windows.

Acts of faithful imagination are to be found everywhere in worship. In the communal enactments of the praise of God, these congregations call on story and song, metaphor and symbol, image and gesture, in order to give expression to the unfathomable mystery of God. The human imagination, enlivened and faithfully shaped through disciplined worshiping communities, learns to discern the presence of God throughout the many aspects of the liturgy. Thus the meaning of Word and sacrament, Fred Holper reminds us, "is discovered again and again in new depth and breadth as sacramental celebration draws us into the mystery of God's covenant relationship with us in Jesus Christ, a relationship whose depth and breadth is never fully exhausted or comprehended. God presents

Godself to us in new ways each time we encounter God in the sacraments no matter how often we celebrate them."[26]

It has been common to be wary of human imagination, fearing that its fruits are "imaginary." Recent research in fields as diverse as philosophy, neurology, and learning theory have repeatedly pointed out, however, that when imagination is understood simply as the act of making present in the mind that which is absent to the senses, the use of the imagination is understood more thoroughly. The natural strategy of the mind is to reach for understanding of the here-and-now by searching for similarities with previous experience and by noticing new patterns of meaning that have not been encountered before. Both the calling on memory and the noticing of patterns are acts of the imagination. In remembering we re-call into the present that which is past. In discovering patterns within present experience we naturally pose imaginative "What if?" questions and explore their implications. When we are called to envision the future our imaginative capacities are oriented to that which is "not yet." In our efforts at meaning making we naturally link past and present in ways that are ever new. They require the use of imagination, our active engagement with the world around us. Understood in this way the term "imagination" does not refer to some outlandish, fly-away mental abandon that will inevitably lead us astray. Rather, the imagination is our active participation in meaning making that allows metaphors to sing and images to resonate with the very presence of God. Imagination works indirectly, bringing various aspects of experience, memory, and expectation together in order to construct meaning. Imagination serves to interpret metaphorical language and image as well as to deepen the symbolic interpretation of concrete experience.

Worship proposes a world that is different from (though not separate from) the world of our ordinary experience. By immersing us in the very presence of God, worship enables us to notice and attend to the presence of God at other times and places. "'Worldmaking' is a prime activity of the artistic imagination," says Leland Ryken[27] and, I would contend, a prime activity of the faithful liturgical imagination. "There is emancipation in the imagination: It frees us in an instant from our time and place and transports us to another world."[28] Theologians in all branches of Christendom agree that proposing and inviting people into an alternative world—a world where all praise and honor, glory, and power are ascribed to the triune God—is a primary intention of worship. But in order to accomplish this—to hold present in the mind those things that are absent to the senses—our capacities for discerning God's pervasive presence throughout creation must be enlivened and disciplined. The God we know is the God of Scripture, especially known in the life, death, and resurrection of Jesus Christ. As we are shaped by scriptural story, image, and metaphor, so our capacities for imaginative discernment of God's presence will become more acute.

Other worshipers sitting near me a few Sundays ago might have noticed the beautifully colored windows. They might have admired them, worried about needed repairs to them, or been irritated by the windows' particular design and colors. It required active, discerning imagination to see the congregation surrounded by the great cloud of witnesses. It is these sorts of sustained, disciplined acts of imagination that worship continually calls forth.

Faithful worship, says Stan Hall, "is service of and in the reign of God as the reign of God is proclaimed by the Word of God, embodied in Jesus Christ, rendered through the Spirit. . . . The church participates in the 'already' and the 'not yet' of the reign of God. . . . Worship according to the Word of God is at once already our engagement in the reign of God, and it is also the sign of that reign for which we pray, which in God's freedom is yet to come."[29] Of course most people do not live, day in and day out, with a consciousness of God's reign. It is in worship that this consciousness is lifted up, shared, embodied, and embraced. In order to perceive the reign of God in worship (and to extend one's perceptions into all of life) sustained, disciplined, faithful use of the imagination is required. Worshipers learn to "see through" the stories, songs, symbols, gestures, and ritual enactments into the reign of God in ways that enable them to discern that reign wherever it appears and pray for its emergence where it does not. Calvin urged Christians to view the world as the "theater of God's glory,"[30] and it is through faithful imagination that the contours of God's glory can be discerned. Walter Brueggemann has said, "The church does its subversive work not by ethical admonition and heavy-handed coercion but by making available an alternative construction of reality which legitimates and makes possible a life more faithful, more obedient, and more joyous." The church's worship, he suggests, does not need to be relevant "as much as it needs to be honest, intentional, and nervy about the practice of reality that is done in this liturgy."[31]

Many, of course, have cautioned against the unfaithful use of imagination, and we do well to heed their warning. Nevertheless, when worship's natural imaginative dimensions are allowed to flourish through Scripture and storytelling, through poetic and metaphorical language, through gesture and enacted praise, through robust use of the church's own symbols, human imagination can be faithfully shaped in ways that give expression to deepening relationships with God.

The Formative Experience of Worship

Let us now shift our attention from aspects of human experience relevant to the practice of worship to a discussion of worship's intrinsic aesthetic qualities and the theological, pastoral, and symbolic questions they raise. The worship wars have so polarized the church's conversations about liturgy that one hesitates to speak about the aesthetics or "style" inherent in worship. But if, as we have claimed, worship both shapes and expresses our beliefs about God and ourselves, we cannot escape such discussions. Added complexity comes from the fact that the environment for worship is made up of so many varied aspects. In addition to the structure and sequence of the liturgy itself, along with its seasonal variations in mood, the liturgical environment is made up of architectural space and how it is used, the decorations and appointments of the space, the rhythm and pacing of liturgical time, liturgical speech and song, and the actions, movements, and gestures of the assembly and its leaders. Each of these aspects contains its own symbolic "language." Gilbert Ostdiek reminds us that "the liturgy is meant to speak to us as one total language, richly and harmoniously varied. It seeks to evoke in us an experience of ourselves as God's people."[32] The aesthetic dimension or "style" of worship, then, is closely related to the symbolic nature of worship itself, with each language revealing the symbolic meanings inherent in liturgical enactment. The emphasis on harmony is of great importance here. Worship-centered congregations want their liturgy to express a consistent understanding of God and themselves, even while that expression is complex, paradoxical, and multilayered. They "think of each sensory language as a unique and valuable way in which . . . experience is opened up to us in harmony with all the other languages being used."[33]

The harmonious blending of all the languages of worship seems like an awesome task, and it is! It is a task that requires of worship planners and leaders nothing but their best and most sustained attention. It also requires the articulation of worship's primary orienting purposes and values as its guiding principles for planning, preparation, and evaluation. These purposes and values are primarily theological and pastoral. In addition, however, the enactment of worship displays symbolic, artistic, and liturgical qualities.[34] Whatever symbolic, aesthetic, and liturgical values inform the planning, preparation, and reflection on worship, we do well to re-member that they are in service of worship's primary theological and pas-toral purposes. As we have said in an earlier chapter, worship begins and ends with God. Recall how the music and worship committee at Latrobe Presbyterian devotes its time to careful planning for and reflection on worship. They understand that their overarching task, amidst the many practical and logistical concerns associated with worship, is to support and sustain the congregation's orientation toward God in worship. All of their efforts are dedicated to this end.

Of equal importance is the "full, conscious, active participation" of the assembly in the worship of God. This is worship's primary pastoral prin-ciple; it grounds all other concerns for taking experience seriously. "The spiritual good [of God's people at prayer] must be the final goal of all our caring for their prayer."[35] In the congregations described here the wor-ship of God is truly the action of the gathered community. People's par-ticipation is attentive and receptive to God's presence among them.

The multiple languages of worship invite particular attention as we consider the formative and expressive nature of worship. "Just as the hu-man reality of Jesus mediates God's presence to us, so too our bodily ac-tions and use of human objects in the liturgy tangibly express and bring about God's sanctifying presence to us and our worship of God in spirit and truth. Liturgical celebration depends radically on the honest use of the full range of symbolic languages and liturgical symbols. These 'signs perceptible to the human senses' either nourish or destroy faith by the way in which they are performed."[36] Thus these worship-centered con-gregations give attention to the full variety of liturgical symbols and sym-bolic languages. They invest considerable care in the way the worship space is arranged and cared for. They choose carefully the vestments, paraments, banners, and communion ware to be used. More and more, people are being encouraged to actively (bodily) participate in worship as they stand for prayers, speak their own prayer concerns, join in the great "Amen," and move out of the pews to come forward for the Lord's Sup-per. Many of these congregations are noticing the ways the rhythm of sound and silence symbolically orient their worship. They notice how the interplay of speaking and singing and the voice of one in contrast to the voices of all give richness to their enacted praise. "We have more silence now," says pastor Debbie McKinley, "and it is active, participatory si-lence, not just dead air."

There is growing concern that all the symbolic languages of worship speak with balance and harmony. There is a natural "interplay and redundancy"[37] among the various symbolic languages of worship to which these congregational leaders are giving fuller attention. At Latrobe, where a renovation of the chancel is under consideration, there is strong support for a new arrangement that will put the pulpit, font, and table on the same level of the sanctuary's platform, indicating the primacy of these three liturgical focal points and their inseparable symbolic significance. The people are learning, too, that they cannot change just one element of their worship space. Changes in the arrangement of the primary symbols of the liturgy have required additional changes to seating arrangements, furnishings, and decorative elements in the sanctuary. Proposals for the new design show continuing attention to the ways each of these symbolic languages speaks uniquely and yet respects the other symbols present in worship.

By its very nature every liturgical symbol and action has artistic qualities, qualities that are called on to serve the community's worship of God. As Ostdiek points out, "liturgy takes its inspiration for symbol and ritual action from the fine arts, both visual arts and performing arts, and welcomes the artistic expressions, both folk and classic, of past ages and of contemporary peoples, when they are able to serve the liturgy beautifully and worthily."[38] Beauty and artistic worth are, of course, notoriously difficult to define, but when objects and performance serve the worship of God, their most necessary qualities include simplicity and honesty. For liturgical objects this means simplicity in design and a clear relationship between form and function. Materials and craftsmanship will show artistic care and simple beauty. They will invite the congregation's use and enhance the symbolic richness of the entire liturgy. As part of Latrobe's continuing liturgical renewal, the congregation has replaced its baptismal font. The new font features a large clear glass bowl mounted on a stand made from the wood of historic liturgical furnishings of the congregation. Its strikingly simple beauty makes the font a visual focal point, and its weekly use in worship as the place of significant liturgical actions enhances its natural symbolic expression. This congregation "lives into its baptism" week by week as they gather around "water and the Word."

The performance of liturgical actions, especially by worship leaders, draws its artistic qualities from the performing arts. However, a subtle but important distinction needs to be made. While worship's gestures and actions are "performed" and while these gestures and actions are led by worship leaders, worship is not a performance in the theatrical sense of that word. The performance of worship's actions and gestures by leaders and people is for the sake of the worship of God. In worship-centered congregations musicians, presiders, readers, and other worship leaders are conscious of their roles in the communal performance of worship even while they reject the notion of worship as "their" performance. Within this framework worship leaders strive for a "noble simplicity" in worship where gestures and words enhance one another, where theological intentions are clear, and where all of worship's elements are within the people's power to comprehend and are free of undue explanation.

Music holds a special place in the performance of worship and has received much attention in the midst of the "worship wars." While it may not be possible to avoid differences of opinion over musical tastes, worship-centered congregations are naturally oriented toward a different starting place. Rather than begining with questions of musical genre, style, and appeal, they begin with the requirements for worship itself and their call to bring nothing but their best to the performance of worship. These congregations have found that when their music (and all of their worship) expresses clear theocentric and artistic commitments, the style of music gains considerable latitude. At Immanuel Presbyterian, organist and choir director Dianne Everson has kept an attentive and discerning eye on the music of the global church. She is able to choose well-written music and texts from Africa, South America, and Asia that the congregation has embraced as their own. In addition, she has introduced the use of African drums and marimbas into worship. On a recent Sunday morning the children and teens of the church led the assembly in worshiping God through music on the marimbas and drums. Their selections were authentic music of Africa and South America, and they conveyed a lively response to the love of God that was entered into by all present. The celebration continued as they played the postlude. No one hurried toward the door. Worshipers stayed to participate in the praise expressed in this lively music.

All of worship's intentions are directed toward praise of God and "the spiritual good of the assembled people."[39] Worship should support the people's prayer and spiritual formation, enabling them to know themselves as the people of God. The capacity of worship to communicate these intentions depends on careful attention to all of worship's verbal and non-verbal aspects and continual critical questioning as to what is being communicated. Symbols have a certain transparent quality in this regard. They inhabit space and time in ways that naturally juxtapose them to one another—even layer them one upon the other—so that the transparency of each naturally enriches the whole. But only careful attention to these specific juxtapositions can move the assembly toward "seeing through" the symbols, which can just as easily stand in contradiction or competition with one another. Such attention also insures that the celebration will be suited to the life of the particular congregation. Worship that is adapted to the culture, way of life, circumstances, and religious development of the people actually assembled to praise God invites an experience of encounter with God. And while the results depend on God's grace (not on our planning and preparation, no matter how careful), God's promises to be with us when we gather are dependable.

Leadership for Worship

Participation in worship is always unavoidably shaped by the qualities of leadership embodied by those who preside at the community's gatherings. One of the most surprising discoveries of this study has been to notice how practices of worship leadership and ritual presiding profoundly affect the spiritual orientation of the congregation. In worship-centered congregations the spiritual participation of worship leaders was always evident. One always has a sense that these pastors and other leaders are sincerely worshiping God as they exercise their role as worship leaders.[40] In Philadelphia Deborah McKinley uses abundant silence to support worshipers' reorientation toward God, and in the process one senses that she herself is engaged in the same reorientation. In Tacoma, Paul Galbreath spent many hours over the course of several months practicing ritual gestures until they became his own bodily expression of response to the presence of God in worship. In Bloomsburg, Marjorie Menaul's calm, generous interactions with the acolytes who serve with her bespeak her own discipline of remaining centered in God through the enactment of the liturgy. Joe Ward and Denise Thorp in Raleigh lead the community in prayer, mentioning by name those whose lives call for celebration and lament before God. In all these ways and more, worship leaders embody a kind of spiritual participation in liturgy that expresses their own response to God and shapes the worship of the people they lead.

What is it that these worship leaders do, or do differently, that gives their worship leadership its spiritual valence? Gilbert Ostdiek offers a helpful starting point when he makes a distinction between "planning" for worship and "preparation" for worship. "We easily lose ourselves in the nuts and bolts of 'planning' and begin to think of our task as one of designing the liturgy from scratch, rather than one of making ourselves, the rituals, the space, and the liturgical objects ready for the moment of public prayer."[41] Rather, he says, preparation includes planning but primarily seeks to enable the worshiping assembly, both leaders and people, faithfully to enact the worship of God adapted to their particular needs and *spiritual* circumstances.[42] The role of pastors and other leaders in being shaped by the liturgy itself is central to this task. "If our pastoral goal is to adapt the liturgy so that the people can hear God's word and pray in their real life situations, the presider-homilist must be there, to shape and be shaped by what is prepared."[43] Thus spiritual preparation for worship leadership is essential and includes prayer, Scripture study, and reflection on the pastoral priorities of the liturgy. It also includes careful planning, rehearsal, and preparation of liturgical space, objects, and vestments. The importance of spiritual preparation, which includes but goes beyond practical preparation, cannot be overstated. All aspects of planning and preparation are given priority in worship-centered congregations.

Worship leadership by laypeople can become an occasion for deep reflection and profound spiritual formation. And laypeople seem to hunger for opportunities to reflect on their experience of leadership in worship. In these congregations pastors understand that asking questions that invite these leaders to describe their experiences—a process of telling their own stories back to themselves in the presence of others who are seeking God's presence—is profoundly formative. Central to these conversations are opportunities to discern God's presence in the midst of preparation, planning, and leading worship. So these faithful pastors ask, in one way or another, "Where is God in this?" Elder Jim Everett of Old Pine Presbyterian recalls the orientation, coaching, and preparation pastor Debbie McKinley provided for him when he was invited to lead worship with her. "It is more than just knowing how to speak to a large group of people. It is about speaking a word from God whenever you read Scripture during worship. Debbie is really good at helping [worship leaders] see all the different aspects. It changes how you participate in worship after you've led worship. It is more meaningful somehow."

Children and Worship

Worship that takes experience seriously by giving attention to the physical, sensory, affective, cognitive, narrative, social, relational, and imaginative dimensions of human experience is naturally child friendly. Children meet life holistically as physical, intellectual, affective, and relational beings. (Part of what it means to be childlike is the way in which various dimensions of human personhood are inseparable from other dimensions. Children have not yet learned the disciplines of adulthood that enable them to identify and differentiate among the various dimensions of human experience.) In a recent issue of a devotional periodical, Jo Ann Staebler gives an account of such a child-friendly church. Baptism is a sacrament of abundance in the congregation she belongs to, she says. "Someone is going to get wet!" Recently a five-year-old who attended church with her grandparents came joyfully and expectantly to the font for baptism. "The pastor managed to get a very ample amount of water into her hands, and it ran down the girl's upturned face and onto her dress. Never have I seen a child in church with such an enraptured expression. Her face radiated pure delight. She barely flinched as the water flowed across her eyes. As she stood there with her hair dripping, her face wet and glistening, her dress spattered, I wanted to stand up and dance my own dance."[44]

Congregations like this one have engaged in some of their most serious debates and decision making around the participation of children in worship. Leaders and members know intuitively that worship that is participatory and multidimensional in its enactment is naturally appropriate for children. Most often their conversations have dealt with issues of adult acceptance of the presence of children in worship and the heightening of worship's naturally child-appropriate aspects. Rarely have they questioned the appropriateness of worship as a place for children. At West Raleigh Presbyterian, the central question for all decisions concerning children, but especially concerning children and worship, is, "What is it we want children to have experienced in the church as they enter confirmation class?" The concern is not so much for children's knowledge about Christian faith as it is for children's participation in the worship, prayer, instruction, and mission of a faithful community. Leaders in this congregation begin by including children in worship. They enhance worship's naturally child-friendly aspects—its mood of anticipation and celebration of the presence of God; its inherent story, drama, and enactment of the mighty acts of God; and its call for heartfelt and embodied response from the people of God. Worship's visual, musical, poetic, and dramatic portrayals of the stories of faith constitute a naturally interactive and participatory arena for multidimensional experience.[45] As with ancient Hebrew worshipers, the objects, actions, and interactions of worship naturally invite curiosity and questioning.

In addition to naturally child-friendly patterns of participation in worship, these congregations offer worship times especially suited to the needs of children, opportunities for parents and children to learn about worship and sacraments, and times of reflection on and preparation for worship. Programs similar to the "Young Children and Worship"[46] program developed by Jerome Berryman and Sonja Stewart, adapted to the gifts and needs of particular congregations, offer children and adults ways to worship faithfully together. If children are dismissed from worship, several values permeate these congregations' planning. First, they want to include in worship the greatest number of children possible (and dismiss the fewest). Second, they want children to be absent from the worshiping community for the shortest possible time. And third, they want children to continue worshiping in ways that are appropriate for their particular capacities even while they are away from the larger community.

Reflection on Worship

Liturgical theologians say we are all theologians as we engage in communal and personal reflection on the liturgies in which we participate, which they call *secondary liturgical theology*. Reflection on worship occupies a necessary but secondary role in relation to *primary liturgical theology*, mentioned above. Following the pattern of relationships between experience and reflection we have been describing in previous chapters, reflection on liturgy serves to deepen our curiosity, insights, and engagement with the church's worship of God. According to Lathrop, "*Secondary liturgical theology*, then, is written and spoken discourse that attempts to find words for the experience of the liturgy and to illuminate its structures, intending to enable a more profound participation in those structures by the members of the assembly."[47] This kind of reflection takes place largely outside of worship. (In fact, when reflection on or explanation of worship comes to dominate worship's theocentric actions and intentions, one might need to ask whether it continues to *be* worship.) The next three chapters will concentrate on a broad range of settings and approaches to reflection on worship—*secondary liturgical theology*. Opportunities to reflect on encounter with God in worship are essential for spiritually maturing congregations.

We have said that worship is the central orienting activity of the Christian life. To say that an activity is "central" implies that other activities occupy particular positions surrounding this central activity and that the relationships of these activities are appropriate to the activities themselves and to worship's theocentric commitments. In worship-centered congregations this means that all other activities of congregational life flow from and culminate in participation in worship. Or, as the documents of Vatican II put it, worship is the source and summit of the church's life. To say it another way, all of the activities of the church are, at least in some measure, occasions for implicit and explicit reflection on what the church says and does in worship. While it is certainly true that there is sometimes great dissonance between the church's claims made in worship and the rest of the life of the church, the intention in worship-centered congregations is to reflect on worship and on all their practices of Christian discipleship so that there is a growing coherence and harmony between what the church proclaims and enacts in worship and the rest of its corporate life. In addition to their reflection on worship, these congregations also engage in consistent reflection on all other aspects of their congregation's life. Thus the dynamic rhythm of experience and reflection on experience is a natural part of the congregation's culture.

Like churches everywhere, these congregations engage in practices of prayer and other spiritual disciplines, study and instruction, mission and ministry, and leadership. Each of these sets of activities offers opportunities to reflect on their life together and to notice ways their practices are (or are not) in harmony with what they do and say in worship. In addition, these sets of practices offer opportunities to give explicit attention to learning the Christian life from their experience of congregational life, as illustrated by figure 3 in the previous chapter.

Experiential learning in congregational life depends on several interactive practices that enhance learning and give it a necessary critical edge. As we have noted before, relationships of intimacy, commitment, endurance, and honesty are essential where "deep learning" consistently takes place. These congregations have largely given up patterns of social reserve that inhibit the exploration of their shared life in Christ. They know how to talk about encounters with God with some precision and specificity because they know the language of faith. In addition, they share a unique congregational vocabulary drawn from their shared experiences over months and years of faith sharing. Within this context of committed relationships and shared vocabulary, members of these congregations engage in mutual questioning, inquiring, and probing in ways that illuminate the details of experience. They know how to ask the right question at the right time, energizing and propelling the experiential learning cycle and establishing its practice in the culture of the congregation.

Chapter Four

Prayer and Spiritual Disciplines

The paradox of encounter with God in worship is that it both satisfies and deepens our spiritual hungers. Being in the presence of God is profoundly satisfying, even as it is unsettling and disturbing. Once we abide with the One who made us and for whom we are made, we find ourselves longing for deeper knowledge of God and for the sustained experience of the presence of God. But corporate worship alone is not sufficient to bring this encounter into its fullness in the Christian life. Such fullness comes, in part, through reflection on encounter with God during practices of prayer and spiritual discipline that have marked the lives of faithful people since ancient times.

According to the experiential learning model we have been following, prayer and other spiritual disciplines offer a particularly rich opportunity for reflection on our encounters with God in worship and in all areas of our lives. In reflection we tell our own stories back to ourselves in order to discover further what riches might be hidden there. According to George Simons, humans have "a need to remember and reflect on value-laden happenings and ideas."[1] In the unrelenting "busyness" of daily life, prayer and spiritual disciplines offer the opportunity to slow down, take time, remember, and explore in ways that are necessary for learning the Christian life. We humans are naturally pattern-seeking, storytelling, meaning-making beings. Prayer and spiritual disciplines offer an opportunity for both personal and communal reflection where the patterns of our lives can be identified and where meaning can be discovered.

One must acknowledge, of course, that not all prayer is reflection nor is all reflection prayer. Nevertheless, in the Christian life practices of prayer and other spiritual disciplines offer abundant opportunities to re-member and explore our experiences in the light of the gospel in order that we might be formed into the likeness of Christ. Marjorie Thompson describes spirituality as the "conscious awareness of, and assent to, the work of the Spirit in us. Spirituality points to a path—to choices of belief, value commitments, patterns of life, and practices of faith that allow Christ to be formed in us."[2] In practices of prayer and other spiritual dis-ciplines Christians demonstrate this awareness and assent. The reflective quality of these practices heightens one's awareness of God's formative presence in other areas of life, while participation in the disciplines them-selves represent assent. Members of the congregations described here know that their own efforts in prayer will not make them more faithful. Rather, it is the work of the Holy Spirit in them to which they submit themselves.

In these worship-centered congregations more and more people are turning their awareness to their own and others' spiritual hungers and to spiritual disciplines that invite them to reflect on their experiences of en-counter with God. These practices have led them into deeper spiritual waters. Pastor Debbie McKinley says she notices a spiritual deepening in her congregation as more and more couples and families pray together and talk together about the Christian spiritual life. Especially from those in "Generation X," Debbie says she hears deeply probing questions about practices of prayer and other spiritual disciplines. These congregations are not seeking some spiritual "high" or novel "spiritual experiences." Rather, they consistently open themselves to faithful Christian spiritual formation through their practices of prayer and reflection. The patterns of reflection present in their practices of prayer and spiritual disciplines allow them to remember and ponder their experiences and to assess the spiritual significance of these events. Members of these communities of faith take time to ask themselves and one another many questions about the experience of the Christian life in all its facets. Memories and de-scriptions are offered and received as gifts given to deepen and enrich the community's awareness of God's presence.

As we have seen, human experience is made up of both external and in-ternal elements. What we see, hear, taste, smell, and touch constitute the multiple stimuli that make up our experience. At the same time, our per-sonal responses to those stimuli are an inseparable part of experience. Thus our feelings, emotions, sentiments, attitudes, and memories are in constant interaction with the world around us. In order more thoroughly to learn from experience, practices of intentional reflection are essential.

In learning the Christian life through the experience of congregational life, practices of prayer and other spiritual disciplines encourage such reflection. The churches described here offer classes and programs that teach spiritual disciplines and support people in their continuing practice. Classes in contemplative prayer, journal writing, group spiritual direction, and the prayerful reading of scripture called *lectio divina* are commonplace in these congregations. In addition, most gatherings, regardless of their explicit purpose, include some form of reflective sharing and prayer. Most notable are the ways practice of personal and communal spiritual disciplines has been woven into the everyday fabric of congregational life.

Settings That Welcome Reflection

The worship of God, especially corporate worship on the Lord's Day, sets the pattern for reflection in these congregations. Carol Holsinger of Covenant Presbyterian Church in Palo Alto, California, speaks for many when she says, "Worship is the focal point of the congregation. That's the one thing that everybody participates in." Especially in Scripture and preaching and in prayer, worshipers reflect on the Christian life in the presence of God and the community. In this setting, joyfully ascribing "all praise and honor, glory and power to the triune God"[3] naturally evokes awareness of oneself in relation to God and reflection on that relationship. This theocentric focus for reflection, established and renewed in all the church's worship, becomes a model for reflection at other times and places. Several congregations began their spiritual renewal by extending practices of communal prayer and meditation throughout congregational life.

At both West Raleigh in North Carolina and Immanuel in Tacoma, Washington, the prayers of the people begun during Sunday morning worship continue in other gatherings. Following suggestions from several popular books,[4] these congregations spend extended periods of time naming their celebrations and concerns in prayer. Communal prayer for one another, the church, and the world, begun in Sunday morning worship, is practiced during weekly noonday prayer, committee meetings, Bible study groups, staff meetings, choir rehearsal, and planning for mission outreach. It is not unusual, especially when some important decision is before them, for committees and mission groups to pause for prayer in the midst of other activities. They embody the understanding that the purpose for programmatic and administrative facets of congregational life is to support the spiritual life of the congregation but are not the spiritual life itself.

We have heard Joe Ward say that at West Raleigh people used to see programs and committees as the "assets" of the church. "Now we see them as the infrastructure that enables the essence of congregational life to go on in worship, study groups, mission groups, prayer meetings, and fellowship gatherings," he says. That "essence" is the Christian spiritual life, supported by what the congregation does and how they do it. In all the congregations described here, the Christian spiritual life is given explicit priority in the church's life. These congregations are comfortable, even eager, to exhibit their participation in and enthusiasm for practices that deepen their relationship with God and to invite others into these practices.

The Christian spiritual life is nurtured in everyone, especially in children and youth. People at Covenant Church in Palo Alto recognize even commonplace practices as formative for the whole congregation. At the close of children's time in worship, the children and the adult leading them join hands and pray in a "call and response" style. The adult prays a phrase and the children repeat it. As one adult commented, "Children are really learning to pray as their language is patterned by the repeated prayer."

Often before these Christians enter into prayer, they spend time in storytelling. They share "joys and concerns," freely and openly naming those areas of their lives where the gifts and struggles of the Christian spiritual life seem most acute. The intimacy of these conversations is sometimes quite profound. How did this culture of familiarity and tenderness emerge and what are its appropriate limits? Leaders in these congregations report that the emergence of close trusting relationships among members did not happen all at once, but that slowly, as times for storytelling became more frequent, people learned to name their experiences of God, their perplexities, and even their deepest doubts. Thus every gathering has become an occasion where attention to the spiritual lives of those present is an appropriate part of the gathering's purpose. Roberta Hestenes writes, "God has called us to be in some kind of Christian community. Community is the gift of God *and* a human responsibility by God's grace and power. The universal community of faith takes form concretely in local congregations, which are called to share life together in ways that bear witness to the love and mercy of God."[5] At the same time, no one is pressured into a level of intimacy with which he or she is not comfortable.

Some gatherings especially lend themselves to the development of intimate relationships wherein the Christian spiritual life is central to the group's concerns. At West Raleigh, mission groups incorporate personal storytelling, prayer, Bible study, and other spiritual disciplines as a part of their commitment to mission. Other small groups formed especially for the purpose of growth in practices of the spiritual life enable members to explore spiritual disciplines, readings from Christian spiritual classics, and contemporary writings in a setting where group members can encourage one another. In addition, most gatherings in these churches have gradually incorporated a variety of spiritual practices into their meetings. Sunday school classes, children's worship leader groups, committees, choirs, governing boards, and Bible study groups continue to be transformed from merely programmatic and institutional entities and to understand themselves as Christian communities.[6] The cultivation of one-to-one spiritual friendships among members is especially important in these congregations. Members mentor one another in the Christian spiritual life, developing relationships of intimacy that extend farther than the more public relationships established in groups. They often form between husbands and wives or other family members.

This transformation has not been universally understood nor embraced, but enthusiasm from a broad range of participants and obvious congregational vitality in worship, study, mission, and fellowship have over time won over many who were initially skeptical or resistant. Patterns of reflection, sharing, and prayer that initially made some people uncomfortable have become the cultural norm in these congregations and are understood as central to the nature of congregational life. Along the way interpersonal relationships have been strengthened and trust has been built, so that appropriate boundaries in congregational intimacy are understood and honored.

Prompting Reflection: The Right Question and the Right Time

Someone has said that what is important to us becomes apparent in the questions we ask. The questions we ask ourselves and one another as we reflect on the Christian life shape the nature and content of our reflections. In these congregations questions inspire reflection on external and internal aspects of experience. Members are especially attentive to discovering the presence of God in all of life. Questions also probe possible areas for further exploration, such as unexamined assumptions and new avenues for wonder. Members of these communities ask one another in many different ways, "Where is God in this?" As we shall see as we explore various practices of prayer, questions for reflection come to us in a variety of ways. While many questions arise from experience itself, the role of the community of faith in formulating questions for reflection is indispensable for both personal and communal spiritual formation.

Questions that prompt memory concerning previous experience take into account both the external and internal nature of experience and include the following:

- What happened, exactly? What did we/I do? What do others remember?
- What do we/I remember most vividly? What seems most important?
- What sights, sounds, smells, words, actions, and/or interactions made up the experience?
- What feelings, emotions, and sentiments accompanied these events?

These questions and others related to them make previous experience available for further reflection. Rather than fading into forgetfulness, past experiences become a renewed arena of God's presence and activity. Like Jacob we may say, "Surely the LORD is in this place—and I did not know it!" (Gen. 28:16).

Reflection on experience often poses questions for us that may not have been apparent in the midst of the experience itself. Memories may be evoked and assumptions called into question by an experience that only systematic reflection can reveal. Peg Sylvester, the organist and choir director at Palmdale Presbyterian Church in Melbourne, Florida, describes the church's recent mission trip to Costa Rica as a "life-changing experience." The trip included living with and worshiping with the people of a small village while the group helped with community projects. Peg is animated as she describes the people, the setting, and the events of the trip. During a mid-week, evening worship service people went forward to place their offering in the basket. One teenage boy gave an amount of money that represented almost all that he had. "The full impact of it didn't really sink in until later," says Peg. "All I could think of was the story of the widow's mite. When I told my friends about it, over and over and over I said, 'I saw it happen!' I get teary-eyed just thinking about it. It was such a lesson to all of us. It was tremendous. The whole week was just filled with that kind of thing." Notice how the full meaning of Peg's experience was not apparent to her until she had time to reflect on it and until a friend said, "How was your trip to Central America?" Only then could she rehearse and relive those transformative moments and begin to understand their meaning.

The following questions enable us to deepen our reflections:

- What memories did/does this experience evoke?
- What connections can we/I make with other areas of life?
- How does this experience call me to see the world differently? What assumptions does it call into question?

The Christian life is intended to inspire our curiosity and wonder. When our children were in grade school, many of the neighborhood children often gathered at our house after school. On one typical afternoon I was making potato salad. I had noticed earlier in the week that several of the eggs in a particular carton had been double yolked, so as I started to chop hard-boiled eggs for the salad, I called the children into the kitchen. I cut what I suspected was a double-yolked egg so that the two yolks were clearly visible. Abby, who lived across the street, looked at me with very wide eyes and asked, "How did you do that?!!" Often experiences, especially novel or surprising ones, make us curious. Our natural sense of wonder, so apparent in children but often suppressed in adults, is awakened by startling new experiences. Even customary routines take on new vitality when we "wonder" about them. We can never discover nor comprehend the depth and variety of God's ways, and so Christian communities do well to ask questions that awaken and reawaken curiosity and wonder. In congregations that exhibit a deep spiritual life, one frequently hears inquiries concerning "What makes you curious?" These kinds of questions are a regular part of the children's worship program at West Raleigh, but increasingly they are making their way into Bible study groups, mission groups, prayer groups, and decision-making bodies. Bible stories and parables featured in the worship program for children include several "I wonder . . . " questions.[7] In this way children are encouraged to reflect on Scripture and enter into the Christian spiritual life.

In these communities is an openness to both asking and being asked questions in order to inspire reflection on experience. Rather than a privatized reserve about the Christian spiritual life, these communities of faith display by their caring and questioning interactions with one another that reflection on the Christian life is a natural expectation. In a variety of appropriate settings, people are free to ask one another questions about their experiences in ways that deepen their reflections and thus their learning. In their book *The Godbearing Life* Kenda Creasy Dean and Ron Foster make the claim that in the activity of "soul tending . . . pastors have permission, and even an obligation, to ask questions others do not ask." They suggest that with teenagers some of the most important questions include "'What's going on between you and God? How goes your spiritual life?'"[8] Members of the congregations included in this study understand themselves, along with pastors, as those called to the art of mutual "soul tending" by explicitly caring for one another's spiritual lives.

There is an atmosphere of hospitality and genuine spiritual regard where these Christians have learned skills in prompting ongoing spiritual reflection. Note that the questions are open-ended and leave abundant room for persons to choose for themselves what reflections they will share and how. Self-disclosure is honored as a deeply personal spiritual practice. Members respect established norms for what may be asked. Likewise they honor the level of vulnerability others wish to enter into. West Raleigh has formalized this process within its Mission Formation Group. When mission proposals are brought to the group, the questioning is often lengthy and deeply probing, but it is pursued in an atmosphere of spiritual discernment where the leadership of the Holy Spirit is actively sought. Questions for clarity of purpose and authenticity of call are understood by everyone to be in service of the spiritual vitality they all seek.

Practices of Prayer and Reflection

If reflection on experience is a way of telling our own stories back to ourselves, then prayer is in part telling our stories to ourselves and to God. Prayer also implies trusting God to unveil for us the spiritual gifts present in those experiences. Prayer places us in the presence of God—our whole and complete selves. Reflection on experience under the guidance of the Holy Spirit opens the way for God to enlighten our understanding and to transform us more and more into the likeness of Christ. In his introduction to the Christian life of prayer, Don Postema lists ways of praying that include talking with God alone or with a group or in public worship; morning and evening prayers at home; observing silence; singing; singing and praying the Psalms; writing psalms of our own; being aware of nature, other people, and ourselves; being aware of the presence of God; saying the Lord's Prayer; contemplating art; reflecting on Scripture and other readings; and listening to music.[9] These congregations use these and additional forms of prayer to seek after and be found by the one true God, for whom their hearts hunger.[10]

Prayer: Together and Alone

The patterns for prayer set in worship inform all other prayers and cover a wide range of human attitudes including praise, adoration, thanksgiving, confession, and supplication.[11] Thus worship, which includes all of these approaches to God, continues to serve what Dennis Hughes and Gláucia Vasconcelos Wilkey have called "the school where we have learned of God's grace and learned to respond though grace-filled living."[12] These congregations are schooled in the prayers of Lord's Day worship so that their prayers in other times and places reflect worship's theocentric intentions. Members of Palmdale Presbyterian report that whereas their prayers used to be loosely structured and often focused on their own needs, they have absorbed patterns of praise, thanksgiving, and intercession that enrich their prayer lives. The rhythm of worship's order, moving from adoration to confession to thanksgiving and intercession, helps these Christians give voice to their own deepest gratitude and concerns. Many members of these congregations publicly pray and willingly lead the community in prayer. There is a natural quality to their leadership that is nurtured in their communal and personal practices of prayer. Preparation for leadership in these congregations includes generous amounts of faith sharing, study of Scripture, and prayer—disciplines they consider more important than the activities of institutional maintenance.

Many have noted the difficulty people have in setting aside time for prayer in their busy schedules. Members of these congregations encourage one another in their personal prayers and share helpful strategies and exercises. Choosing a consistent time, place, and set of prayer practices can be helpful, they say. Renewed interest in daily prayer, including praying the Psalms, has relieved many of the necessity to invent prayer practices for themselves and to join the whole church in prayer. Arthur Paul Poers says, "This practice can provide a way of prayer that will help some—perhaps many—pray."[13] The choir, organist, and pastor of Immanuel Church in Tacoma have produced an audiotape for Daily Prayer as outlined in the Presbyterian *Book of Common Worship* that contains sung and spoken responses to accompany Scripture readings. Many in the congregation use the tape daily, turning it on as they begin the service of prayer, pausing to read and meditate on the daily Scripture passages, and returning to the tape to conclude with sung responses. The reality of their companionship in prayer is made audible as they listen to familiar voices on the tape and remember other families who are praying along with them.

Prayer: Spoken and Silent

We note in Scripture how often prayer takes the form of conversation with God, with God and the people of God both speaking and listening. We also notice how our practices of prayer seem to favor our own speaking over listening for God's "still small voice." In these congregations there is a healthy balance between speaking and silence. Prayers give expression to reverent yet intimate relationships with God where everyday language serves to gather and articulate the gratitude of the people. At the same time the poetic, imaginative, and metaphorical language of worship has shaped their understanding of themselves and of God. Scriptural metaphor, especially, is present in prayers by a variety of congregational leaders. Sermons and prayers are full of poetry and imagery drawn from Scripture that enliven the imagination and enrich the natural sensual qualities of worship.[14] In an Advent sermon Immanuel's pastor Paul Galbreath points out the generosity of God's gifts of metaphor and image when he reminds the congregation of occasions when there has been dancing and artistic expression in their worship. "As we begin to see, experience, and feel the movement of the Spirit," he says, "we connect with the Gospel in new ways. We need the gifts of movement, dance, drama, and music to open our hearts and imaginations to engage all of our senses in the story of the birth of the Christ child among us."

As we have noted, in these congregations a spirit of prayer permeates all aspects of the congregation's life. Their awareness of God's constant presence among them means that when someone invites a group to pause for silent and/or spoken prayer in the midst of study or decision making, an atmosphere of communion with God emerges quite naturally. Especially in their ability to keep silence, these congregations demonstrate their communion with God. "Listening is the first expression of communication in prayer," says Marjorie Thompson.[15] At Old Pine in Philadelphia, pastor Deborah McKinley speaks with admiration of the ways the congregation has learned to pray. "When I say 'Let us pray,' I pause and give people a chance for their attention to come into the time of prayer. If you don't, they won't be with you. The prayer will be finished and they'll finally be listening. But if you pause and just let it be quiet, the people begin to pay attention, and they begin to pray with you. They don't just listen, but they're actually praying." Deborah expresses the knowledge that silence is essential if people are to become aware of God's presence and open themselves to encounter. As Marjorie Thompson writes, "The breathing, quieting, and 'centering' so frequently recommended in prayer are simply ways of helping us focus on the One we wish to be with."[16] With this in mind, people in these congregations, in their personal and communal prayers, eagerly enter into silence and anticipate entering into the presence of God. Their spoken praise, confessions, and intercessions are often combined with times of deep contemplation as they seek God's leading in their lives. In a world that is often too busy and too noisy, silence is sometimes hard to come by and may make some people uncomfortable. Among the members of these congregations, silence is a welcome gift that is treasured as a threshold to the presence of God. Members of Old Pine described a recent occasion when a number of visitors were present for the baptism of a family member. Many of the visitors did not know how to enter into silence, which heightened the awareness and appreciation for silence among regular worshipers.

Spiritual Reading and Lectio Divina

Many in these congregations have explored the ancient practice of *lectio divina* or, as it is sometimes described, reading Scripture with heart and mind. This centuries-old practice rests on the faith that the same Holy Spirit that was present in the inspiration of Scripture will offer enlightenment as Scripture is carefully read and pondered. In describing the use of *lectio divina* for reading the spiritual classics, Richard Foster and Brian Smith note that "each phrase is pregnant with meaning and it is best to read at a measured pace, pausing often to reread, rethink, reexperience the words until we not only understand their meaning but are shaped by the truth of them."[17]

This deep engagement with Scripture is addressed to the whole person, mind and heart, not favoring one over the other. Rather than give preference to the heart and have sentiments, emotions, and feelings overwhelm our approach to scripture, *lectio divina* aims to balance mind and heart. For the reverse temptation is real as well. Our habit is to analyze and master the information in what we read. According to Henri Nouwen,

> to take the holy scriptures and read them is the first thing we have to do to open ourselves to God's call. Reading the scriptures is not as

easy as it seems since in our academic world we tend to make anything and everything we read subject to analysis and discussion. But the word of God should lead us first of all to contemplation and meditation. Instead of taking the words apart, we should bring them together in our innermost being; instead of wondering if we agree or disagree, we should wonder which words are directly spoken to us and connect directly with our most personal story. Instead of thinking about the words as potential subjects for an interesting dialogue or paper, we should be willing to let them penetrate into the most hidden corners of our heart, even to those places where no other word has yet found entrance. Then and only then can the word bear fruit as seed sown in rich soil. Only then can we really "hear and understand."[18]

Lectio divina as practiced by ancient and contemporary Christians is composed of four related phases or movements: reading *(lectio)*, meditation *(meditatio)*, prayer *(oratio)*, and contemplation *(contemplatio)*. The aim is not to read lengthy passages of Scripture but to open oneself to relationship with God through spiritual reading. Thelma Hall writes, "Lectio . . . engages the whole person: mind, heart, spirit—the intellect and imagination, the will and the affections. All are at some point activated by grace, reaffirming the fact that Lectio Divina is . . . an organic process which takes place over a period of time. . . . "[19]

In the first movement, *lectio* or reading, the approach to scripture (or other classic devotional text), is gentle and reflective and encourages lingering over particular words, phrases, or descriptions. Thompson says, "You allow the words that are pregnant and weighty with meaning to sink in and expand and nourish your heart."[20]

In the second movement, *meditatio* or meditation, the holistic intentions of *lectio divina* are deepened. Unlike other forms of meditation that seek to empty the mind, meditation as practiced here activates the mind as well as the heart in an attitude of receptivity and discovery. Thompson continues:

> The type of mental work is quite specific. It is not the critical, analytical, or formulating work of Bible study, which may inform meditation but remains distinct from it. The mind work of meditation moves us to reflection on where we are in the text. Active imagination can sometimes help us find connections between our life stories and the great story of God's redemptive work with us.

Meditation engages us at the level of the "heart" in its biblical sense, where memory, experience, thoughts, feelings, hopes, desires, intuitions, and intentions are joined. This is where we are likely to discover what a given passage means in our lives personally or as a community.[21]

The third movement of *lectio divina* is prayer or *oratio*, where prayer naturally flows out of our meditation. "*Oratio* is the direct cry of the heart to God that rises when we have heard ourselves personally addressed through the Word."[22] Through meditation on Scripture God can touch our deepest joy, pain, longing, and desires. In *oratio* these honest responses from deep in the heart can freely flow in expressions of praise, confession, repentance, lament, reconciliation, and adoration. "*Oratio* allows a full range of human responses to tumble forth in heart-felt prayer to the One for whom we were made."[23]

The word *contemplatio* or contemplation evokes images of the loving gaze, the restful abiding in the presence of the Beloved. In contemplation, when the fruits of reading and meditation have been expressed in prayer, one can simply spend time in God's presence. Thompson concludes: "Contemplation is essentially rest, play, Sabbath-time in God's presence. . . . Here we allow ourselves simply to be, welcoming God's own way of being with us in a 'Now' that transcends time."[24] In this four-part practice of praying with Scripture, Christians through the ages have opened themselves to the formative presence of God. According to Dom Marmion, in *lectio divina*

we read	(*lectio*)
under the eye of God	(*meditatio*)
until the heart is touched	(*oratio*)
and leaps to flame.	(*contemplatio*)[25]

The congregations described here often engage in *lectio divina*, both in their personal practices and when they gather. Those who regularly engage in its practice are eager to teach others, so that as its practice expands to include more people and groups, the congregation is increasingly shaped by Scripture. In a recent newsletter article, pastor Joe Ward invites the congregation to pray for members of the confirmation class as they participate in their spring retreat. He describes the discoveries the class has made and points out all the important facets of the decisions concerning church membership these teenagers will soon make. He closes with a description of the Christian life that could point directly to the practice of *lectio divina:*

> But, most significantly, we have discovered that the key ingredients [of the Christian life] are the practice of prayer and familiarity with Scripture. From these we'll hear the call of Christ. Through these, we'll see models of the other marks of discipleship. The reality is, we 21st Century Christians are going to be less and less an alternative to the spirit of the age, unless our lives are shaped and sculpted by the stories, poems, prayers, songs, and expressions of faith that are contained in the "unique, authoritative witness to Jesus Christ as Lord and Savior," the Bible—Old and New Testaments. Reality is that some other institutions out there can offer people what the Church has offered: recreation, learning, medicine, even comforting words, . . . and they can often do a much better job than the church. The one thing nobody else has to offer is a community of prayer. We begin with prayer and Scripture.

The pattern of prayer and Scripture offered in *lectio divina* is, as Joe Ward points out, unique to the church's ministry and profoundly formative for the Christian life.

Self-Examination

As John Calvin reminds us, knowledge of God and knowledge of ourselves are inseparable, and so we turn to practices of self-examination. Most orders for worship begin with an act of praise to God, followed closely by an act of congregational self-examination. Thus worship makes the connection between knowledge of God, knowledge of ourselves, and the importance of self-examination. Other more detailed practices of self-examination have been common throughout Christian history. Self-examination, understood as the practice of reflection on experience that leads to learning, is especially useful. Understood in this way, self-examination includes honest assessments of our human condition as well as grateful acknowledgment of the presence of God in our lives. The process of self-examination usually includes five steps: gratitude for God's gifts of grace, prayer for the gift of insight, self-examination, acts of sorrow, and a statement of resolve of future faithfulness.[26] Self-examination undertaken in the context of thanksgiving and expectation of God's guidance especially invites Christians to ask, "For what moment today am I most grateful? For what moment today am I least grateful?"[27] These questions are helpful in sensitizing us to God's abiding companionship and moving us away from morbid self-absorption.

In self-examination we are brought to *awareness* and *confession*.[28] These two aspects of self-examination have been called "examination of conscience" and "examination of consciousness." In examination of conscience we trust in God's loving and thorough knowledge of us in order to gain insight into ourselves. "We rely on the grace of God to give us insight into who we are and how we behave," says Thompson. "God knows what we are ready to look at and when we need to do so."[29] In examination of consciousness we are concerned to notice when we have been aware of God's presence in our lives and when we have not. Here our attention is thoroughly on God's presence throughout our experience. By reflecting on those times of acute awareness we become more adept at recognizing them again. Reflecting on times when the presence of God has been more hidden or when our awareness has been less acute, we discover how God has been present even when we did not think so. "The whole point of self-examination is to become more *God-centered* by observing the moments when we are or are not so."[30]

In these congregations the practice of self-examination occurs in a variety of settings, sometimes in periods of personal prayer, in small prayer and study groups, in programmatic or decision-making gatherings, and in corporate worship. Especially because these congregations are worship-centered, their weekly practice of corporate confession in worship opens them naturally to the practice of self-examination. During Lent, when the whole church is in a season of repentance, congregations seem to be especially attentive to self-examination. "Lent is our time to come to terms with the anguish of God and with the anguish of our journey with God, toward God, and in contention with God," says Joe Ward. In a Lenten newsletter article he encourages "everyone to make the journey again, as if for the first time. Face the cross and hear the Word that speaks silently to us of the heartbreak our world has imposed on its maker." It is the poets and painters, he says, who give us language for this anguished and astonishing realignment of relationships that is the Christian life.

Journal Keeping

All of the spiritual disciplines included in this chapter (and other disciplines, too) encourage us to remember and reflect on our experiences and to learn from them, a necessary part of the experiential learning cycle described earlier. Reflection finds its most concrete expression in the discipline of journal keeping, where one makes a tangible record of experience and one's reflections on experience.[31] One journal keeper puts it this way: "That's why I keep a diary—because it all comes back—the details of those treasured experiences my brain would forget if I didn't have the magic passwords in my trusty diary to trigger my untrustworthy memory. Diary-keeping is memory-keeping."[32] Without a written record many of our most important experiences may be forgotten or only dimly remembered and thus unavailable for reflection and meaning making. "As history serves the purpose of giving identity, meaning and value to tribes and peoples, so the private journal provides these same boons to the individual."[33]

Journal keeping as a spiritual discipline has as its guiding principle a desire to come closer to God through writing. According to Anne Broyles, there are many approaches to journal keeping as a spiritual discipline, no one of which is a "right" way. "One person may journal in response to Bible study. Another may take a meditational walk or have a time of silence and then record the thoughts and prayers that occurred during that time. Someone else may record daily events and then see the hand of God in that dailiness."[34] In all we open ourselves to the presence of God. Journaling becomes a spiritual discipline whenever our faith in God and our openness to God's presence are strengthened.

To keep a journal is to engage in an activity that results, at least in part, in a tangible object. Writing allows experiences, memories, emotions, and insights to take concrete form in our hands and before our eyes. When aspects of our lives remain only in memory, we are less likely to discover the depth of their meaning. "Few of us can hold together all the different threads of our lives," says Morton Kelsey, "unless we put them down one by one. It is strange how we can forget very important parts of our lives until we sit before a blank piece of paper and put them down one by one. In order to gain objectivity before any important decision or many minor ones, it is valuable to take time to reflect."[35] Journal keeping offers the opportunity to work through our confusion and come to some clarity about our lives. In addition, journal keeping offers a way to structure our time and attention in ways that seem necessary for deepening the Christian spiritual life.

Ed Walker, pastor of Westover Hills Methodist Church in Richmond, Virginia, first experimented with journal keeping during a classroom project in his Doctor of Ministry program. As he and the congregation explored an arts ministry at their church, his own reflections became increasingly important in discerning the direction of the ministry. "In a journal I can jot things down and then come back to them later. The journal helps me get some distance from my experience and reflect more deeply on it. Every experience has a lot of layers to it. A journal helps me take the layers apart and reflect on each of them." During the early phases of the arts ministry, Ed says his journal has been especially important in his own personal reflections on the ministry. It has also been a rich source of insight into the congregational dynamics of the new ministry.

Members of the Westover Hills church have recently started a spiritual formation group that uses a journal as one of its disciplines.[36] Participants have remarked that the journal questions not only deepen their reflections but also help them make the transition from the discussion of the group to their own personal reflections. "After a few minutes," says one participant, "it was like I was all alone. The journal helped me concentrate and not be distracted by other things." Ed agrees. "I always need to make a shift from being the 'teacher' or leader of the group to a more personal focus. The journal helps me do that."

Many members, leaders, and pastors in these congregations fruitfully keep journals as a way of reflecting on encounters with God and deepening their awareness of God's presence. They agree with Morton Kelsey, who says, "Christians believe that God, the divine lover, seeks our friendship and companionship. We can experience this encounter in outer events or rituals, through human contacts, or through our inward turning. When we do not make some record of our experiences of God, it is almost as if we devalue them."[37] Rather than seem to devalue these experiences of encounter with God, these Christians commit their memories and reflections to paper through journal keeping, where they can be remembered and pondered anew.

Storytelling as a Congregational Spiritual Practice

During one of my visits to West Raleigh Presbyterian Church I visited the men's Sunday school class that has faithfully met for all of the church's seventy-five-year history. (I may have been the first woman ever to be included in their Sunday morning gatherings, and their hospitality was warm and gracious.) After the class was over I asked several of the men to describe West Raleigh church for me. Immediately they said, "You've got to talk to Buck Flinton!" I sat down next to Buck and heard a most remarkable story. It was the late 1960s, said Buck, and he was serving as a deacon. One of his responsibilities was to make the deacon's report to the governing board, and so he just happened to be present to witness a pivotal moment in the life of the church. A mixed-race couple had requested membership in the church, and the decision was on the docket for that evening. Buck's eyes sparkled as his memory took him back to that night. The discussion had been lengthy, but from the beginning there was a strong consensus that the couple should be welcomed. Someone said, "God didn't make it easy! A black couple would have been easier." Nevertheless the session was unanimous and adamant that "race shall never be a determining factor in membership in West Raleigh Presbyterian Church!" All of the men sitting around Buck and me nodded in agreement, affirming the story as a clear indication of what kind of place West Raleigh is. With stories like these, repeated as the church makes difficult decisions about its future, the people of West Raleigh come to know who they are and to express their hopes for who they will be.

We may not be accustomed to thinking of storytelling as a spiritual discipline, but at West Raleigh and other congregations in this study, it is. It is a shared communal practice that enables the community to tell its own story again and again in ways that preserve and treasure their shared life. At the same time storytelling creates a vision of who these communities might become, as their congregational life is ever more faithfully shaped according to the gospel. Memory and vision are integrally linked in congregational life. According to Bruce Birch, "Memory is oriented to activities of remembering what God has done and how faithful response has been made to God's action. Vision is oriented to activities of anticipating what God is yet doing in the world and aligning congregational life to serve that action of God's grace."[38] Sharing stories of personal, family, and congregational encounters with God offers glimpses of who we are and who we want to become together before God.

Storytelling in congregations, along with other modes of conversation, serves as an "undercurrent" that provides energy and direction for congregational life. Organizational and programmatic elements of congregational life are apparent on the surface, but in storytelling and conversation the depth and quality of a congregation's life can be discovered. The inherent narrative quality of the stories seems almost irresistible in human communities. As Charles Foster suggests, "they intensify our sense of belonging to each other and help link us to the dreams, struggles, and accomplishments that distinguish our social identities from those of other congregations and denominations."[39] The intimate relationships that seem necessary for effective spiritual formation can be brought into being through shared experiences and ongoing storytelling.

Leaders in these congregations use a variety of occasions to tell stories and promote conversation in the congregation. At Immanuel Church in Tacoma the annual "Saints of Immanuel" luncheon is a time for much storytelling, as long-time members are individually honored for their faithfulness. In several of these churches stories of faith are shared in new-member gatherings, in officer training sessions, and in shared joys and concerns during Sunday worship. Storytelling in these congregations serves many of the same purposes as journal keeping might serve for an individual. The life of the congregation can be recounted and reflected on as stories are told and retold over time. And as we have seen, reflection on shared Christian faith enhances learning.

Spiritual Friendship and Spiritual Direction

The term "spiritual direction" may be new to many Protestants, but it has a long history and heritage in the Christian tradition. Protestants may be more familiar with spiritual friendships that spring up during the natural course of congregational life. In many of the congregations in this study, covenant groups and prayer partners offer spiritual direction in patterns of mutuality and common concern. Natural patterns of discernment, encouragement, and accountability emerge as people pray together and alone. At Immanuel Church an element of spiritual direction increasingly appears in committee meetings. According to Anna Ayers, "We are becoming intentional about including worship in our meetings. We stop and listen and reflect on what we've done as a committee. We put prayerful discernment into our committee work. With the pastor's prompting, we often ask, 'How is God present in this? Where do we see God's hand?' It began with [pastor Paul Galbreath] asking these questions again and again, but now it is a natural part of the life of the congregation." Increasingly members of the church ask themselves and one another that basic question of spiritual discernment and direction: "Where is God in this?" As a result their ability to act as spiritual friends to one another has broadened and deepened.

Spiritual friends serve as spiritual guides in their ability to listen carefully to one another during times of reflection on the Christian spiritual life.[40] In *Soul Feast*, Marjorie Thompson writes, "A spiritual guide offers hospitable space for us to speak and be heard. Often we do not fully know our thoughts or experiences, our questions or unresolved issues. We do not know until we have had a chance to put them into words before an attentive and receptive ear. A spiritual director can 'listen us into clarity,' helping us articulate our thoughts, feelings, questions, and experiences in relation to God."[41]

A spiritual guide also helps us notice things, directing our attention to the ways God is working in our lives. At the beginning of this chapter we noted how humans are naturally pattern-seeking, meaning-making beings. Spiritual friends can help us notice patterns in our lives and in our relationship with God and can support us as we struggle to make meaning amid the complexity of contemporary life. Spiritual mentors within congregations continually direct the attention of individuals and groups to moments of grace throughout seemingly ordinary events. Sometimes their guidance comes in the form of questions that prompt others to notice how God is working among them. At other times the telling and retelling of stories about times when God has seemed particularly near serves to shape the ways people perceive and understand their life together. Attentiveness to the presence of God is a gift of spiritual direction.

Reflection on Practices of Prayer

This chapter has been concerned with some of the practical disciplines and practices of spiritual formation, especially those that encourage Christians to reflect on their life in God. A spiritual director helps Christians discern particular disciplines that are appropriate for their spiritual growth and offers support as people learn new disciplines. In the congregations described here a variety of spiritual disciplines have been explored and practiced. At West Raleigh a classroom dubbed "The Well" has been set aside for learning contemplative prayer. It is in a particularly quiet location, so the ability to focus on the presence of God is uninterrupted. Regular classes and interest groups learn new practices of prayer and support one another in their personal spiritual lives. They come together to share the ways God is at work in them and to receive guidance in discerning God's leading. At both Old Pine and Immanuel, retreats have been important occasions where new disciplines can be introduced and where spiritual mentors can offer "guidance on ways of prayer that attune us to God's presence."[42]

Those charged with caring for our souls, our spiritual mentors, offer their most significant gift when they love us and pray for us. As Marjorie Thompson says, "the love of a spiritual director for the one directed is always maintained by the love of Christ. It is agape love. The ongoing expression of that love is faithful prayer, both within and beyond meeting times."[43] Spiritual mentors in these congregations are, above all, faithful in prayer and in practicing spiritual disciplines. They demonstrate a level of maturity in faith that is the fruit of their own experience of the presence of God in their lives. They are not perfect, of course, but demonstrate humility, compassion, and perseverance as they faithfully respond to the call of the gospel. Those who seek them out for guidance in the spiritual life sense their trustworthiness and their ability to keep confidences. Their lives are marked by a compassionate honesty, wherein the challenges of spiritual growth can be named and addressed. The people around them sense that their trust is in God, not just in the forms of spiritual practices. Their steadfastness comes from their deep faith in the Creator of heaven and earth, and all spiritual searching, uncertainty, and discovery are in God's hands.

Many people in these congregations recall "the way it used to be" in contrast to the way the congregation is now. In the introduction we heard Lorraine Burd, chair of the worship and music committee at Latrobe Presbyterian, describe how the worship committee in her church used to be responsible for washing and ironing the linens for communion and hosting formal teas. Now the committee is at the center of the liturgical and spiritual renewal in the congregation as they lead worship, reflect on their practices and patterns of worship, learn more about liturgical theology and history, and experiment with new ways of worshiping God. The change has been difficult for some whose commitment to patterns of social formality outweighed their interest in the Christian spiritual life. The reorientation of congregational life from programmatic and institutional concerns toward their shared life in God has been difficult for some. But with the encouragement of the congregation's spiritual leaders, people have been led to respond to God with greater freedom. The congregation now enjoys a rich liturgical life that has become the foundation for their spiritual renewal. The spiritual mentors in these congregations have been bold in demonstrating, encouraging, and initiating new ways of acting and being. "It is hard to let go of old habits and ways of being," writes Thompson. "Out of [encounter with God], God calls us to a new sense of purpose and mission in life. A spiritual director can encourage us toward a fuller freedom to respond to God in loving obedience."[44]

The spiritual masters tell us that reflection on our practices of prayer is an essential step along the pilgrimage of the Christian life. And, not to put too fine a point on it, participation in practices of prayer are *experiences*. So to take up again the experiential learning cycle, if we want to learn from our experiences of prayer, we can reflect on our practices, observing the ways they shape us into the likeness of Christ. We can study about new practices of prayer, investigating their movements and dynamics, their history and usefulness in the lives of others. And we can complete the learning cycle by preparing for and experimenting with these new patterns. Ongoing reflection, learning, and experimentation insure that attentiveness to the work of the Holy Spirit in our lives is maintained. In these congregations, learning the Christian life from the experience of congregational life, including the experience of prayer, is a pervasive part of congregational culture.

Chapter Five

Study and Instruction

I t is Sunday morning and, not surprisingly, a group of adults is gathering in the library of Immanuel Presbyterian Church in Tacoma. A similar group is in the conference room of Old Pine Presbyterian in Philadelphia. Another group gathers at Covenant Presbyterian in Palo Alto. On Wednesday nights at Northminster Presbyterian in Seattle, the church parlor buzzes with conversation around a book the group has read. In Bloomsburg, Pennsylvania, people of St. Paul's Episcopal Church crowd into rector Marjorie Menaul's study on a weekday morning. What makes these groups remarkable is not just *that* they gather but *why* they gather and *how* they go about achieving their purposes. Adults in these congregations gather for study, serious study. They exhibit eager curiosity about many things, especially those things that center on the Christian spiritual life. Often they study Scripture. At other times they study creeds or the works of theologians or the lives of important figures in church history or practices of worship and prayer or topics of current importance in the world. The questions they bring to their study often center around their need to understand why they are doing what they are doing as Christians and as a congregation. They are not satisfied with established, unreflective "habits" of personal and congregational practices. They hunger for ways of engaging in the Christian life and in congregational life that are authentically practiced and critically reflected upon. Thus they have an almost inexhaustible supply of lively questions that bring them to these opportunities for study. They expect to learn something, to be sure. But more than that, they expect to deepen and broaden their communal and personal participation in the Christian spiritual life. They expect to grow in faith.

At Old Pine the group is studying short fictional pieces gathered for the theological questions they raise.[1] The reading for this Sunday is particularly challenging and raises many questions about the nature of suffering and its spiritual significance. Most everyone in the group of about fifteen has come well prepared. They have read the assigned stories and have given some thought to the study questions provided. Pastor Debbie McKinley guides the discussion, using thoughtful, probing questions. She lets the discussion take its own course, depending on the rich insights of participants to provide significant learning for all. Among this group of adults are long-time church leaders and shy newcomers, well-educated individuals and those with little formal education, people from all walks of life, including a mentally ill man who is a frequent participant. Also present are several people who, I learn later, have experienced profound physical and personal suffering.

The discussion in this group is frank, respectful, probing, and open-ended. The group's conversation is marked by an implicit assumption that "understanding suffering" is *not* their purpose. Rather, they intend to explore suffering together, noting its shape, dimensions, dynamics, and effects. They intend also to surround their explorations with the questions that Christian faith raises. In their conversation one notes a high degree of intellectual flexibility, with one searching question giving rise to another. Thus they are not surprised that their explorations do not result in a list of "principles of suffering" or some such set of answers. They seem to view the paradox and ambiguity of suffering (and all of human life) as normal. Their stability comes, they say, from the presence of the living God in their lives, who provides a foundation of faithfulness within which to face even the paradox of suffering. Spiritual growth takes time, says one participant. "You can't be pulling up the carrots to see how they are growing."

In the congregations described here serious study is a community norm. There are opportunities for study and instruction for children, youth, and adults, with adult learning given a particularly high priority. Opportunities for study among church leaders abound, with study, along with personal reflection and prayer, a regular part of committee meetings, planning sessions, and the meetings of governing boards. Especially in these settings, topics for study are carefully chosen for their pertinence to the purposes of the group. At Latrobe Presbyterian, where study of the liturgy is seen as especially important, pastor David Batchelder often begins worship committee meetings with a bit of liturgical history and invites the group to explore its relevance for their own practices of worship.

Within a context of spiritual searching, such study opportunities can lead congregational leaders to ask questions, analyze current practices, and propose alternative patterns for the congregation. In these and many other settings church members and leaders are given the opportunity to understand their experiences within larger frames of reference, using mental models that they themselves devise or models from some other source. Someone has said that at least half of what we learn in school we will never need—but nobody knows which half. With that in mind, these congregations are not interested only in "relevant" topics. Their interests are wide-ranging and demonstrate their commitment to knowing the Christian tradition as a foundation for their practice of Christian faith.

As congregations learn the Christian life from the experience of congregational life, study and instruction are cultural practices that support the construction of a uniquely Christian worldview within the congregation. It is this process to which this chapter is dedicated. And while the model of experiential learning we are proposing begins with experience and places study and instruction within the context of reflection on experience, the church has never felt obliged to engage in instruction as a response to experience *only*. Leaders need not wait until an experience prompts members of the congregation to seek further study of a topic. Pastors and educators in these congregations use study and instruction as opportunities to introduce new ideas and to engage in serious reflection on Christian practices. Study and instruction provide settings where leaders can propose conceptual frameworks that will help to orient the congregation's attention toward the presence of God among them.

Study and Instruction in Experiential Learning

The congregations described here exhibit at least four significant qualities that we have noted before. They take experience seriously, especially the experience of encounter with God in worship. They invite and nurture enduring, trusting, and honest relationships among members. They use a unique vocabulary—a congregational "native language"—to name and explore their experience of encounter with God. And they engage in frequent questioning, striving to ask the right question at the right time in order to discern the presence of God in all they do.

In the cycle of experiential learning, lived experience, especially the experience of encounter with God in worship, is of central concern. Learning from that experience, however, is likely to be weakened without investigations that take us beyond our own time and place. Humans have the well-developed ability to think abstractly—to employ words, images, and metaphors to express concepts—to organize concepts in relation to one another, and to analyze the merits of conceptual systems. Engaging in study and instruction offers explicit opportunities both to engage in original concept formation and to entertain the ideas of others. Thus we are exposed to the many ways others have sought to express the meaning of their experience through the use of abstract concepts. Our experiences are open to interpretation through the meaning others have made from similar experiences.

The process of forming concepts most often occurs in congregational life during opportunities for study and instruction. The task of these study opportunities (which include but are not limited to what we commonly call "Christian education") is "to engage the faith-story and the experience of living into a dialogical relationship from which meaning for living emerges."[2] Thus the relationship between experience and the conceptual interpretation of that experience is a reciprocal, mutually illuminating one. "The faith-story and experience must necessarily be related. The faith-story is a tool to interpret and test one's existence, in the same way that experience helps one to understand faith anew in different cultural epochs with different cultural needs."[3]

The resources for building the conceptual structures necessary to understand our lives "Christianly" begin with Scripture. In the congregations described here the study of Scripture is an ever-present feature of congregational culture. The more they know of Scripture, they say, the more deeply they can enter into the worship of God. On Wednesday nights at Old Pine Street Presbyterian in Philadelphia, pastor Debbie McKinley leads a group in a study of the coming Sunday's lectionary passages. Members of this group prepare for the study with prayerful reading of the passages beforehand. Then the group explores the passage together, with Debbie's exegetical preparation as a foundation. According to Charlotte Cady, "It prepares you for the worship service in a different way than if you haven't [been a part of the study]. We've really talked about [the Scripture] and understood its meaning in a little more depth. . . . It helps me look more deeply into Scripture and into my faith." The mutual benefit of this kind of study for both pastor and congregation is confirmed by stories told at Old Pine Street. Debbie says she always gains insights from members of the study group, and she draws on their wisdom as she prepares the sermon. Members of the study group say they "listen in a whole different way" on Sunday, anticipating echos of their Wednesday night conversation. The conceptual structures introduced and proposed on Wednesdays are modified and strengthened on Sundays.

All of our human intellectual capacities can be marshaled as we engage the breadth and depth of the Christian tradition and explore the various conceptual approaches others have taken. The knowledge we gain about Scripture and the history of the church serves as a context, a kind of background knowledge, in which worship occurs. The more congregations know of that "great cloud of witnesses," the more fully they can enter into encounter with God in worship. References to the exodus of the children of Israel out of slavery in Egypt are not likely to connect with worshipers who do not know the story. Quotations from John Calvin or John Wesley will miss their mark with congregations who are not familiar with aspects of church history. Poetic allusions to scriptural stories in the texts of hymns only make connections when people know the Scripture. So the acquisition of basic biblical and historical literacy enhances participation in worship.

Over and above basic literacy, however, the ability to analyze, synthesize, and evaluate knowledge is also a task central to study and instruction. In the congregations described here the accumulation of information is not an end in itself. Neither can the style of study and instruction be seen as "indoctrination." There is not a strictly enforced set of principles that must be adhered to. Rather there is a culture of intellectual curiosity, investigation, and love of learning within these faithful Christian communities wherein the nurture of faith is encouraged and supported.

At Covenant Presbyterian in Palo Alto, where a love of learning is demonstrated through the adult education programs, in "Family Cluster" small-group meetings, and in the excellent church library, people take joy in the opportunities they have to share their personal faith stories and to learn from one another. "There is a really wide spread of opinion on social and theological matters," says Diane Jones, a longtime member. "Politically, we have some very liberal people and some very conservative people, but it doesn't seem to get in our way. Who we are as Christians is more important than our political affiliations or other kinds of personal categories." Members of the congregation are active in presbytery, synod, and national church activities and take advantage of the learning opportunities those connections provide. But, says pastor Isaiah Jones, they are committed to "bearing with one another" and being the body of Christ together. With these values in mind, they put their differences of opinion aside and let their curiosity and love of learning take the lead. This stance is supported by the congregation's multicultural character and by study opportunities such as the study of Luke-Acts that focuses on multiculturalism in the New Testament church.

In this congregation and others like it, study and instruction encourage and support the life of the mind, which they understand as a necessary element in Christian faith. We have noted that Christian faith includes a belief conviction, a trusting relationship, and a lived life of agape.[4] In the activities of study and instruction, the belief component of faith is given explicit attention. According to Thomas Groome, "While Christian faith is more than belief, there is certainly a belief dimension to it as it finds embodiment in the lives of people. . . . That Christianity makes certain historical, moral, and cognitive claims and proposes them to people as a way of making meaning in their lives is beyond doubt. The *activity* of Christian faith, therefore, requires, in part, a firm conviction about the truths proposed as essential beliefs of the Christian faith. Insofar as these beliefs are personally appropriated, understood, and accepted by the Christian, there is therefore a cognitive, or . . . 'intellectualist' dimension to Christian faith."[5] In this context the word "belief" is both a noun and verb.[6] We use belief as a noun when we refer to the ideas and concepts employed to articulate Christian faith. We use belief as a verb when we refer to that activity of personally understanding, accepting, and appropriating the ideas and concepts that make up Christian faith. Faith requires, then, both knowledge *about* the beliefs and practices of Christian believers as well as personally appropriated convictions that these beliefs point toward truth.

In chapter 2 we introduced a process of learning that theorists call "building cognitive structures," a process given explicit attention in study and instruction. Calling on the human capacities for abstract thinking, comprehension, analysis, synthesis, and evaluation of ideas in symbolic form (words and images), educators offer knowledge about Christian faith within a context where that knowledge can be understood and personally appropriated.

The formation and reformation of Christian conceptual frameworks requires the use of a specialized vocabulary built up in the Christian tradition over many centuries and uniquely adapted in each congregation's culture. Ethnographer James Spradley notes that "language is more than a means of communication about reality: it is a tool for constructing reality. Different languages create and express different realities. They categorize experience in different ways. They provide alternative patterns for customary ways of thinking and perceiving."[7] We have noted that the congregations described here all have distinctive vocabularies, distinctive sets of words and phrases that reflect their unique worldview. Brant Copeland, pastor of First Presbyterian in Tallahassee, calls the acquisition of a Christian vocabulary "putting on the linguistic garment of salvation":

> The Christian faith uses a specialized vocabulary and a particular collection of images and metaphors, most of them drawn from Scripture. The culture outside the church doesn't resonate with these metaphors or understand many of these words because they make reference to a reality the culture does not acknowledge. The challenge of Christian catechesis is not merely to translate the specialized language of faith into rough cultural equivalencies. The challenge is to acculturate disciples into a new world altogether, to transform them into native speakers of Christian.[8]

Opportunities for study and instruction in these congregations intentionally engage this vocabulary and encourage members to become "native speakers." It may be awkward for some to begin using specialized words such as "discernment," "call," "spiritual journey," or even liturgical words and phrases like "The peace of the Lord Jesus Christ be with you," "This is the Word of the Lord," and "Thanks be to God." But without this specialized vocabulary we are less able to name our experience of encounter with God in Christian terms and to reflect in ways that are spiritually formative. Thus study and instruction in worship-centered congregations is a kind of "language school" that enables participation in the worship of God and in the Christian spiritual life.

Conceptual structures are made up of ideas and images clustered together in intricate mental frameworks. We noted in chapter 2 that individuals exhibit a wide variety of patterns in the ways their conceptual structures are constructed and employed. Concepts can be closely related to one another, forming an integrated system of beliefs, or concepts can be loosely related, even compartmentalized from one another. It is not unusual, in fact, for people to hold an array of contradictory beliefs. In addition, not all beliefs play equal roles within a belief system. Beliefs can be described as central, intermediate, or peripheral, indicating their significance within the structure of a conceptual belief system. Central concepts are those that are essential in the construction of a belief system. Intermediate and peripheral beliefs, by contrast, are important but play a less pivotal role in the belief system and its embodiment in action. Moreover, people hold beliefs with varying amounts of conviction. Some beliefs, even central beliefs, are held tentatively by some and with great certainty by others. There are differences, too, in the flexibility and/or rigidity with which belief systems are constructed. Some people, we have noted, hold their beliefs so rigidly that they fail to note the distinction between themselves as persons and the beliefs they hold. To quote John Hull, rather than *having* beliefs, such people *are* their beliefs,[9] making the process of exploration a threatening, even terrifying one. For others the process can be exciting and liberating.

In the congregations described here the task of examining and constructing conceptual belief structures is carried on in an atmosphere of trusting exploration, where beliefs and practices can be examined in considerable depth and detail, knowing that all of the explorations are grounded in faith in God, not in the conceptual constructions of beliefs themselves. Individuals are supported and encouraged to continue their explorations, even when they feel unsure about where that exploration might be leading. Group members model for one another a tolerance for ambiguity as they resist the temptation to let anxiety overwhelm them. Thus participants tend to develop flexible belief systems. They are eager to understand central as well as not-so-central aspects of Christian faith and to explore the relationships among those beliefs. Thus they aim toward coherent and integrated Christian faith where belief undergirds action and where action inspires further exploration. These congregations, by the careful strategies they employ for their study together and through the connections they make among worship, prayer, study, and mission, demonstrate *how* to study the Christian faith. Longtime member of West Raleigh Ann Myhre describes it this way: In this congregation, she says, there are lots of people who want to keep "learning and caring" together. For them it is not just a matter of being interested in the subject matter or loving to learn. Rather, says Ann, learning inspires caring, and caring for others prompts questions that make people eager to learn more.

Educators have been accustomed to think of the cognitive functions employed in the construction of conceptual structures as logical, linear, cause-and-effect processes. While these are indeed necessary, the process of concept formation and the construction of conceptual structures and belief systems is now understood to include much more. In fact, all of the dimensions of experience described in chapter 3 (physical/sensory, affective, cognitive, narrative, social/relational, and imaginative) play significant roles in the construction of belief systems. Of particular importance here is the imaginative dimension of learning.

Shellie Levine, a researcher into children's spirituality, argues that in addition to linear logic, children (and presumably adults, too) exhibit what she calls "metaphoric logic" in their engagements and appropriations of the world and use it extensively in making meaning.[10] Faith, she says, is "the cognition of the possible"[11] known both through hypothetico-deductive reasoning and through the use of metaphors enacted during children's play. When children engage in pretend play, what is possible *and* the child's faith in that possibility are acted out by the child. Levine uses the example of a child using a broom for a horse. Children, she says, routinely take into account the reality of the broom—its length and width, the materials of which it is made, its spatial location, and so on—while also exhibiting faith in the possibility that it *is* a horse. "During the metaphoric cognition of play the child is exquisitely sensitive to dual realities. . . . During play the broom is truly a broom while simultaneously being a horse."[12] Or to use a more familiar definition for metaphor, the broom both *is* and *is not* a horse.[13] The capacity to engage in imaginative, metaphoric thinking along with logical reasoning, says Levine, forms the foundation for spirituality in children and in adults. Metaphoric logic enables us to comprehend, embrace, and enact faith according to the possibilities found in God's grace.

Cognitive structures are expressed in symbolic forms—in words, images, gestures, and actions, and in their juxtapositions, seen especially in worship. To call again on Fred Holper, *how* does Christian faith mean? It means symbolically. Or to use the church's language, "No merely human symbols can be adequate to comprehend the fullness of God, and none is identical to the reality of God. . . . Yet the symbols human beings use can be adequate for understanding, sharing, and responding to God's gracious activity in the world."[14] As congregations enter into study of Scripture and tradition, they do well, as these congregations do, to recognize conceptual structures for what they are: necessary, helpful symbols by which Christians throughout the ages have sought to describe their experiences with God while not intending to equate those symbols with the triune God they seek to worship. During times of study and instruction natural curiosity calls us to inquire about *what* these symbols mean. In pursuing such questions, however, we find symbolic, embodied answers. Thus we are once again reminded that in all our teaching and learning the "facts" of Christian faith, "teaching that" is in service of "teaching how" to enact that faith in worship, prayer, and service.

The complex mental frameworks constructed in the natural meaning-making process of experience and reflection on experience serve as interpretive lenses that shape how we perceive the world.[15] We see what we expect to see most of the time because past experience has taught us what to notice and what to ignore. Even so, our ongoing experience and meaning-making reflection call for the formation or rather the re-formation of our mental frameworks. Every experience is an opportunity to encounter the world afresh and to reconsider life's meaning in light of that experience. Of course, most of us live lives that flow within fairly predictable boundaries so that the routines of daily living often serve to mask the uniqueness of the ordinary. Sometimes, maybe more often than we think, opportunities arise that allow us to look at life from an alternative perspective. Life is full of experiences that open up gaps between what we expect and what we encounter, and we are startled into seeing things in a new way. Especially during life's major transitions and unexpected crises, our customary ways of perceiving and understanding are challenged. Leaders in the churches described here say that these are the times when opportunities for learning are especially fruitful.

At West Raleigh, where practices of spiritual discernment permeate the culture of the congregation, members face life crisis situations in ways that reflect their openness to new learning. Henry Wynands, an engineer who recently found himself unexpectedly looking for a job, says that in the midst of the uncertainty of unemployment, the process of spiritual discernment practiced in the church helped him approach his job search in a more systematic and concentrated way. "Mission discernment is important for what's going on in the church," he says, "but it is also really important for me personally." He is less anxious about the uncertainty of his situation, and he is open to a variety of possibilities.

The gap between what we expect and what we actually encounter is called by social scientists *cognitive dissonance*.[16] Sometimes the dissonance can be so mild that it is barely noticeable. At other times it is so great that it disturbs the entire structure of our mental framework. Cognitive dissonance always takes the form of "otherness," wherein an encounter with a situation, person, opinion, or point of view is something other than that which we expect. And it is natural to want to resolve that dissonance. According to Laurent Daloz, "there is an intrinsic human need to close such a dissonance, to harmonize it again with our own inner selves."[17] That drive for resolution of dissonance, he says, is what learning is all about. Teaching involves opening up the gaps and then supporting learners as they strive to close them. Teachers "toss little bits of disturbing information in their students' paths, little facts and observations, insights and perceptions, theories and interpretations—cow plops on the road to truth—that raise questions about their students' current worldviews and invite them to entertain alternatives to close the dissonance, accommodate their structures, *think* afresh. . . . Transformation demands a deep rethinking of our fundamental assumptions and . . . the role of the 'skillful teacher' is to enable that to happen."[18] Teachers in the church, whose orientation is toward spiritual formation, have the explicit task of proposing the gospel of Jesus Christ in ways that intentionally raise questions about the congregation's current worldview while also inviting learners to entertain faithful alternatives.

When I was a twenty-something, stay-at-home mother of two young boys and singing in the choir of the church down the block, a personal comment by the pastor during a sermon seriously rocked my world. I had been raised in a conservative Baptist tradition, but my husband and I were living in a community with no Baptist churches, so we joined the Methodist church. During an Advent sermon that first year our pastor William F. B. Rodda said, almost as an aside, that while the virgin birth was a centrally important matter of faith to many people, for himself it was not all that important. First I doubted my own hearing. Had I heard him correctly?! Then I set about trying to reason his comment through. I thought I understood how God worked: God did this (send Jesus to die on the cross for the sins of the world), you did that (repent, confess, and be baptized), and everything was hunkey-dorey for all eternity. Neat and simple, I had been taught. Now this wise and wonderful man was saying that Jesus' virgin birth—the basis for his ability to save—was not that important! What could all of this mean?

While continuing to care for my family and sing in the choir, over the next six months I pondered and puzzled over these matters. Finally, on a very hot summer day, I called Dr. Rodda's office and asked if I could come to see him. As I walked to his office, I carried a fistful of scraps of paper. All during the winter and spring new questions would emerge out of my pondering (sometimes at the strangest times and places) and would push my thinking along. I had questions scribbled on the backs of old grocery lists, the corners of torn paper bags, the backs of envelopes. I attempted to put the questions into some logical order and lay them at the feet of this wise saint, my pastor. If "salvation" consisted of thus-and-so, we Christians should be involved in certain kinds of ministry. But if "salvation" was something more comprehensive, then how were we Christians to know what to do?

Dr. Rodda, a patient and wise teacher, spent all afternoon with me, working through my questions and posing many more. At the end of that time I was more ready than ever to spend a lifetime pursuing whatever questions came along, sure that "salvation" rested in the hands of the Creator of heaven and earth, whether I understood it completely or not. The questions, I have found, are more important than the answers most of the time, and it was a "skillful teacher" who taught me that.

As we have noted, the process of reforming the mental models through which we understand the world can be a difficult one for some people. Lawrence Daloz, in the words of Dante, has called it "the deep and savage way,"[19] a journey into seemingly uncharted territory that requires the suspension if not the relinquishing of familiar patterns of belief. It is a journey that not everyone is willing to complete. Adequate support for learners from leaders and fellow learners is essential in the process.

A pattern of navigation through this process of "perspective transformation"[20] is often evident. When learners are faced with new information or with an unfamiliar situation that forces them to look at things from a startlingly new perspective, their first response is often shock and immobilization. This state of numb surprise accompanies an out-of-the-ordinary encounter, whether one receives it with gladness or with suspicion and resistance. Researchers have found as they study accounts of adult decision making that it seems to make little difference whether the reaction is positive or negative; there is still a period of immobilization as individuals try to comprehend unfamiliar cognitive territory. Often this stage is followed by a period of denial, where people are inclined to think, "This just *can't be true!*" The impulse here is to anticipate the difficulty of "changing one's mind" and to suppress those potential conflicts. Yet even while resisting a new perspective, the mind is active in reflecting on its features and possibilities, a task that requires considerable energy. (Recall the switchback patterns of reflection noted in chapter 2.)

When perspective transformations are particularly demanding, the period of denial may be followed by a period of depression or regret as persons grapple with possible disruptions in their accustomed patterns of interaction and commitment. If their priorities change as a result of new insights, they fear that relationships may be disrupted. It is at this point that many people abandon a new perspective and return to their former perspectives. Whether they continue in the process of transformation or abort its progress, there is a period of "letting go" of options. Transformation always involves a necessary period of "saying yes" and "saying no" to particular sets of possibilities. Often people describe a kind of grief or mourning over possibilities, commitments, projects, and relationships that will be left behind, no matter which path they choose.

As people proceed further toward fully integrating a new perspective, they begin to test options and search for new relationships and commitments. Questions abound here. Intellectual explorations may include a broad range of subjects as people explore the implications of new knowledge. They may try out a number of activities and reach out to a variety of other people for friendship. All of this activity is directed toward incorporating the new perspective into all aspects of their life. Commitments may be short-lived as they try one thing and then another before finding a good "fit."

As the tensions inherent in reforming one's perspective are resolved, there comes a time for integration, when people review the journey they have been making and search for meaning in the experience. They tell their stories back to themselves in order to discover the importance of their transformation. They construct an explanation of the circumstances that brought about the change and of their choices during the transition. All of this leads to a more thorough integration of the new perspective into emerging commitments and life choices.

This process of perspective transformation repeats itself again and again throughout the lives of Christians who take seriously the call to spiritual formation. As the likeness of Christ is formed ever more deeply in us, we are called examine the beliefs we hold and the ways they orient our perceptions, values, and actions. The process may be gradual and incremental. Occasionally it is sudden and disruptive. In all cases, however, the role of the community of faith is integral to the process. There are very real fears and dangers inherent in our conversion into the likeness of Christ, and the role of a supportive and challenging community is essential in this process.

Among the striking features of the congregations in this study are the social and relational elements inherent in their approach to study and instruction, which are seen in the ways individuals and groups relate to one another. People are open to knowing one another well and are committed to one another for the long haul. Their relationships exhibit noticeable levels of trust and honesty that have developed over time. Thus they provide an adequate "holding environment" for experiential learning, where there is support *and* challenge *and* trustworthy communal stability. Members of these congregations and especially the groups who study together routinely entrust their exploration and learning to others as they investigate Scripture and the Christian tradition together and subject its proposals to rigorous questioning. Individuals trust one another to allow them to explore, to challenge their ideas lovingly, and to help them discern the path of faithfulness to Jesus Christ. Leaders in these study groups emerge out of their demonstrations of knowledge and wisdom in matters of Christian faith and their own lived faithfulness (not their social status or personal achievements). According to Dale Ziemer, "the fruitful conversation of the Christian community is a work and gift of the Holy Spirit. It is both evidence of the presence of the Spirit in the midst of the community as well as a key aspect in the formation . . . [of] community. . . . The 'principalities and powers' of the present age manifest themselves in a complex web of issues, challenges, and opportunities—a situation in which no one individual 'knows the answer.' The only viable option exists among groups of people who gather together to think, inquire, probe, pray, and deliberate together to discern God's will for their life together as they seek to engage these realities."[21]

At Northminster Presbyterian in Seattle, pastor Dennis Hughes says, "We take it for granted that people will have questions and come to different answers, but we have a common commitment to seeking those answers with some integrity." With that in mind the church has taken on some difficult topics together and has grown through the experience. During one recent Sunday morning classroom conversation, an elderly man responded enthusiastically to learning about the ancient roots of Christian worship. It was obvious that this knowledge was beginning to reshape his understanding and appreciation for the practices of the church, when suddenly he became indignant. "Why don't our pastors tell us these things?" he asked. "How is it we've been to church all our lives and no one will tell us these things?" Reflecting on that exchange, Dennis says, "There are people who have been afraid to talk about tough questions. We delight in it." Elder Connie Fraser remarks that "all of us talk about the fact that we don't always see eye to eye but we all get along." At Northminster they know they don't have all the answers, members say, but that is okay. It is pursuing the questions that is the intention here.

Welcoming the Questions

We have noted how reflection on experience often results in more questions than answers. In congregations with a lively intellectual climate, questions are welcomed and taken seriously. Assuming that it is natural to be curious, these communities often ask, "What are you curious about? What do you wonder about?" Often people's questions are simple "information" questions through which they seek to comprehend the Christian story more fully. Once the information gaps have been filled, however, a deeper meaning-making level of questioning emerges.

- How might we "explain" our experience?
- What theories might we propose? (Why did it happen this way?)

While our own hypotheses are important and can be the source of new theological insight, the church has a rich treasury of reflections on encounter with God at its disposal, beginning with Scripture. In searching for conceptual frameworks to illuminate experience, Christians turn first to Scripture. And so leaders often ask

- What events in the story of God's people might help to illuminate our present circumstances?

Likewise leaders, as resident theologians and spiritual mentors, call on specialized training and experience to put congregations in touch with the theological resources of the church from throughout history and around the globe, including voices to which the church has not always listened. Leaders entertain questions like

- What theological concepts are relevant to our experience?
- What is their history and meaning?
- What can we learn from the church through the ages and around the globe?
- Whose voices have we not yet heard? The poor, the homeless, the ill, people of other races and ethnic groups, those to whom we seek to minister?
- What might those with whom we disagree say?
- How might these "outsiders" understand our experience? What will be necessary in order to hear their voices?

In addition to scriptural and theological frameworks are a number of other disciplines on which the church can fruitfully draw in order to understand its circumstances. These disciplines, necessary and helpful as they are, are always in service to the larger scriptural, theological, and spiritual orientations of the congregation.

- Are there theories from the fields of economics, political science, psychology, sociology, organizational development, leadership theory, and so on, that might be helpful in understanding our current circumstances?
- What is the relationship of these theories to the church's theocentric claims?

"Soul tending" is understood to be a universal and mutually shared responsibility of all the baptized. And so perhaps the most pervasive question, articulated in many different ways, is "Where is God in this?" This question, drawn from practices of spiritual direction, is the question toward which all other questions move during times of study and instruction. It is not intellectual curiosity alone that energizes study for these congregations, but the desire to know God. Intellectual pursuits enable these congregations to understand their faith more fully and enter into the experience of encounter with God more deeply.

Intellectual curiosity and a welcoming of questions pervades the entire culture of these congregations, not just programmed occasions for study. One mark of this hunger for knowledge is the presence of a good church library. These libraries include reference books; Bible dictionaries and atlases; biblical commentaries; theological dictionaries; classic works of theology, history, and Christian spirituality; study materials; devotional books; and fiction. Often there are large collections of children's books that appeal to a broad range of ages. At Northminster in Seattle, the library occupies attractive shelves along the wall of the church parlor. When people gather there for coffee hour, week-night study group, or a committee meeting, they are likely to visit the shelves as a part of their exploration of questions inherent to the Christian spiritual life. These churches also have collections of curriculum materials for children, youth, and adults, carefully catalogued and shelved for convenient access. Their commitment to study and instruction is reflected in their budget allocations, where substantial (sometimes generous) resources are set aside for books, curriculum materials, and guest speakers.

Why would congregations choose to put their library collections in the most frequently used space in the church rather than a quiet, out-of-the-way corner? The presence of these collections signals to members of the congregation that the life of the mind is valued and supported. These congregations know that "everything the church does teaches," even the presence and placement of resources for study and instruction. For them learning about the history, theology, practices, and biblical grounding for the Christian life is not limited to the Sunday school hour but is an integral part of the whole process of learning the Christian life from the experience of congregational life. Seeking more knowledge and a deeper understanding of their Christian heritage is a natural part of what it means to be the church. And so they welcome questions, even the most probing, difficult questions, and they support and encourage the search for knowledge these questions inspire.

In the aftermath of the terrorist attacks in the fall of 2001, St. Paul's Episcopal Church in Bloomsburg, Pennsylvania, began searching for ways to help its members and others gain insight into the significance of these events. One area of concern was the realization that people in a small rural town had little or no contact with Muslim people and little knowledge of Islam as a major world religion. Rector Marjorie Menaul worked with members of the church to design a series of study sessions that would serve as an arena for sharing their knowledge and discussing their concerns. Interest and enthusiasm built for the study as people read critically and did further research on their own. The group began by reading *An Introduction to Islam for Christians* by Paul Varo Martinson[22] and then expanded their engagement by reading other books and articles, exploring Internet websites, and watching documentary presentations and interviews on television. People came to the meetings well prepared with information, questions, and insights. Naturally many points of view were represented in their discussions. "I was delighted," says Marjorie, "that people were able to question and challenge each other in an atmosphere of mutual respect and genuine searching. There was a consensus that no one had all the answers and that everyone's insights were valuable, even when people did not agree." In this most unsettling time this congregation was able to invite, even welcome, their most difficult questions and to explore the implications of those questions in an atmosphere of mutual respect and intellectual engagement. At the end of the study they invited leaders from the nearest Islamic center fifty miles away. Their study had prepared them well to ask substantive questions and show genuine respect for these religious leaders.

Teaching in Congregational Life

Congregations that take experience seriously are attentive to the many elements of congregational life. So it is not surprising that educational leaders consider seriously how teachers and learners will experience instruction and plan environments that will support spiritual formation. Beverly Mills has been a member of West Raleigh Presbyterian Church for about ten years. Her spiritual awakening has its roots, she says, in the women's circle of which she is a member. Her eyes light up as she exclaims, "We studied worship for a whole year!" In addition there were some adult classes on worship during the Sunday school hour. "It was really enlightening because it is not something that you fully understand, just intuitively. There's some education that has to go on." Through this focused study Beverly says her spiritual life has grown. The more she understands about worship, she says, the more thoroughly she can enter into the presence of God with the gathered community.

Congregations train, nurture, and support those involved in educational ministry in many ways, and the resources for this support are plentiful.[23] Teaching expertise is supported by a large array of resources for teacher training, an expanding repertoire of teaching strategies, careful curriculum evaluation and selection, and ongoing program planning and evaluation. Even more important in these congregations, however, is the recognition that teaching in the church is an experience that calls for reflection and can result in fruitful experiential learning.

In my years as a director of Christian education, I often held teacher training events in the congregation, to which almost no one came. The congregations I served participated in regional training events that depended on a few participants from a number of churches for their success. While these strategies still have an important place in preparing teachers for teaching in the church, additional aspects of educational leadership and ministry can enhance these programmatic efforts. The responsibility of educational leaders in congregations is, among other things, to nurture the spiritual formation that is inherent in teaching in the church. With that in mind, leaders need to ask themselves, "How can I support teachers in discerning God's presence in their teaching?"

In order to address this question educators might organize teacher training on a rotating schedule, classroom by classroom, program by program. All groups would naturally be planning, teaching, and evaluating their programs, and leaders should systematically join teachers in those activities. There would be many opportunities to learn teaching skills, expand the teaching repertoires of teachers, review curriculum materials, plan for learners' needs and abilities, and evaluate ongoing teaching practices. In addition, each group's time together would include the study of Scripture, personal sharing and prayer, and reflection on God's presence and activity in teaching. The intimacy of a small group focused on shared responsibilities holds the possibility, I think, for spiritual formation to become an integral part of teaching in the church.

While the churches in this study do not use this model, educational leaders willingly take on their roles as program administrators and skills trainers for program leaders because they know that these tasks provide opportunities for initiating the processes of spiritual formation inherent in teaching in the church. Teaching in the church provides opportunities for encounters with God and with the people of God that call for deep spiritual discernment. Teaching is deeply formative when leaders ask, "Where is God in this?" Most churches are, on some level, program oriented and task focused, and while programs and tasks are an integral part of these congregations' lives, they know that programs are *not* the point. Spiritual discernment and formation provide the foundation for all programmatic work. So leaders in worship-centered congregations weave the spiritual nurture of teachers into every encounter. All of the organizational and programmatic tasks are surrounded by communal prayer. Evaluation of individual teaching sessions as well as whole programs always give spiritual discernment a central place. (Whether or not a particular program went well or poorly, the presence of God can be discerned and teachers can be formed by that presence into the likeness of Christ.) Thus in these congregations involvement in Christian education is understood as a call and as an opportunity for faithful formation.

Reflection on Study and Instruction

Educators are trained to reflect on practices of teaching and learning in whatever settings they occur. In the congregations described here, these patterns of consistent reflection, grounded in intentional spiritual discernment, are among the many gifts educators bring to congregational life. With the guidance and example of capable educators, these congregations have adopted consistent practices of reflection and spiritual discernment as a part of their congregational culture. What has emerged in this chapter is an account of communal and personal spiritual discernment that arises from study and instruction but is not a purely individual affair. It is inherently relational and interactive throughout. The mental models Christians use for perceiving and interpreting the world begin and end in social contexts, and Christian faith is no exception. Thus the role of the community of faith in the articulation, exploration, critique, and reformation of the conceptual structures of Christian faith takes on a centrally formative role.

Chapter Six

Ministry and Mission

Contractor Steve Wright kneels at the threshold of my front door and completes extensive porch repairs while he tells me how his life has been changed forever by a trip to Honduras four years ago. I noticed early in the porch project the church logo on the front of his shirt (Wesley United Methodist Church, Bloomsburg, Pennsylvania) but have just today noticed the slogan in big letters across the back: "Shut Up and Dig!" "What's with the slogan on the back of your shirt?" I ask. So Steve spends the next half hour (while he works) telling me about his call to participate in a mission trip. "I knew God wanted me to go, but I kept making excuses," he admits. As he continued to pray he became confident that God would lead him to the right response and that his wife Kathy would be an instrument of God's leading. "That very night I was in my office with the door closed, praying, when Kathy knocked and said, 'You've got to come see what's on television.'" What he saw was the devastation of Hurricane Mitch on Central America and immediately he knew he was needed. Months later his church's construction team was one of the first mission groups, other than medical teams, authorized to go to Central America to assist the Hondurans. Steve puts the finishing touches on the doorway, but he hasn't finished his story. He jumps to his feet and says with passion in his voice and in his eyes, "I'm not the same man I was! I'll never be the same again!" Since the first trip Steve has gone on four more mission trips and has spoken to dozens of church and civic groups about his experiences.

The next time Steve comes to the house he brings along the photo albums and diaries of his trips. "The spelling is terrible, but I don't care. If

129

you read them, maybe you'll see what the trips were like." He is right! The power and immediacy of his experience radiates from each page. He has keen powers of observation and has recorded detailed descriptions of places, situations, and especially people. In the village where the team worked, a little girl, Estebana—her name in Spanish so much like Steve's own name—captivated him with her big brown eyes and playful ways. A boy, Mateo, worked alongside the men. A Nicaraguan stonemason's only means of livelihood, a worn and fragile trowel, fell to pieces during their work together. Steve was pleased to have given him (against the rules) an expensive new trowel that could sustain his earning capacity for years to come. These detailed descriptions, offered in the midst of vivid story-telling, give rise to emotions and personal reflection that make Steve wonder about many things. Why are these people so poor? Are our efforts really making a difference? Does all this work really help? How will this affect my life when I return? Will I be able to describe what I've learned to those back home?

Steve's church has a long tradition of mission involvement. Over the last several years the church has sponsored almost a dozen overseas and stateside mission trips. Staff member Marcia Kent Coleman, who has supervised many of the trips, says she always hopes that participants will come away with a larger worldview and an ongoing relationship with the poor. Otherwise, she says, the effort may not be worth it. "We were planning a trip to Honduras right after Hurricane Mitch when one of the members of the church here, a bright, capable professional man, asked me, 'Why can't I just write a check? Why should I go to some strange place to help?' I said, 'You can't pay enough to duplicate our presence, the fact of our being there in this crisis.'" It is this ministry of presence that inspires Marcia's efforts. In fact, she says, it may be that North Americans are affected more than the Central Americans by the experience.

The Bloomsburg Food Cupboard is housed on a quiet side street a block and a half off Main Street in a recently vacated volunteer fire hall adjacent to St. Columba's Catholic Church and school. The cupboard is open on Tuesdays and Sundays, and on this particular August Tuesday there is an evident cheerfulness about the place. A three-week heat wave has broken overnight, and the temperatures are almost cool. All the doors to the building are open, allowing the breeze to flow through. Lively conversation goes on, as clients and volunteers exchange greetings and updates on "how things are going." Martha Sheehe, the director, says, "This is not as much about food as it is about friendship and caring." There are people here, says Martha, who are at the lowest end of the social and economic ladder. She mentions a current book that describes the lives of the working poor (*Nickled and Dimed* by Barbara Erenreich) and says that it pretty accurately depicts the lives of the people coming through the doors of the food cupboard. Many of them are struggling with illness, have few job skills, or are raising grandchildren on a fixed income. "I often get asked if we serve the 'deserving poor,'" says Martha. "I always invite people who ask that question to come down and volunteer with us. Then I ask them, 'How many of these people could you hire?'" Martha teaches sixth-graders in St. Columba's Sunday school and is active in parish life. One of the most formative experiences for her was studying the Old Testament with the children. "I get frustrated," she says. "Poverty and hunger have been with us since Old Testament times, but it is hard to understand how it could still be going on." Martha has put her considerable organizational skills and her expertise as a nutritionist to work to help answer that question. The volunteers who work with her share her commitment and dedication to helping alleviate hunger in their community. "There is an affinity among people from all the churches around here. They feel called to this ministry and are here faithfully, week after week."

Martha Sheehe and Marcia Kent Coleman both echo a kind of skepticism about the relationship of privileged Americans to the poor. Martha notices some families who come to the food cupboard seem to be trying to live a middle-class lifestyle even though their earning power is minimal. She understands that desire, she says, but thinks it says something about what most Americans understand as "the good life." Marcia says she hopes the mission involvement of people at Wesley Methodist will help people to ask "What is this game we are playing in suburbia?"

When Steve, Marsha, Martha, and all who work with them respond to God's call to be in ministry in the name of Christ, they do so in a concrete, bodily way. Steve is involved body and soul and mind in digging foundations, laying concrete block, and teaching other workers the skills he has learned as a contractor. Martha's energetic tackling of the tasks of feeding the hungry, as well as her genuine welcome of them, makes her ministry truly incarnational.

The church has always understood the incarnational activities of ministry and mission to be grounded in the worship of God. According to Robert Martin, "It has been the historical self-understanding of the great Christian traditions—Anabaptist, Orthodox, Roman Catholic, Reformed, Anglican, Pentecostal, etc.—that the worship of God is . . . fundamental to the life and all ministrations of the church. As the bedrock of Christian discipleship, worship orients the church's pastoral and lay ministries . . . beyond mere action to their true origin, source, and goal as the praise and glory of God."[1] Worship grounds all that goes on in congregational life and serves as the incarnating compass point for the church's ministries, both within its walls (ministry) and outside its walls (mission).

According to Darrell Guder the incarnational nature of ministry, which has its origins in God's creation of the universe and in the incarnation of Jesus Christ, orients the church to the *why* and *what* and *how* of mission and ministry. "*Incarnation* . . . is a noun that summarizes the 'what' of the gospel, rooted in the 'why' of God's compassion for creation and purpose to bring about its salvation."[2] Because this is so, says Guder, the very shape of the church's ministry is patterned after God's own in-breaking presence in creation.

> There is a fundamental pattern to God's self-disclosure throughout all the scriptures. The way in which God acts is itself an essential dimension of God's mission. We discover what God is like as we experience God's love in action. The what and the how of God's mission, as it unfolds, are congruent and always shaped by the why of God's love. The plot of God's salvation history cannot be reduced merely to propositions about God. Rather, the story reveals both what God intends and how God wants his saving purposes accomplished.[3]

God's intention for humankind, the *why* of ministry and mission, has been articulated in that well-known first question from the Westminster Shorter Catechism, an articulation that resonates well with worship-centered congregations:

> Q: What is the chief end of [humankind]?
> A: [Humankind's] chief end is to glorify God, and enjoy [God] forever.[4]

According to Guder, "it is God's purpose that all humanity should be reconciled with God in Christ and experience forever the blessings of divine grace and favor. That is, to use the technical term, the eschatological purpose of human existence; this is the goal toward which God's saving activity is moving."[5] Since God's ultimate intention for humankind is to glorify and enjoy God, the intention for Christian ministry and mission endeavors should ultimately correspond with this intention. Ministry and mission in the congregations described here are understood to lead toward the worship of God, both for those who initiate mission and those who receive it. Marty Leming, who helps in the children's worship program at West

Raleigh Presbyterian, says her own worship life has been enriched through helping children worship. The quiet atmosphere of the children's worship program has nurtured her sense of reverence, she says. But more than that, her whole understanding of worship was changed by a four-year-old. Each Bible story is followed by a series of "I wonder . . . " questions. "One day I asked," says Marty, "'I wonder how we get closer to God?' and a child answered, 'We don't get closer to God. God gets closer to us.'" Many participants like Marty, who are active in ministry within the church and mission outside the church's walls have noted how they always receive more than they give, for which they give thanks and praise to God.

The worship-oriented intention for ministry and mission also determines the *how* of ministry. Glorification and enjoyment of God imply relationship with God, relationship that has its origins in the life and ministry of Jesus Christ. Guder says, "The relationship that the first disciples had with Jesus continues in every particular community of faith in its relationship with its Lord. Here is the heart of Christian worship, especially the Eucharist as the concrete experience of Christ's presence, receiving us into his presence in order to send us out as his people. How to do Jesus' mission, then, is learned from Jesus in every generation of the church through all the ways God's Spirit enables us to hear Christ's word and respond to his call."[6] Congregations that incarnate Christ-like relationships in their ministry and mission extend the concrete experience of Christ's presence to those they serve.

In order to discern the *what* of Christian ministry and mission to which a congregation is called, members and leaders must develop skills for perceiving the needs of the communities they serve and skills to identify the gifts necessary to meet those needs. Guder calls this the "boundary-crossing capacity of incarnational ministry."[7] A call to participate in a particular occasion for ministry or mission calls for a compassionate and informed understanding of the needs of others and a clear sense of the community's gifts. The gift and the call cohere in action that incarnates God's love in a particular time and place.

Mary Frances Cheek, a newly ordained elder at West Raleigh, says that spiritual hungers that have led to greater attention to the Christian spiritual life have also changed the way people understand the church's mission activities. "Instead of saying, 'We've just got to have warm bodies here feeding hungry people,' people now say, 'Where is God calling you? What are your gifts for ministry?'" The mission discernment process has focused on bringing together people's gifts for ministry with their growing discernment of God's call, she says, and it has helped to energize the congregation's mission efforts.

The congregations in this study demonstrate a strong commitment to mission, both local and global. Pastor Isaiah Jones of Covenant Presbyterian in Palo Alto says that it is the spirit of mission that attracted him to Covenant. "It has been a very mission-minded church, locally as well as globally. Presently the church is involved in many mission projects." The church is host to the local food cupboard. Members of the church are active in the denomination locally, regionally, and nationally. And the annual budget of the congregation shows a high percentage of giving to mission causes.

The congregations featured in this study seek to achieve coherence among the *why* and *how* and *what* of ministry as they respond to God's call to ministry and mission. They know that genuine liturgical renewal must lead to renewal of the church's life and witness in the world. Otherwise it is not genuine renewal. As Fred Holper reminds us,

> Our service of God in the sanctuary flows into and out of our call to serve the needs of God's people in the world. Congregations must commit themselves to an intentional and continuing process of conversion to a "liturgical piety," in which every aspect of their life and witness comes little by little to be shaped by the compelling, but also dangerously subversive, story of God's intentions for the world remembered and acted out in their corporate worship. That process of conversion—that process of letting God's encounter with us in worship form and transform every dimension of our corporate life and witness—must be at the heart of each congregation's efforts at liturgical renewal. Only then can we come to see *clearly* just how many places at the table *God* wants us to set.[8]

Becoming a "Sign, Foretaste, and Instrument" of the Reign of God

Whenever the church enacts its commitments to extend the worship of God to all creation, it gives witness to the lordship of Jesus Christ. Inagrace and Paul Dietterich at the Center for Parish Development write that every ministry of the church can be understood as a *sign* of the reign of God, a *foretaste* of that reign, and an *instrument* for bringing about an element of the reign of God here and now.[9]

> As a sign . . . the community of God's people is called to point beyond themselves to the power and the glory of the almighty God. The testimony they are to give is not to their own holiness or goodness, but to

the gracious love of God. The reign of God does not fall from the clouds; it is mediated historically. It is established by shining forth from one concrete people and thereby revealing its nature in the world. Precisely to the degree that the people of God lets itself be grasped by God's rule it will be transformed—in all dimensions of its existence. Only in this way will God's people become a light and sign to the nations.[10]

Especially as Christians participate in worship they enact the coming reign of God, and life together becomes a *foretaste* of that reign. Kevin Seasoltz writes, "Liturgical celebration is like a dress rehearsal for the end of time. We put on Christ and act and relate to one another as Christ relates to us."[11] This enactment of right relationships established in Jesus Christ is not limited to liturgical enactments alone, to be sure. In congregations all interactions and relationships come under the power of Christ's transforming love enacted in worship. "It is by the quality of their communal life that God wills the church to be a light to the nations . . .," write the Dietterichs. "It is by the character of its communal life that the church witnesses, that it proclaims the gospel, that it serves the world."[12] The quality of the communal life will naturally be different from the society that surrounds it. "It is a community separated to a different style of life and to new forms of life which realize what God wants society to be."[13] The distinctive kind of common life to which the church is called, and of which worship is a foretaste, calls congregations to deep introspection and self-criticism because the church is, naturally and of necessity, an institution. As Guder puts it, "The problem is not *that* the church is institutional but *how* it is institutional. . . . The question that the incarnational understanding of mission places before the institutional church is this: Is our communal institutional life an embodiment of the good news? Does the way we live, decide, spend money and make decisions as organizations reveal both the character and purposes of God for humanity?"[14] In order that people may "taste and see that the Lord is good," all aspects of congregational life can be examined and shaped according to worship's own commitments. Recall Joe Ward saying our first job is to listen to God's leading.

The church as an *instrument* for bringing about the reign of God in particular historical circumstances has been a central task since the church began. When the church acts as an instrument it takes experience seriously, especially the experience of the poor. Thus all of the aspects of experience—the physical/sensory, affective, cognitive, social/relational, and imaginative aspects—are active in the lives of those to whom the church ministers as well as in the lives of Christians engaged in ministry and mission. To engage in ministry and mission is to engage in "a reality in which the actual circumstances of human life are treated seriously. . . . The church is challenged to take seriously and deeply involve itself in the affairs of the world. As an instrument of the reign of God, the church is to announce the coming kingdom of peace and justice, of love and life, the consummation of God's purpose of love with humanity and [the] universe—to announce the undefeatable fulfillment of creation."[15] This announcement comes in the form of proclamation, of course, but also in actions that establish justice, demonstrate compassion, and conform the actual circumstances of human life to the intentions of God enacted in worship. One of my friends says the church has saloon doors. They swing both ways. When we hear the announcement of "The gifts of God for the people of God," we immediately think of those who have no bread, and we are compelled by worship's intentions to share what we have. Likewise when we encounter others in our acts of ministry and mission, we are brought again and again to encounter God in worship.

Jim Everett is a deacon at Old Pine Presbyterian. When his father died, Jim was determined to find new meaning in his loss. "I wished there was a way to make it so that there was some good that could come out of this. I just thought maybe I, from having watched my dad go through that, maybe I know a little bit about it that would make me a better visitor to somebody that had [cancer]." So every Sunday after worship Jim goes to a nearby hospital cancer ward. He asks the staff if there is someone who would like a visit that day. "I tell them I'm on my way home from church and is there anyone who might care to have a visit. They are very good at hooking you up with someone. I just spend a little while. Most of the people I call on don't have the energy to talk real long. I ask them about their church, and they often want to talk about that. And I look for them the next Sunday if they're still there and try to see them as often as they're still in the hospital." For Jim, worship inspires him to visit and, in turn, the visits lead him back to worship.

The image of the church as a *sign*, a *foretaste*, and an *instrument* of the reign of God in the world gives these congregations a way to evaluate the church according the worship's enacted vision. Congregations consider how their life together points beyond themselves to the power and glory of God. They ask how the experience of congregational life is a foretaste of the coming reign of God. And they ask how their activities and ministries help to bring about that reign.

Steadfast in Ministry with Heart for Mission

In preparation for calling a pastor, many congregations enter into a mission study process where they describe as clearly as possible the character of their congregation and its ministry. Recently such a description crossed my desk, and it amazed me. The list of programs that support ministry among church members and programs that extended the mission of the church beyond its own walls covered five single-spaced pages! The opportunities to be involved in the life of this church of about four hundred members covered a broad range of options, including choir and music ministries, and worship leadership such as ushering, greeting, and reading Scripture. There were opportunities for teaching children, youth, and adults and for participating in outreach to youth community wide. Mission opportunities included a job-referral service as well as food and clothing assistance for those in need. Outreach to students at a nearby college was encouraged through transportation and home-away-from-home programs. Financial support went to ecumenical campus ministries, local social service agencies, and international missionaries sent by the denomination. This congregation seemed on the verge of programmatic exhaustion.

In the worship-centered congregations described here, on the other hand, opportunities for participation in living out the Christian faith pervade all of congregational life. But such opportunities are consistently understood as an extension of encounter with God in worship. Members know that worship leads them into mission and ministry, and they are equally well aware that ministry and mission lead them directly back to the worship of God. Some members support ministry and mission efforts financially, others personally and actively, and others with their prayers. Whatever the type of participation, these congregations are conscious of the call to incarnate the ministries of the church in the ways they discern God leading them. Their experience of engagement in ministry and mission provides ample opportunity for reflection, study, and new insights that lead to more faithful involvement. Whether they find their call to ministries within the church or to mission outside the church, all those who discern God's call are supported and nurtured in reflection on their experiences of ministry. Care for the spiritual lives of those who incarnate the church's ministries is a priority in these congregations. Opportunities for reflection on the experience of Christian ministry abound in planning meetings, in study sessions, in debriefing conversations, in prayer, and in worship. Leaders in these congregations consistently plan for formal opportunities and grasp informal opportunities wherever they present themselves to ask choir members, Sunday school teachers, mission volunteers, lay worship leaders, ushers, food pantry workers, homeless shelter hosts, and the kitchen cleanup crew, "Where is God in this?" Without this, they say, the church is more like a private club or a social service agency.

Ann Myhre at West Raleigh says emphasis on the experience of participation in ministry and mission, along with the resulting opportunities for reflection, is a welcome change from former patterns of doing program and mission in the church. "We used to do it by committee. The committee would come up with a consensus about what to do. Then the session would rubber stamp it, and then the congregation had to deal with it. That is not the way we are looking at it now. This new way of spiritual discernment and prayer and reflection on our mission involvements takes a lot more effort." It is threatening to some people, says Ann, but she is convinced it is the right way to go about things. "I have very strong feelings about God leading us to be where we are while we work out what God wants us to be."

Throughout this book we have been advocating an experiential learning model for congregational life. In educational circles this style of education has most often been called the action/reflection or *praxis* model.[16] And we have been describing congregational life as a series of actions or activities on which members and leaders are called to reflect. This is how we learn the Christian life from the experience of congregational life. Often the intention of the action/reflection model is "transformation," a term that points toward the ways we humans are always changed—transformed—by experience. The changes may be gradual and so slight as to be almost imperceptible, but humans are, nevertheless, changed by experience and are more profoundly changed through the process of experience *and* reflection. As Socrates pointed out so long ago, "The life which is unexamined is not worth living."[17] These congregations engage frequently in reflection on their ministries. And, equally important, individuals and groups within the church see their mission and ministry involvement as significant experiences on which they themselves are called to reflect as they seek to be formed into the likeness of Christ.

When Christians engage in ministry and mission activities, they naturally move into unfamiliar territory. They place themselves at the disposal of those they seek to serve and must necessarily begin to see the world from the perspective of the "other," whether the "other" is nearby or far away. Pam Wilson, a member of West Raleigh Presbyterian, says that about ten years ago she thought the church was dying. "We were full of experiences without much of an opportunity to reflect on any of it. That kind of reflection is not just an intellectual exercise. It's a spiritual, prayerful, worshipful exercise. That's what I think makes West Raleigh a different place. Part of the culture here is that we are trying to become new while we maintain tradition. Some of our culture is the old and the new. We are learning a particular way of translating the new. We are trying to coexist or blend the old and the new, and that is shaping our culture. You can't be here very long and not feel it in some way." These new patterns of ministry inspire deep reflection in members' lives, which contribute to the overall spiritual formation of the congregation.

Merietta Wynands reflects this same sentiment when she describes her own growth in faith through leadership in the children's worship program. "It has changed my awareness of the gifts and talents that God has given me. Now I understand that God was growing my faith and growing my gift of teaching and of nurturing leaders. I understand that now. The body of Christ needed me to use those gifts, and I hadn't been able to up until that point." Merietta says this way of living out her ministry is a three-way relationship. "My relationship with God has been strengthened in that, just being affirmed that I am God's child; I have been given gifts. God has given me the Spirit and the power to use these gifts to feed the body of Christ."

Steve Wright encountered this alternative way of seeing the world during his trips to Central America and discovered that it was both rewarding and frustrating. A contractor by trade, Steve learned to see from a different point of view while building a concrete block building in Nicaragua. Builders there do not use plumb lines or levels as they lay concrete block, but square and level the building by sight as they go along. Steve, as the outsider, had to step back and follow their lead as the building went up. "It was very hard," he says, "but it helped me see how you have to do things differently where you don't have much to work with." Steve returned from Central America with a passionate love for the people there and a new respect for their way of life. He has questions of faith that he says never would have occurred to him without the experience of working alongside people who are different from him.

Transformation that comes as a result of the experience of encounter with the "other" can follow a discernable pattern.[18] First there is the experiential immersion in an encounter that challenges long-held assumptions. The surprise and strangeness of a different vantage point on the world can seem threatening, but those who welcome it as an opportunity to explore find that they can tolerate the tension. They are willing to be vulnerable to the risks of something different and open themselves to it. An essential component of this openness and vulnerability is the support of the community of faith and its built-in mechanisms for accountability. People are not left to work out the tensions of strange patterns of ministry and mission on their own but are encouraged by those with whom they minister. Together they discern the path of faithfulness within the complexity and particularity of their unique situation. They lovingly hold one another accountable to the overall purposes of their ministry and to their call to service.

Those who accept a call to ministry within the church or to participate in the mission of the church outside its walls find their ministries most fruitful when they understand as clearly as possible the social and economic circumstances surrounding their ministry. To support this understanding, Georgeann Wilcoxson points out, the church needs skills in social systems analysis, ways to understand the actual circumstances of the lives of those in need of God's reconciling love.[19] They enter into fact-finding, study, and analysis of the situation in order to learn how they might effectively focus their ministry efforts. Thus their involvement in ministry becomes more fruitful for those to whom they minister and for their own growth in faithfulness.

When pastor Dennis Hughes of Northminster Church in Seattle began thinking about possible mission involvement in the congregation, he says he was hoping to find an ongoing project that was too big for the congregation to do alone. "About that time I got a call from an old friend in Catholic Community Services housing ministry. She said, 'Dennis, I need you to start a homeless shelter for mentally ill people in your neck of the woods.' I just about fell off my seat, and I said, 'Come on over and talk to us. I'll get the group together. That sounds like just the kind of thing we might be able to do.'" Catholic Community Services provided them with information about the larger contexts of mental illness and homelessness in the Seattle area, and with insights into how their church could help address some of these systemic needs. "Every month or six weeks we have volunteer meetings where all the volunteers are brought together to reflect along with the partners from the mental health community who do the screening and referral of our guests. We sit down and talk about the lives of the people we serve, the issues that we run into with them." With this kind of systemic approach and support, the ministry has run smoothly for several years.

At West Raleigh, where hands-on ministry with the hungry and homeless is complemented by active leadership in organizations that work toward alleviating the root causes of these and other social problems, such social and economic analysis is central to effective ministry. Some of their ministries are focused on addressing immediate needs while others are working toward broader social justice goals. Thus their ministries mutually support one another. Dieter Hessell refers to this as an "alternative intelligence system" where "the church's socially engaged groups often have enough experience to know what is really happening to ordinary folks and possess important information about the impact of public policies on families, community life, and mental health—enabling faith communities to offer competent policy proposals and to participate in innovative programs. Congregations that make good use of member know-how plus denominational and ecumenic connections actually can make a public difference. . . . "[20]

Participation in public policy efforts is new in some of these congregations. For others it is a well-established orientation to the world and the needs of others. In either case, involvement in searching larger systemic answers to human need fosters questioning and learning. At West Raleigh Presbyterian, a church with a long history of involvement in systemic social change, social justice concerns came naturally. Elder Jack Cover has been active for several years in helping to change the church's attitudes toward gay and lesbian people. Recently he became coordinator for a Sunday morning forum class that for many years has initiated conversations about a variety of social concerns and justice issues. "Doing this 'Hassis Class' thing has been a challenge, a spiritual challenge for me." It is helping him bring together his ongoing concern for social justice with spiritual and theological aspects of those concerns. "When you talk to people they'll talk to you about things that are happening in spiritual terms, will deal with a problem in spiritual terms. One of the reasons we joined this church was that we liked that. You have the feeling that the Spirit is in this church. It's a terrific thing." Jack's passions for social justice are being used through his leadership in the Hassis Class, and his own spiritual life is being deepened as he puts together those concerns with their theological and spiritual aspects.

Like Jack, longtime West Raleigh member Mary Rose Raefer has been active in issues of social justice, with roots in her childhood. "My grandmother was a suffragette; my mother marched in the Mothers for Peace march; and I marched in the Million Moms March. I think of my religious life involving outreach and social issues, more than just contemplation.

My husband, Bill, is very much interested in politics and is a volunteer in a lot of agricultural assistance organizations." According to the writers of *Common Fire: Leading Lives of Commitment in a Complex World*, people who are engaged in an active way in their communities often grew up in families, churches, and communities where an enlarged sense of the world and of one's responsibility was the norm. Early in their study, the writers say, they "began to hear about important encounters with others significantly different from themselves." These encounters gained significance as people were able to make "constructive engagements" with those different from themselves. "What distinguished a simple encounter from a *constructive engagement* was that some threshold had been crossed, and people had come to feel a *connection* with the other."[21]

Mary Rose's activities include the League of Women Voters, the Peacemaking Committee, and the Local Ministries Committee of the church, and extensive mentoring at the state Women's Correctional Center, a minimum-security facility with a work/release program. Mary Rose describes the work/release program and the ways prison policies make success for released inmates almost impossible.

> The work/release program has different levels. Level One means you're probably working in the cafeteria, cleaning or whatever. Level Two means you might be working in state offices or the governor's mansion or somewhere around Raleigh, and you get paid about a dollar a day. Then when you reach Level Three, which is the highest level, you have to find your own job outside of the prison and start paying room and board and restitution, if that's possible, and saving some money for release. This presents a terrific problem for the women. First of all, they can't call out of the prison except to make collect calls, so you can't call a future employer that way. Then there's the staffing shortage in the prison. There's only one woman coordinating the program. There are about 190 women in the prison. She does the best she can. So most of the women are working flipping hamburgers or cleaning in motels, doing unskilled work, which will not support them when they get out of prison.

Mary Rose and others in the Community Volunteers program at the prison work under the supervision of the chaplain. "We take the women for interviews. We try to work with their families. We try to help them find housing and jobs and transportation—all of the things that have to be done. The state does not have an adequate aftercare program for these women."

For Mary Rose, integrating the Christian spiritual life with work for change in the systems that affect the everyday lives of the poor is complete. "I find the Word of God in a lot of different places and people. To me, I see how people triumph over things that are wrong. I see it just about everywhere, in everybody." There are plenty of groups who provide prayer and Bible study at the prison, she says. "But you also need people who will write their Congress people and march in front of the capitol. I would like them to say, 'Hey, I'll become a mentor at the prison.'" It is hard, she says, to know precisely what the will of God is. "But in fear and trembling we hope we're doing the right thing."

For Mary Rose, like Jack and many others at West Raleigh, the Hassis Class is an important center for that spiritual and systemic integration. "It is a place where we talk about social issues in relationship to our beliefs. It is very important because we may read the paper and we may not really think about these things enough unless somebody inspires us to wonder about it. That's been the joyful thing to me about that class, that though we may disagree, we take these issues seriously. Do we really love our neighbor? Do we really pray for our enemies? Do we try to love our enemies? What are the consequences of supporting political parties or issues? What about the death penalty? How does a Christian look at that? We've dealt with campaign finance reform, feminist theology, gay and lesbian rights, the positive and negative aspects of foreign missions, and racism. We talk about a lot of different things." Mary Rose knows that "you just can't be in a vacuum. You're in relationship with other people, groups of people." Pam Wilson, who works for a nonprofit organization concerned with social change, says West Raleigh's sustained conversations about the connections between the spiritual life and contemporary issues has given her "a way to marry the spiritual side of myself and the worldly side of myself in a very concrete way. This church has helped me to take the spiritual part beyond the walls of this congregation and in fact to bring that to the work that I do."

According to Elaine Saum, "Politics is really about the care and management of humans living together, sharing the resources of the world. . . . Politics is love in action. It is the inevitable means by which we as individuals as groups love our neighbors. To love our neighbors is to work toward a time when the law of love coincides with the law of the land."[22] With such orientations in mind these congregations seek to combine acts of charity along with consistent advocacy for equitable public policy. Jane Ives quotes someone as saying, "'Our real work is to be the face and hands of Jesus for people we don't even know yet and to see the face of Jesus in them.'"[23]

Many of us live in a "middle-class cocoon" that reinforces our lack of understanding and interconnectedness with the poor.[24] This cocoon begins with our comparative affluence that allows us to live in neighborhoods where our contact with the poor is limited. We can afford transportation, medical care, and other services that insulate us from the day-to-day concerns of those who are not equally affluent. The media reinforces middle-class lifestyles and a kind of "civil religion" where the dreams and aspirations of the American middle class are "sacrilized" as God-given rights. Family life is organized around consumption and upward mobility. The educational system helps to duplicate the existing social and economic order. In the workplace social arrangements and the distribution of power are rarely questioned. Even religion can become so privatized that community and global concerns receive little attention.

In the congregations described here are explicit strategies for breaking through this cocoon, bringing the needs of the world to the attention of the community of faith, especially during the prayers of Lord's Day worship. Steve Wright remembers the first presentation he heard, where the possibility of going on a mission trip was introduced. The presentation, he says, was a no-nonsense introduction to the realities and rewards of hands-on mission involvement, and it raised important questions for him. "I had never thought of doing anything like that before, so I had to really think it over. There were lots of things I needed to think through before I was ready to get involved." The speaker didn't gloss over any of the difficulties a mission team might encounter. At the same time he described the needs and the contribution a mission team might make in the lives of people who are in need.

At Northminster in Seattle, where mission involvement is close at hand, associate pastor Karen Breckenridge remembers how the youth of the church overcame their initial fears of the homeless mentally ill. "We make and serve dinner once a month for the guests, and boy, that's been an experience. When we first started doing it, these kids were so nervous. A couple of them were fifth and sixth graders, and they wouldn't talk to our guests. They wouldn't run upstairs to invite them down for dinner. They were just really scared. Within a couple of months they got used to the idea of providing a meal and sharing a meal with homeless people. We sit and eat with them. Now it is to the point where if I have to cancel our scheduled involvement for some reason, the kids ask if they can do it another week rather than to just forget it." The young people now look back and remember how scared they were. "We had a conversation about it after we had been serving dinner for about six months, and they talked about how scary it was. They needed some distance from it to be able to talk about it." Face-to-face contact with the homeless mentally ill has helped these young people see the world and their place in it in a different light. Karen says they now have a more realistic understanding of the needs of the poor. They also see themselves as people who are able to extend hospitality. "These kids are usually the ones who are waited on. Most of their needs are met by their parents. They don't often have the chance to play host and hostess. We serve this meal as if we're having company for dinner, with special menus, table decorations, and candles. It's an opportunity for them to be gracious and hospitable in ways that they don't get to do very often."

When people return from mission trips and work camps, they sometimes wonder whether their efforts have made a difference to the people they have sought to serve. Contractor Steve Wright asks himself this question explicitly in his diary, written during his second mission trip to Nicaragua. On the way from Managua to the village where he and others from Wesley Methodist Church would work, he writes that he began to question his own motives. He was homesick for his family, and he was overwhelmed by the devastation left by the recent hurricane. "I started to think about why I came on this trip. I was very depressed. I thought to myself, Did I come for the wrong reasons? Like wanting people to think I was a good person? . . . Maybe by the end of this week I will be able to answer this honestly, but not right now."

In Seattle, where the homeless population is quite large, the Northminster congregation regularly assesses its efforts with the homeless mentally ill. According to pastor Dennis Hughes,

> We have nothing to offer here but hospitality. It is a ministry of pure hospitality. But it is 'therapeutic' because we genuinely care. We greet our guests by name and get to know who they are. We share some of our life with them. It is all focused on our guests' lives so it draws us out of ourselves, which I think is the essence of spiritual formation. It relieves us of the burden of self-centeredness and the agony of egocentrism. This ministry frees us to concern ourselves with someone else, which gives us a deep, rich connection with God through the life of other beings. . . . Our guests are sometimes very fragile when they first come to us. They are pretty isolated and withdrawn into themselves. Our volunteers know how to let them know that if they want to talk, that is okay. We play games like checkers

with them. And we see them over the course of weeks come out of the isolation of homelessness and mental illness into a social world.

All of this makes Northminster's mission with the homeless mentally ill worthwhile, a reality most evident when a guest is no longer homeless. "A woman who had been our guest for several months made an announcement the other night. She got up and said, 'I'm getting an apartment on Monday.' Well, the entire group stood up, came over, and hugged her and patted her on the back. I'm talking about mentally ill homeless guests encircling Karen and congratulating her. It is wonderful to see how they are able to fantasize about what life is going to be like when they have their own place. 'Karen, you're going to be able to cook your own dinner every night. Sit down in your own kitchen with your own plates. You're going to have a place to wash your clothes and a bathroom. Your own bathroom!' Really, it is a fantasy of hope." In these and other ways members of the Northminster congregation are encouraged to notice ways this and other ministries make a difference.

Jo Ann Van Engen explores the dilemma of genuine helpfulness in an article titled "The Cost of Short-Term Missions."[25] While she does not doubt the sincerity of those who sponsor, plan, lead, and participate in these trips, she wonders whether some adjustments might be advisable. First, the trips are expensive, requiring money for air travel, accommodations, and materials. Could the money be better spent by the third-world poor themselves? Second, in areas where employment is scarce, work done by first-world workers might more profitably be done by the people themselves. In addition, a great deal of effort is required of host communities to provide for mission volunteers. The efforts may, in the end, send the wrong message. "Because short-term groups often want to solve problems quickly," says Van Engen, "they can make third-world Christians feel incapable of doing things on their own. Instead of working together with local Christians, many groups come with a let-the-North-Americans-do-it attitude that leaves nationals feeling frustrated and unappreciated."[26]

Instead, Van Engen suggests that we "start thinking of [short-term missions] as a responsibility to learn."[27] She suggests congregations focus on learning, not doing, by sending representatives to find out what those in the third-world are facing, what we can do to help, and how we can build long-term relationships. "Preparing for your trip means more than packing your suitcase and getting your shots. Read as much as you can about the people and culture. Find out what some of the problems are. Learn a little of the language you will be hearing. . . . Show respect for people by knowing something about their lives before you arrive."[28] Van Engen further recommends that groups plan for long-term relationships that build on learning and partnership. Be ready to participate as a "global Christian" in a first-world context by finding out how the actions of the first world affect those in the third world. Approached in this way, short-term mission involvement might further break down the middle-class cocoon that keeps many Christians unaware of the plight of others.

The Episcopal diocese in central Pennsylvania has established a mission partnership with a sister diocese in Brazil. There have been visits from Brazilian pastors to the United States and American pastors to the churches in Brazil. Marjorie Menaul, rector at St. Paul's Episcopal Church in Bloomsburg, has both given and received hospitality. A Brazilian pastor was Marjorie's guest for several weeks, and she spent almost two weeks in Brazil during Advent, 2001. The partnership, says Marjorie, is based on mutual interest and respect between the two dioceses. "We are learning what it means to be the church in Brazil, and that affects how we understand ourselves as the church here. They see themselves as called to serve the poor. They have so little and most of it goes to serve the poor." Rather than trying to supply the Brazilian church's needs, the diocese here is opening itself to new understandings and shaping its relationship with the Brazilian church around this new knowledge. Paternalistic attitudes are being replaced by deeper insight, and a three-way partnership that includes a nearby regional medical center is emerging. With the two dioceses acting as a communications network, the medical center hopes to be able to identify children and adults who require medical treatment not available in Brazil. Local churches would be called on to help with transportation and hospitality for families who accompany patients to the United States for treatment. The Brazilian diocese would assist the medical center in finding placements in health clinics for medical residents and other personnel during overseas service assignments. "Everyone has something to offer here, and the mission of service to the poor is at the center of the partnership," says Marjorie.

The Christian community must be "culturally bilingual," grounded in the Christian tradition, faith, and practice, while also learning the "plausibility structure[s] of the world in which we are called to be Christ's witnesses. . . . "[29] In this way Christians are able to "translate" the gospel for those they seek to serve and to invite them to share in the life of God. As Guder says, "Such translation is not just a matter of language, although that must be included. It implies the learning of a cultural system so that the gospel can be embodied within it in understandable (which is not necessarily reductionistic) ways."[30]

Reading the Bible with the people of the Nicaraguan village where he was working gave Steve Wright an opportunity to reflect on this bilingual necessity in both a literal and a metaphorical way. Americans and Nicaraguans had "worked our guts out" digging a foundation for a new building. Their work was interrupted by a moment of deep communion, even though they spoke different languages. "Francisco, one of the men we were working with, noticed a little Spanish Bible sitting on my backpack. And he started to read it. So I went over to talk to him, and we started to read the Bible together. He would read his in Spanish, and I would read mine in English. We read Psalm 145 and Psalm 93 and 1 John 2:18–23. We drew a crowd. It was very wonderful and inspiring." In his journal Steve writes, "We are really getting close to these guys. I think they really like us. [After reading the Bible together,] we went back to work praising God for grace and mercy. We work very hard at times and are bonding as a group and getting something done." Through his friendships with the people he worked, prayed, and read Scripture with, Steve learned something about the village culture of Nicaragua. He developed a growing appreciation for the Nicaraguan people.

Worship and prayer surround all of these ministry and mission efforts. In most congregations when leaders are chosen and installed, it is through some liturgical rite. Mission volunteers, teachers, those who visit the sick, governing board members, and many more are singled out for prayer and commissioning during Lord's Day worship. Beverly Mills describes the ways worship and prayer surround and permeate all of congregational life at West Raleigh. "The Mission Formation Group begins their meetings with worship, sometimes with communion. They studied Exodus together when they first formed the group. They took a lot of time to study Scripture thoroughly, but it was integral to their journey. We begin session meetings and deacons meetings with Scripture and prayer. At the officers retreat we started with *lectio divina*. We are putting a more theological and worshipful foundation under all the work we do." This shift toward a more spiritually centered approach to ministry and mission has really changed the character of their life as a congregation. Many members remark on the change and the inclusion of the "inward journey" along with the "outward journey." Beverly says that there were some folks who were mission oriented but gave little or no attention to the Christian spiritual life that undergirds mission. There were also people who were focused on the spiritual life with no engagement in mission. "You had the outwards with no inward, but you also had your inwards with no outward." Now, she says, the church is beginning to see the need for both in every Christian's life. According to associate pastor Denise Thorpe, the gospel calls for both.

These congregations continue to pray for those involved in mission when they gather and when they pray in families and alone. In several of the churches the lists of those to be remembered in prayer, along with the ministries they carry out, are included in Sunday bulletins and newsletters. Thus the process of transformation that results from involvement in ministry and mission begins with encounter and a willingness to become vulnerable; moves to study, analysis, and fruitful ministry; and always leads back to worship, prayer, and thanksgiving.

When these congregations participate in ministry and mission, they do so out of a broad range of motivations and levels of involvement. As they participate and then have opportunities to reflect on their experiences, these Christians become aware that they themselves are changed. Whatever the outcome of their efforts, their lives will never be the same as a result of their encounter with the "other" in Christ-like service. West Raleigh church, whose language of "the journey inward and the journey outward" is part of the congregation's natural vocabulary, offers frequent opportunities for reflection on experiences in ministry and mission. Fran Albro says, "Mission is about being in relationship. It's not just putting food on the table. It's establishing a relationship with that person you are serving. Mission groups commit to being on this journey together for a certain amount of time. They become involved in each other's lives. Mission is about their relationship with God, their relationship with each other, and their relationship with those people whom they are seeking to serve." Reflection on mission activities with a priority for noticing the activity of God helps make these efforts spiritually fruitful.

At Old Pine Presbyterian, the Saturday for Seniors program has been a part of the congregation's mission for many years. Church members say that they participate as much for the sake of the relationships they establish with other members and with the senior citizens they serve as they do for the sake of the feeding ministry itself. Deacon Jim Everett says, "I'm generally there three out of four Saturdays. Everyone volunteers to help prepare the food, to prepare the sack lunches and serve, and then to clean up. I try to volunteer there as often as I can." Relationships built up in this way provide the foundation for the deep spiritual searching and questioning that accompanies worship-centered congregational life.

Questions That Energize Ministry and Mission

God's call to faithful ministry and mission is heard in these congregations through many of the ordinary activities of congregational life. People begin to ask deeply probing questions as they worship, pray, study, and lead the congregation together. In these congregations there is receptivity to such questioning and support for members as they seek clarity about God's call. Most often people seek to explore the implications of encounter with God in worship and the deepening of that encounter through prayer and study. They begin with questions such as these:

- What difference do the insights gained from worship, prayer, and study make? If we take these insights seriously, what will need to change? In us? In the church? In the world?
- How do we discern God's call to renewed engagement in worship, prayer, study, mission, and leadership?
- What ministries of ministry and mission is God calling us to now?

Once a direction for ministry and mission has been discerned—a call has been heard and answered—there is a necessary time of planning and preparation. Questions to be asked here include

- What will prepare us spiritually for renewed engagement in ministry and mission?
- How shall we plan and prepare for engagement in ministry and mission?
- What resources do we need? What resources do we have? Where might other resources come from?
- What expertise do we need? What wisdom needs to come from the needy, the poor, those to whom we seek to minister?
- How shall we organize and train for participation in ministry and mission?

Always these congregations are seeking deeper participation in the life of God in all they do. The question they most regularly ask is

- Where is God in this?

Reflection on Ministry and Mission

The congregations and individuals we have described take seriously the experience of participation in ministry and mission. In organized and programmatic ways as well as casual encounters that are part of the congregation's culture, these Christians treasure opportunities to recall, savor, decipher, and understand their experiences. And they open themselves to the anticipated transformation God may work in them. Describing mission volunteer trips, Jane Ives says, "Participating in team orientation meetings, reading about the area where we will be working, and praying both for our team members and for persons where we are going to serve—all help keep us focused forward into the experience. Mission team commissioning services, both during annual conference sessions and in local church worship settings, have blessed me with deep peace and an assurance of God's will for my life, confirmed by the supportive prayers of our church community."[31] Her phrase "focusing forward into the experience" is an apt one, highlighting the need to treasure the experiences associated with participation in ministry and mission.

Relationships built in the midst of carrying out the tasks of Christian ministry and mission have a particular kind of honesty and resilience to them, possibly because they are forged under circumstances surrounded by prayer and requiring a certain kind of improvisation in order for the tasks to be successfully accomplished. People learn to trust one another and to value their work together rather than being overly concerned with a perfectly completed project. There is a balance between mutual support and challenge that establishes fruitful truth telling and integrity. Because their larger vision and purpose are what bring these Christians together, they are committed to working through any difficulties and maintaining mutual accountability.

In an earlier chapter we described how at West Raleigh Presbyterian, when the child care center was closed and the congregation no longer had an identifiable mission focus, many said, "Just pick something and let's get on with some mission work." After some deep soul searching and experimentation, however, the church adopted a slower, more spiritually focused process for discerning mission callings throughout the congregation. They were not satisfied with an organizational structure that allowed the mission of the church to become separated from its worship and prayer life. Now a discernment pattern is practiced broadly across the congregation. People are learning to "focus forward" into all the experiences of the Christian life. They treasure the questions that arise out of the many events of their lives that carry God's call to ministry and mission. They "focus forward" by immersing themselves in what is going on and by remembering, pondering, and praying over the events later. These Christians know that there will be dependable times, places, and relationships where the memories of their experiences can become the focus of undivided attention. With that in mind, they can give their full attention to what is happening *now*.

Hearing God's call to ministry and mission is a responsibility given to every Christian in baptism for which the church calls on the gifts of spiritual discernment. "Today's world requires discernment as a way of being, not just as something in which to engage in times of crisis," says David White.[32] In the program he heads, the Youth Discipleship Project at the Claremont School of Theology, he tries to help young people internalize the skills and practices of discernment in order to imagine the world as God would desire it.

Discernment as a way of being is evident in the congregations described here as they undertake their call to ministry and mission. They "yearn for the will of God, even as God, in love, yearns for them."[33] In these churches a culture of discernment has been established in such a way that more and more people are included among those who yearn for God's will. At West Raleigh, educator Fran Albro is very conscious of the need for both challenge and support. When she introduced some new mission endeavors to the congregation, she included explicit discussion of the "fear factor" that is always present when we venture into unfamiliar activities. In small groups church members were given opportunities to be honest about their own fears and to explore their meaning. According to Amy Simes, "just the opportunity to actually name the fears and discuss them was very important. We still have to figure out how to deal with them, but we didn't just brush them aside and move on. We took fear seriously." Talking about fears together demonstrates both support and challenge. Christians are challenged to participate in mission efforts even though they may be fearful. At the same time they are supported as they face those fears and the situations that evoke fear.

Discernment, according to Charles Olsen and Danny Morris, includes a number of attitudes and activities or, as they say, *being* and *doing*. First, spiritual discernment must be grounded in the commitments of the gospel and framed according to particular situations. Discernment is not a once-and-for-all activity but must be entered into anew according to life's changing circumstances. Communities then lay aside any extraneous matters (ego, false assumptions, predetermined conclusions, etc.) in a process called "shedding." Theological themes, images, and metaphors drawn from Scripture root discernment in the Christian tradition. "The tradition may confront, confirm, nudge, or even transform the direction of the discernment process."[34] It is then time to listen to the prompting of the Spirit and explore imaginative possibilities. Consultation and prayer improve our initial intuitions until the discernment of God's will "becomes the best that we can imagine it to be within the yearning of God."[35] We must then test options and choose a course of action in response to God's leading. Last of all, "resting tests the decision by allowing it to rest near the heart to determine whether it brings primarily feelings of consolation (a sense of peace and movement toward God) or desolation (distress and movement away from God).[36] These ways of being and their related practices (doing) make up a "reflection pool" with "stepping stones" toward spiritual discernment. The steps are not necessarily sequential but, taken together, represent a group of activities and attitudes of openness wherein the Spirit of God can be at work.

Chapter Seven

Leadership in Worship-Centered Congregational Life

Worship inspires more worship. The worship of God draws communities and individuals ever more deeply and broadly into worship as both the vertical and horizontal dimensions of the Christian life become expressions of life in God. Deepened participation in the Divine life with God brings forth the truest praise of which humans are capable. At the same time more and more dimensions of our lives are lived before God, so that over time daily activities become acts of praise to God. Within the church, persons of courageous faithfulness and extravagant affections show the way for others to join in this incarnated praise of God. Outside the church, praise is often expressed in action for the sake of others so that their well-being brings glory to God. All activities of the Christian life draw on a variety of compassionate and practical motivations, but the ultimate goal is to include all of creation in acts of praise to the living God. Worship inspires more worship in ourselves, in our communities, and in all creation.

Congregational leadership has its roots in the worship of God as pastors, educators, and other congregational leaders are ordained and commissioned to particular roles in orienting all of congregational life toward the deepening and broadening praise of God. Ordination and commissioning of leaders are a part of the assembly's worship of God, and historical sources indicate that congregational leadership has been for the sake of the worshiping assembly from the beginning.[1] At West Raleigh Presbyterian Church the ordination of elders and deacons is a splendid and celebrative occasion in the life of the congregation. Months of prayer, conversation, and discernment have preceded the day's solemn festivities. Long before the call to leadership and the willing response of these women and men, the entire congregation was engaged in discernment. Elder Mary Frances Cheek was surprised by the training retreat for new elders and deacons. "It was not at all what I was expecting. I thought it would be all about proper procedures, things like that. But instead it was about our stories, about times in our lives when we felt the presence of God with us. There were things about these people I did not know. I was so touched by several of the stories. Then we celebrated communion together. As Joe [Ward] says, it is the greatest thing you get to do, serve someone communion."

The following Sunday, when the time for the service of ordination arrives, the elders and deacons gather on the chancel platform where vows are taken. Then, with the congregation standing, one by one these elders and deacons kneel, many hands are laid on, and a generous prayer of ordination is spoken for each one by one of the pastors. The spiritual gifts of each elder or deacon are richly described, and God is praised and thanked. The Holy Spirit is called on to sanctify each one for spiritual leadership in the congregation. Mary Frances reflects on her ordination, saying, "It was momentous in my life. You feel the weighty touch of people who have gone before in the laying on of hands. I felt God's hands just kind of descend on me. It was wonderful." Elder Pam Wilson says, "It is a meaningful experience to have a prayer that has been thoughtfully written just for you as an officer. It made me feel like I had gifts and that those gifts were recognized and appreciated. I think that is important to do."

Structural and Interpersonal Leadership

Leadership in the church operates at both *structural* and *interpersonal* levels.[2] *Structural leadership* encompasses the many administrative tasks and responsibilities that come with leadership in any organization. Schedules and buildings, policies and personnel, programs and materials must be organized and managed, and it is the responsibility of leaders to see that these things work well. *Interpersonal leadership*, on the other hand, involves Christians in a web of relationships that personalize. As Robert Martin says, "To personalize means that individuality is recognized, called forth, and celebrated. . . . Individuals are welcomed and incorporated into the faith community and are granted freedom to discover and be more fully who they are . . . in communion."[3] It is the web of personalizing relationships, including especially the divine "Other," within which congregational leadership is exercised. Congregational leaders seek to establish a congregational culture where the welcome of the community can be extended and where relationships that contain the possibility of Christian transformation can be formed. The relationship between structural and interpersonal leadership is complementary but necessarily asymmetrical. "The proper relationship between structural and interpersonal [leadership] is an asymmetrical complementarity whereby the structural is put in service of the interpersonal for the sake of entering into personalizing relationships with one another."[4]

In the congregations described here the exercise of structural leadership is consistently for the sake of interpersonal leadership. We have seen how many of these leaders surround the structural dimensions of their leadership responsibilities within personalizing practices. At both Old Pine Street Church in Philadelphia and Immanuel in Tacoma, prospective new members of the congregation meet with the pastor and other congregational leaders over a meal at the pastor's home. Rather than spend time talking about the organization of the church and its programs, the group spends time getting to know one another, studying Scripture, and reflecting on the presence of God in their lives. "We always do new members class at my home around a shared meal and Scripture," says Paul Galbreath. "We reflect on our journey and what brought us here and how the story from Scripture intersects with our own story. . . . I have a deep conviction that runs contrary to some literature on pastoral leadership. I really do believe that pastoral ministry is about relationships and it's about friendships with people. I'm convinced that the biblical model, particularly the model of Jesus' ministry in the gospels, is about the friendships that are formed in this odd group of people that come together. I'm acutely aware of the dangers of that, but I'm willing to run that risk because if it's not about relationships and it's not about building friendships that will last, then I don't want to do it."

Deborah McKinley remembers when, after several years at Old Pine, she became aware of a shift in the quality of her relationships with the congregation and their relationships with her. "Connections deepen with people as I participate in people's lives through births, deaths, hospital calls, and pastoral counseling. After I had been here about three years, I said to my husband, 'I'm finally the pastor here.' It takes that long for you to gain that pastoral authority from simply being present with people and listening to their stories and participating with them as their pastor."

These leaders see themselves within, not above or apart from, the personalizing web of relationships within the congregation. Spiritual renewal is the goal. Their relationships with members and other leaders are essential components in this personalizing process. Paul identifies a range of risks and unhealthy codependencies, but his awareness of these keeps him critically self-reflective. "And," he says, "there are some people I can check with who will be really honest with me about these issues, so I can check things out from time to time."

Leadership: The Authority to Define Reality

The worship of God draws one into a view of the world that is religiously and spiritually defined. In congregations there are formal and informal leaders who have the authority to describe this worldview in compelling and definitive ways. According to Scott Cormode, "the authority to craft the categories people use to describe the experiences of life is the power to define reality."[5] At West Raleigh we have seen how a particular vocabulary used by many church leaders and members has served to define reality for this congregation and has shifted the meaning of mission from organizational efficiency in response to a need to include practices of prayer, Bible study, and styles of relationship that nurture the community's spiritual life. Interest in the inward journey and the outward journey has, according to Chris Simes, "taken the traditional approach to mission and turned it upside down." Rather than appointing a committee to study a need and organize the congregation to address it, the new way of discerning a call to mission begins with the spiritual lives of particular members. Chris continues:

> It is not efficient. The mission group does not just take a service project and run with it. The idea is that you spend about half your time working on the project and the other half of your time is for prayer, for forming a bond in your group. And we do a Bible study at every meeting. As the mission group evolves there's expected to be a real sense of openness and accountability with each other. It is a place where we learn to speak the truth in love. There is an intimacy that grows over time. Now, I'm an engineer. Engineers make lists. We do things. We plan. We organize and get on with it. In the Wheels for Hope mission group we learn to try to do mission on God's timetable. We learn that the journey is as important as the result. And doing it through the group with everybody being involved in it. All that is worth the inefficiency. These are all things that I have had to have demonstrated to me.

Christians know that pastors and other leaders occupy special positions within the congregation. Ordination as minister or lay leader brings with it the public recognition of some unique status and responsibility within the community. It sets one apart. Whitney Grissafi at Immanuel Church in Tacoma recounts an amusing conversation with one older member of the congregation that highlights the nature of this difference. Under Paul Galbreath's leadership the church began ordering its life around worship at the same time they enriched the experiential elements within worship. After they had been "passing the peace" each Sunday for about a year and a half, Whitney asked one of the long-time members of the church how she felt about it. "Well, I feel a little awkward about it. It just feels strange to me. It's not something we've done. *You know, sometimes I think Paul's more religious than I am.*" At West Raleigh a retired college professor comments on the spiritual renewal taking place in the congregation and says, "I think they want us to be just like Jesus' twelve disciples." The pastors and leaders in these congregations are communicating a vision for Christian discipleship that is significantly different from a kind of civic Christianity that has marked much of contemporary religious life.

According to Scott Cormode, "A religious leader's first responsibility is to define reality theologically and spiritually. Religious leaders inhabit a world of interpretation, a 'rhetorical reality' where defining the categories people use to interpret their lives is extremely powerful."[6] In the congregations described here pastors and leaders are attentive and creative in taking advantage of the many opportunities that come with leadership to exercise this conceptual framing. David Batchelder in Latrobe asks, "What time is it?" and invites the congregation to enter the mood of each seasonal celebration. Paul Galbreath makes frequent references to the church's oneness in Christ through baptism and to the need to be fed by Scripture and the bread and wine of Eucharist. The tangible symbols of the baptismal life—the Christ candle, a bowl of water, a chalice—are present at every meeting of church leaders. They serve as material reminders of theological and spiritual realities while Scripture is read and explored and prayers are offered to God. Anna Ayers, a deacon at Immanuel, says the pervasive presence of these tangible symbols has shaped the way she understands her ministry as a deacon:

> It is not an accident that the [communion] cup and the bowl [of water] are with us when we start a deacons' meeting or that we light a

candle and ask God to be with us. It's all very intentional. For me that has changed my view of going to worship from being something I do as a passive participant to something I actively and intentionally engage in. . . . We gather in prayer at the end of our meeting and mention the cares and concerns of others and pray for others while we're there. We pray out loud for people, express our concerns out loud, and ask others to hold these same people in their prayers. You know people are actually going home and intentionally praying for those folks because of the way they are participating in the prayers at the end of the meeting.

The worldview of worship that pervades the rhetorical framing of congregational leaders uses a distinctive religious vocabulary and draws attention to the differences between a theocentric worldview and some other worldview. We have seen how Joe Ward, in his work with the nominating committee, introduced practices of spiritual discernment rather than "filling the slots" by saying, "Your job is really to listen to God. Our first task is to listen to what God is saying to us and to trust that we will hear something." Such spiritual and religious framing reoriented the committee's self-understanding and played a role in the deeper cultural change that has happened at West Raleigh.

Cultural Change and Adaptive Work

Changes such as these require what leadership specialists call adaptive work. When the circumstances of a congregation change, as they always do, members and leaders are faced with gaps between the ways they have always understood themselves as the church, the values this self-understanding implies, and the practices that the congregation embodies in giving expression to those values. Leaders are also faced with multiple ways of adapting themselves and the church to the new situation. Those who lead the way have the ability to shape the way these new circumstances are understood and thus to shape the responses of the congregation. "Adaptive work," says Ronald Heifetz, "consists of the learning required to address conflicts in the values people hold, or to diminish the gap between the values people stand for and the reality they face. Adaptive work requires a change in values, beliefs, or behavior."[7]

In the congregations described here the process of liturgical renewal that has gone hand in hand with spiritual renewal has required significant adaptive work on the part of members and leaders. Each congregation faced circumstances that compelled them carefully to examine their values, beliefs, and behavior in order to discern what their faithful response should be. Immanuel Church in Tacoma held a prominent role in the community for many decades. More recently the church experienced a significant decline in membership and influence. The causes were multiple and were both internal and external. When the church embarked on its present renewal, with Paul Galbreath as its new pastor, leaders in the presbytery said they felt that if significant changes did not come within five to eight years, the church would probably have to close its doors. "Looking back, I think that was overly optimistic. I don't think we had that long. Renewal has happened because there was a core group of people who were really dedicated to being part of the church coming back to life. There was energy and there was a longing for something new. . . . There are people here who had never even heard of a lot of the [liturgical] stuff we're doing. But they said, 'You know, we're not going to make it unless we try something, and so we're willing to take a chance. We're hoping it will be in a direction that is respectful of the past here and connected to the past here but is open to the future.' . . . The amount of change that this congregation has gone through has stretched all of us."

We have seen how, when individuals reorient the frameworks for understanding their world, an adequate holding environment contributes significantly to the transformation. Likewise in congregational life the presence of an adequate holding environment plays a key role in the congregation's ability to face necessary changes and do the kind of adaptive work necessary to meet them. Congregational leaders provide this indispensable holding environment for the congregation and for one another as the congregation moves into the future. They set the tone for the congregation as they articulate a vision for the future and indicate the necessary steps for bringing that vision into reality. The holding environment that leaders provide functions primarily to contain the stresses of adaptive work. In the face of the uncertainty of change, even constructive and eagerly desired change, there are stresses that require attention lest they overwhelm the change itself. Since the anxiety that comes with change is unavoidable, when leaders are able to direct the energy of change into productive avenues rather than allowing the tension to abort the process of change, the congregation is strengthened.

At Immanuel the presence of children in worship was an issue that required significant adaptive work on the part of the congregation. Leaders were able to establish a holding environment and balance the necessary issues in such a way that over time the congregation could adapt to its new circumstances. Paul Galbreath says, "It was the hardest thing we've done."

Like many mainline congregations, the Sunday schedule at Immanuel called for children through early adolescence to be dismissed from worship for child care. "Families with children started coming to the church, and the children left the worship early in the service after the prayer of confession, before any of the readings. Then it was playtime. We had an accident waiting to happen. It was not safe, the kind of things that were going on. We worked on it and worked on it, and we made no progress whatsoever." After a year of little progress, the issue was brought to a head when key congregational leaders, including the educator and the pastors, decided that during Advent children would remain for the entire worship service. An experience of children's participation in worship during Advent, they hoped, might be a suitable introduction for both children and adults.

"All hell broke loose when we did it! People were livid with us for saying that during Advent we want children to be present in worship." In response the ministers and educator and other leaders met with those who were concerned with the change.

> In the end we had three factions. There was the staff and other lead-
> ers who longed to have a wholeness in the congregation during wor-
> ship. There were parents who were worried, who said two things.
> They said, "This is the one hour that I get to worship and I just need
> that time." And they said, "My kids don't want to be here. They say
> it's boring. You're going to lose my kid. They're not going to come
> to church any more if you do this. They say it's boring.'" Then you
> had older members who had never had children in the sanctuary
> from day one in the life of this church, as far as I can tell. They said,
> "Why do we want the disruption in the sanctuary when there are
> children here? They are distracting. They are not quiet." So every-
> one was in an uproar about it.

The leaders of this congregation moved quickly to create an environment where the stresses of the presence of children in worship could be brought to the surface and addressed constructively.

"I don't know if I'd do it again. I certainly wouldn't recommend it," says Paul Galbreath,

> but by forcing the issue it caused all of us to look at it a little differ-
> ently and to work hard at trying to find some kind of compromise.

We worked really hard for more than a year on it. That is really a pretty short period of time, but for us in leadership it was a really rotten period of time. The initial compromise we made was to lengthen the time the children are in worship so that they hear at least two of the three Scripture readings and they hear the choir. Music is really important for children in this congregation. We want people, including the children, to absorb the music.

They also established a children's corner at the front of the sanctuary where children could go during the service to get things to play with. As children learned to participate in worship, and because the children's corner became a distraction, they were able to remove it. "Largely what it took was parents who were willing to sit with their children," says Paul. They were able to reengage parents to be with their children in worship and to provide some support and supervision. At the same time long-time members of the congregation have gradually adjusted to the fact that there's movement and there's some noise.

"On most Sundays when I look out there I see parents sitting there with their children. And I see enormous growth in the lives of the children," says Paul. Children have learned the structure and rhythm of the service in ways that contribute to their liturgical spiritual formation. The long-time members recognize that there is some long-term hope in the congregation, signaled by the presence of children. "I am in awe of that," says Paul. "They take great pride in counting how many children go up for children's time on Sunday morning. That is an important sign for them that the church can have renewal. Worship is now intergenerational in the best sense of the word. Children are included, even in leadership, and regularly take important roles in worship."

We can hear in Paul Galbreath's story that the people of the congregation were called on to engage in significant adaptive change in order to include children in worship. Leaders introduced a number of strategies in order to enable the congregation to change its culture and maintain the level of commitment and relationships that had characterized the church's identity.

Strategies for Adaptive Change

Congregational leaders have several strategies at their disposal for channeling the stress of change, including *directing attention toward relevant issues* and the plans for addressing them, *gathering information and regulating its flow, reality testing, framing issues, orchestrating conflicting perspectives,* and *choosing a decision-making process.* According to Ronald Heifetz, by appropriately using these strategies leaders are able to provide an adequate holding environment within which individuals and organizations can engage in the necessary adaptive work that comes with change.[8]

Leaders are able to *direct attention to relevant issues.* In congregations there are many issues that require the attention of pastors and leaders. At Immanuel the liturgical and theological vision held by key leaders inspired them to propose a bold experiment by including children in worship during Advent. The stress this decision engendered was substantial, but in the end leaders were able to lead the various "factions" to a workable compromise. Incremental change had not produced results, so the leaders were decisive in making the issue inescapable, thus forcing the congregation to engage in some necessary adaptive work that the congregation had avoided and resisted for many months. They directed the congregation's attention to their concerns about excluding children from worship and were able to insist that the issue not be avoided.

Immanuel Church did not engage in a technical "programmatic" change with the many pragmatic adjustments such change brings. They were not satisfied with the idea of instituting a new program for children during worship. Rather, the leaders were steadfast in their view that what was needed was a profound cultural change in children's participation in worship, of which programmatic and practical adjustments were only one part. In a similar way at West Raleigh you will remember the significant role played by the children's worship program in instituting and furthering the congregation's growing hunger for spiritual nurture for themselves and their children. Mary Frances Cheek, whose children grew up at West Raleigh before the changes came, says, "A lot of the spiritual energy has come from the young families that are in the church with young children. Praise God because they wanted more for their children than some of the rest of us even knew to want for ours. They became hungry for spiritual development for their children." In both congregations some changes were programmatic, but most were cultural changes wherein spiritual values became paramount in the life of the whole congregation. Leaders were able to keep attention focused on the spiritual dimensions of cultural reorientations even while they addressed practical issues.

Congregational leaders have *access to most all the information* about a congregation's life. Their unique vantage point allows them to "see the congregation whole" in a way that most other members are unable to see.

Weighing information from various sources allows leaders to engage in reality testing in such a way that future courses of action are more clearly discerned. Leaders must consider what information to share, when to share it, in what form, and with whom. With responsibility to the whole congregation, not just one particular segment of it, leaders learn to balance the needs of various groups for the sake of the whole congregation.

At Immanuel the parents of children, the long-time members, and the leaders of the congregation each had points of view and genuine concerns that needed to be addressed. Each group had suggestions about how their concerns might be met. "We met with everyone concerned, but we met at length with parents of middle-school children," says Paul Galbreath. By listening to their concerns congregational leaders gained important information that could be used as the adaptive work progressed. Relevant information also included the church's history and values, which could serve as resources in understanding the congregation's present dilemma and finding an appropriate solution. Paul says, "Part of what I do is listen to people and look for moments from the past that can be resurfaced both as a way of bringing people into institutional identity and as a way of reinforcing values from the past and asking people to expand on those. Those are the gems that one looks for." In this way Paul gathers information from the past that can be shared with the whole congregation. Older members who are eager for congregational renewal used this information to gain a new image of the church and adapt to new circumstances.

Using their access to information and the vantage point it provides, congregational leaders are in a position to *manage information and set the pace of change*. Issues can be given particular urgency in light of the congregation's circumstances, or they can be allowed to "ripen" over a longer period of time. At Immanuel leaders chose the season of Advent to focus attention on an issue, to press its importance in order to initiate change. In liturgical renewal at Latrobe David Batchelder uses the metaphor of moving the furniture. "There are two ways to change the room. You can move all the furniture at once, in which case you've got the room the way you'd like to have it but you run the risk of someone sitting on the lamp, thinking that's where the chair is. The other way is to move furniture strategically, a few pieces at a time. This is the way we've tried to do it here in Latrobe." At a recent worship and music committee meeting, for example, David reported on a conference concerning welcoming the unchurched into worship and congregational life, a topic he has raised several times over a two-year period. "I want to say just enough about welcoming new Christians to plant the seeds. I want people to begin thinking about how welcoming new Christians is harder to do now than it was before and to know that we're going to be thinking about it, so if some changes come down the road people won't be totally surprised." Notice how David manages information, sharing important facts and perspectives at a pace that allows the committee to absorb and adapt to the information but not be overwhelmed by it. Issues carefully chosen for their cultural significance and framed in ways that highlight the theological and spiritual values at stake encourage congregations to engage in the adaptive work of becoming worship-centered communities of faith.

Leaders also have a responsibility to *communicate and celebrate the adaptive work* of the congregation. Paul Galbreath, a natural storyteller, heard a story from new members that he could share with the congregation to celebrate their inclusion of children in worship:

> The most interesting thing to me about this whole arduous process was that about a year later we were doing a new member class. As we were going around the table, there were two or three mothers of families that were joining the church who said, "The reason that we come here and the reason we love this church is because you embrace children and they're welcome in worship." Well, Jenny, the associate pastor, and I just stared at one another. These people perceived that including children in worship was a long-term institutional value that was here. We hadn't even fully absorbed the change as leaders in the church, but the perception of new people was that it was just a part of the congregation's culture.

Hearing this story told again and again in coffee hour and committee meetings, the congregation has been able to get an image of themselves as successful in a very difficult adaptation and transition. It communicated a feature of Immanuel's identity that had great appeal for these young families. Members of the congregation were able to incorporate the inclusion of children in worship into their self-understanding and become more open to further inclusion.

Leaders in the congregations described here have learned to participate in processes of change as a "less anxious presence,"[9] acknowledging the stresses of change but calmly articulating a firm belief in God as the guarantor of the life of the church and subordinating all cultural practices to communal discernment of the leading of the Holy Spirit. With their own anxiety in God's care, leaders can *orchestrate conflict* and contain disorder.[10]

In the midst of cultural change, conflict is inevitable and can become a source of creative energy for adaptive change. Remember how Paul Galbreath and the other congregational leaders used the conflicting views about children in worship to help generate a creative energy field where new ideas could come to light. During an open forum after worship they calmly listened to the many concerns raised by each group and helped them arrive at a suitable compromise. They used newsletter communications to articulate the vision and importance of children in worship. They were attentive to coffee-hour conversations. The pastors heard the concerns, especially from long-time members during home visits. Ideas from the staff and others were woven together and experimented with until the congregation's culture of children in worship found a suitable adaptation.

Leaders can act as mediators and arbitrators among conflicting points of view within the congregation. Acting as *mediators*, congregational leaders help insure that all sides of an issue can be heard and areas of common agreement can be identified. They use their authority to support and protect others as they describe various points of view, identify benefits, and explore potential problems. As *arbitrators*, congregational leaders help the community prioritize options according to their theological commitments and come to decisions.[11]

Acknowledging that all of us operate with our own unique set of "mental maps," leaders can encourage participants to hold their own and others' views somewhat tentatively in order to test their viability. In an environment of trust, church leaders can momentarily set aside their own assumptions and examine issues from a variety of points of view. These leaders describe and demonstrate how one can suspend one's own point of view, at least temporarily. They have the ability to conduct brief thought experiments—exercises in "What if?" Leaders use their authority to remind participants that their approach must remain tentative and exploratory until all sides of an issue have been examined. Once this point is reached, the group can move into deliberations during which various ways of framing issues can be articulated and particular solutions can be advocated. It is the authority of leaders that can help to insure respectful and constructive conversations. The holding environment provided by trustworthy congregational leaders makes adaptive work possible. Ronald Heifetz writes, "People cannot learn new ways when they are overwhelmed. But eliminating the stress altogether removes the impetus for adaptive work. The strategic task is to maintain a level of tension that mobilizes people."[12]

Bringing various groups together for these kinds of exploratory conversations means "working across boundaries." Leaders recognize and respect the various ways groups frame and articulate issues and seek to find ways to make the boundaries more permeable and open to realignment. According to Heifetz,

> groups that come together to address an adaptive problem generally consist of representatives from interested parties that act as factions. To exercise leadership in such a group, one needs to understand the constituent pressures on each of those representatives and the relationships among their organizations. . . . In essence, one wishes to form a new coalition with these people, where the coalition entity has a purpose that redirects the previous purposes of the parent organizations. If successful, then the coalition will achieve a self-perceived boundary of identity and a cohesion of self-interest. This is the beginning. Then, each representative must lead his or her own faction in its own process of incorporating what the representative learned in the coalition. Clearly, this is an interactive process in which individuals import and export perspectives across boundaries as their own constituents adjust their views.[13]

Leaders have a responsibility to *orchestrate conflict* and use its energy well. At the same time they must *contain the disorder* conflict can sometimes bring. At Immanuel the congregation's leaders held lengthy conversations with the groups involved where their role was to listen. They supported parents, teens, and long-time members as they described their hopes and fears concerning children in worship. Values and emotions that might have sewn the seeds of extensive conflict were welcomed into open discussion where respect and discernment set the tone. "I'm really fascinated by the way change happens and the way, in some instances, it can be absorbed into the congregation pretty quickly in terms of memory," says Paul Galbreath. "I'm also fascinated by the way significant changes require changes on the part of leaders, require repeated conversations, require compromise on all our parts."

Honoring the Past in the Midst of Change

Every congregation is rooted in a particular history and set of traditions. But times have changed for most churches, and new occasions call forth new duties. In the congregations described here is a healthy balance between the history and traditions of the congregation and energetic explorations into new practices. These congregations are focused on the present and the future, not fixated on the past. At the same time they have a respectful regard for the heritage embodied in the congregation's faithful members. Great care is taken to acknowledge and celebrate this heritage, even while the church examines all its practices in light of a worship-centered orientation. Immanuel Church in Tacoma has an annual celebration of the "saints" of the congregation. On the Sunday nearest All Saints Day, the congregation selects two or three of its faithful long-time members and honors them as "Saints of Immanuel." These saints are included by name in the prayers of thanksgiving during worship. At the luncheon that follows the service, the life and ministry of each one is described and each saint is given a candle. "That's not much for someone like Bob Arpke, who has sung in the choir for sixty-five years. Every Sunday!" says Paul. "Every candle has a cross on it, and I always say something like 'Because you have shared the light of Christ with us, this is the light of Christ to you.' We want it to be a sign of their faithfulness (not just an appreciation of them personally). I'm astonished by the power of those moments in people's lives. Why wouldn't you honor and respect those who have kept this church alive through their faithfulness and loyalty? And respect the virtues that we all long for?"

Adaptive work that moves congregations into the future is difficult and challenging. These congregations, even the ones that have been severely eroded, find spiritual resources for their renewal in their traditions and history. Tradition and history serve as touchstones for the future and contribute to the congregation's identity in ways that give it the courage to change.

Leadership, Authority, and Power

The work of leadership for adaptive change requires a careful balancing of the uses of power. Leaders can and do exercise authoritative leadership, but in the process of adaptive change those times may be rare. Rather, leaders understand their authority as a warrant for building and maintaining an adequate holding environment within which congregations can engage in the adaptive work of cultural change. This requires trust and timing. Leaders in the congregations described here are proactive in addressing the anxiety that comes with change in ways that build trust. At West Raleigh the session makes use of several forms of communication as they seek to keep the congregation informed about emerging mission initiatives. In addition to newsletter articles and summaries of session minutes, the congregation uses "listening sessions" and town hall meetings to insure that everyone is informed and that all voices are heard. When the building renovation committee began its work, patterns of spiritual discernment within the committee were apparent for all to see, and the progress of their work was freely shared. The congregation was able to understand and support the committee's working, so that when the discovery of large amounts of asbestos significantly reshaped the project, the congregation absorbed this news with understanding and resilience. Pam Wilson, a member of that committee, recalls it this way. "The building committee started every meeting with communion and Bible study that really invited God to be a part of what we were doing, whether we were looking at designs or architecture or money, no matter what it was." Even when anxiety and resistance to change overwhelmed a few, the *holding environment* established in the committee's regular worship and prayer was able to contain the tension so that the committee itself was not overwhelmed.

Creating Personalizing Relationships

Someone has said that no one cares how much you know until they know how much you care. This is especially true in the church. Leaders in these congregations address anxiety and build trust through a broad range of practices that demonstrate their care for persons and their spiritual lives above all other goals they may have for the church. Paul Galbreath recounts a hospital visit where the power of caring was made especially clear. There had been conversations in the congregation around a number of issues about which there was disagreement. "When I came into [this member's] hospital room, he said, 'I didn't think you would come to see me because I knew that we didn't agree on [an issue].' I said, 'Of course I'd come to see you!' I don't have to say any more than that. The fact that I'm there already says it, and it already transforms the nature of our relationship." Paul says that what the congregation tries to do is "have a variety of times and places that call people together so that relationships are anchored in shared experiences. Then when we go through a period of congregational change or personal crisis, there's a reservoir to draw from."

In order to develop the kinds of trusting relationships we hear Paul describing, pastors and other congregational leaders will need to engage in some serious prioritizing and decision-making. The congregations described here are doing what Eugene Peterson calls making "much ado about the significant."[14] Rather than let their leadership gifts and energies be spent in administrative and programmatic activities, these congregational leaders understand that their first call is to *spiritual leadership*. With this in mind they are attentive to both personal and communal spiritual disciplines. They cultivate practices of prayer and spiritual discernment in themselves and in one another by the ways they organize their meetings, approach decision-making, and engage in mutual accountability. By building skills in the practices of prayer, spiritual discernment, and the study of Scripture, they are able to invite other members of the congregation into the Christian spiritual life. Their example and mentorship of others deepens the spiritual and worship-centered orientation of the congregations. At the same time it contributes to a growing reservoir of trust that can help contain the anxieties that come with change.

Leaders in these congregations demonstrate many spiritual gifts in their exercise of leadership. They have a clarity of vision about the congregation and its future, a vision grounded in the experience of encounter with God in worship. As Paul Galbreath says, "We're increasingly clear here that what we're doing is about spirituality. . . . The end on Sunday morning is to glorify God, and it is for us to be transformed by that process." Their confidence in God's leading, even when they cannot fully see into the future, gives rise to qualities of patience, courage, and commitment. These leaders are generous in their explorations of the many possibilities and options before the congregation. They are able carefully and energetically to investigate opportunities before them and make courageous decisions in response to their discernment of God's leading.

In congregational life leadership is exercised more as mentoring than as executive administration. We have seen how in addressing the need for adaptive change leaders are restrained in their use of authoritative leadership. They seek instead to establish relationships wherein an ethos of trust and challenge can thrive. Whether the relationships are formal (in covenant groups or on a committee, for example) or are informal spiritual companionships (that develop naturally within friendships), within the culture of the congregation is the expectation that spiritual care for one another is a primary feature of all relationships. We have heard Paul Galbreath say, "If it's not about relationships and it's not about building friendships that will last, then I don't want to do it."

According to Lawrence Daloz, "mentors seem to do three fairly distinct things: they *support*, they *challenge*, and they *provide vision*."[15] In providing *support* congregational leaders create a context wherein trust can be developed, and individuals, as they develop, can experience the security necessary to examine some of their most closely held beliefs and practices. Leaders also exert a necessary amount of *challenge*, disturbing the comfortable equilibrium or entrenched resistance to change that can lead to stagnation. In either case the role of congregational leaders is to find an energizing balance between support and challenge wherein congregations can engage in fruitful adaptive work. An imbalance of support and challenge can thwart a community's efforts to adapt. Increased challenge without adequate support can cause communities to retreat from change. Conversely, abundant support coupled with weak challenge is perceived as an implicit confirmation of the status quo. As we have seen, the necessary discernment of the balance between challenge and support is perceived through relationships leaders have with members of congregations. Within the context of commitment and trust, leaders are able to discern and exercise over time a fruitful combination of support and challenge that opens the way for a deepening spiritual life.

Mentors also provide vision. Daloz says, "Mentors hang around through transitions, a foot on either side of the gulf; they offer a hand to help us swing across. By their very existence, mentors provide proof that the journey can be made, the leap taken."[16] In helping others look ahead, articulate a dream, draw their own maps, mentors offer a credible chance that success is possible. Congregational leaders as spiritual companions and guides support and challenge even while they help to name the vision toward which the congregation is moving. Part of this envisioning is also to look back and see significant progress that has been made and to name and celebrate it.

Resilience of the Social System

When initiating cultural change in congregations the *resilience of the social system* is a crucial factor that requires careful consideration. We have noted how in the congregations described here relationships of commitment, affection, flexibility, and courage that have endured over time form an environment where courageous truth telling can occur. In congregations where liturgical renewal and spiritual renewal have gone hand in hand, hospitality and generosity have been cultural norms. The ability to entertain differences and welcome change depends in some measure on a web of relationships that help a community maintain its equilibrium.

In order for cultural change to endure in congregational life, the work of adaptation must be taken up by the people themselves. Thus the work of creative adaptation to changing circumstances becomes a cultural characteristic of the congregation. In this environment decision-making processes become broadly participatory as responsibilities shift to the primary stakeholders, members of the congregation. According to Elizabeth Price, "these kinds of disciplines can create a culture, time and reality, in which a community can be self-directing, that can take charge of its learning, that focuses on the learner rather than on the teacher, whose members are skilled to work corporately in partnership in the processes of self-directed learning."[17]

Cognitive Complexity and Congregational Leadership

The multilayered thinking exhibited by leaders in the congregations described here requires simultaneous attention to several levels of meaning. According to Scott Cormode, the three primary areas of attention for church leaders are pastoral, organizational, and theological: "Religious leaders must address each situation they encounter at multiple layers. They balance pastoral concerns for individuals against organizational concerns for the community, all the while maintaining an eye on the larger theological implications of the situation. If a religious leader stops working at any one of these levels, she loses part of her vocation."[18] The complexity of this kind of balancing may seem daunting, but in the congregations described here the abilities and priorities called for are part of the culture of spiritual leadership nurtured throughout the leadership development process. Recall how at West Raleigh when parents of young children wanted a safer environment with spiritual nurture for their children, Marita Wynands took the lead in helping to find an appropriate program. They looked first of all for a program that showed pastoral sensitivity to the spiritual needs of young children. They also kept in mind the liturgical and spiritual focus they wanted. Then they considered the organizational, spatial, and material needs of the program, which were considerable. By balancing all of these considerations, the group was able to discover and adapt a program that met all of their needs.

At West Raleigh and the other congregations described here, the culture of the congregation has been thoroughly influenced by the kind of "fourth-order thinking" their leaders exhibit.[19] Some have called this "systems thinking"[20] wherein multiple perspectives and the relationships among them are balanced, considered, and evaluated. While not everyone in a congregation can or will develop these reflective analytical abilities, the culture of the congregation is deeply influenced by their leaders' manner of exercising leadership. As Elizabeth Price writes, "A congregation that proceeds in a fourth order way of making meaning may not necessarily have a large number of people with complex cognitive skills; instead the influencing factor may be a history or ethos of the congregation that holds this way of thinking as conventional."[21] Congregational leadership requires that leaders "see the congregation whole." In order to balance pastoral, organizational, and theological issues in the midst of the many activities and relationships that make up congregational life, congregational leaders need ways to understand not only the various dimensions of congregational life but the interrelationships among those dimensions. It is the responsibility of leaders to become keen, compassionate, and critical observers of congregational life. In caring for the pastoral, organizational, and theological dimensions of congregational life, giving priority to the pastoral, leaders serve as initiators of and active participants in the spiritual renewal of the congregation.

The spiritual renewal of these congregations is not the same as church growth. Rather than broadening the scope of the church's influence through numerical growth, worship-centered spiritual renewal seeks to deepen the congregation's participation in the Divine life. The critically reflective culture implied here may not attract everyone. For these congregations, however, its fruitfulness gives witness to its faithfulness.

Incarnational Leadership

Many have noted that leaders have unique opportunities to "model" the Christian life within the congregations they serve. While this is undoubtedly true, in the congregations described here something more is going on. The presence and action of the Holy Spirit in the lives of these leaders makes it possible for richer spiritual dimensions to be revealed. Robert Martin notes that "in the spiritually charged relationships within . . . congregational settings, people [are] attuned to realities lying beneath the surface, and they [are] able to see these spiritual realities in the discipleship of others."[22] He calls this kind of leadership "incarnational" and "iconic." Drawing on the Orthodox theology of the icon, he notes how "the nature and meaning of the painted image [icon] is derivative of the living icons of Christ and human beings." Christ as the image of God ("Whoever has seen me has seen the Father," John 14:9) and humankind created in the image of God incarnate the presence of God in human experience. This incarnation is qualitatively different from the Christ's incarnation, but it is incarnation nonetheless. In this way all Christians through Christ participate in the divine life, a kind of participation we call communion. To understand leadership iconically, then, is to ponder the ways leaders participate in, incarnate, and reflect epiphanies of God's presence as they exercise the structural and interpersonal dimensions of leadership. "That we are living in an incarnate reality where God is truly Emmanuel is one of the most fundamental truths of Christianity, and iconography is meant to communicate exactly that truth," says Martin.[23] More than role models, leaders become icons of communion with God in which persons see Christ and see themselves in Christ. "This is the fundamental ground of ecclesial leadership upon which all of the tasks, roles, and practices of leadership are based and in which they find their fulfillment."[24]

In the congregations described here, while leaders do not use the language of iconic and incarnational leadership, their exercise of leadership has become an incarnation of their life in God and a reflection of the congregation's identity as the body of Christ. Throughout this study many members and leaders in congregations described friends and spiritual companions who grew continually into the likeness of Christ, a likeness that was evident to all around them.

In describing a similar congregation and its leaders, Robert Martin says,

> People were relating to one another in such a way that they became images and icons; they reflected more to others than they were in themselves. Coming at it from another perspective, people were seeing in one another more than the person or group in front of them. They were discerning a two-fold spiritual depth: a revelation of the life of God and of themselves in God. This reflective-disclosive quality is important for a theologically adequate understanding of ecclesial leadership. For what is Christian leadership but a more prominent form of discipleship? And what is discipleship but an embodied image of the divine life? Thus, an ecclesial leader is a disciple in whose life others see Christ and sense the meaning of the divine life in their own.[25]

Leaders in the congregations described here understand their exercise of leadership as ministry. Kenda Creasy Dean and Ron Foster write, "Ministry is the grateful response of God's people, whose activity in the world and with one another suggests a new way of being alive. Ministry is not something we 'do' to someone else. It is a holy way of living toward God and toward one another."[26] To live in this way is to live a "Godbearing life."

At Immanuel Church it was a long evening for the governing board. Their agenda included a detailed report filled with probing questions from the committee charged with calling a new associate pastor. The building and finance committee reported on an extensive engineering assessment of their education building, noting that there were significant structural concerns. A major earthquake had jolted the area just weeks before, and while the building was not damaged, its inherent weaknesses raised questions about its overall safety. The committee asked the board to consider the possibility of constructing a new building. The worship committee proposed a revised schedule for communion, indicating the manner of distribution for each celebration. Everyone understood the boldness of their proposed schedule, which included more frequent communion but fewer occasions for being served in the pews. But before they began this weighty agenda, the board gathered in a semicircle around the fireplace of the church library. An order for evening prayer awaited them as they gathered. Amid lots of laughter and good humor, the Christ candle from the sanctuary was lighted and placed next to a bowl of water and a chalice. The group sang and prayed and heard Scripture. They shared their celebrations and concerns for the congregation and prayed again. As they moved to the conference table to take up the agenda, a deep calm seemed to move with them. Reflecting on the meeting later, Paul Galbreath says, "I can't imagine people going home from the meeting saying, 'There was no source of life in this for me.' That's just not what is going on. It is part of the transformation of the culture of leadership in the church that causes people to want to be there. We have brought people into what is alive."

Congregational leadership has its origins in worship. In an earlier chapter we have heard Galbreath describe the transparency of worship leadership: "I think that all of liturgy is about transparence. It's about whether you're willing to be transparent when you're in front of people, because whether you like it or not you *are* transparent when you're in front of people doing the liturgy. It is about being transparent to the sacred. The end is for people to see and taste and touch the divine." It is the responsibility of congregational leaders to lead congregations in discerning the presence of the sacred, according to Galbreath, to be windows on the sacred on the congregation's behalf.

Reflection on Leadership

Throughout the process of exercising leadership, pastors and lay leaders in these congregations regularly reflect on the experience of leading.

Leadership for them is an exercise in experiential learning where they *draw on the concrete experience* of leading, *reflect* on their experience, *study various concepts* related to leadership, and *experiment* with new ways of leading. These leaders practice a variety of spiritual disciplines that include opportunities to examine the ways they lead and the responses from those around them. Some leaders keep personal journals. Most include periods of meditation and prayer in their daily routines. At West Raleigh minutes of meetings serve this purpose for some groups. Rather than reading like objective reporting, minutes often have the quality of a collective prayer journal in which the spirit of the meeting is clearly evident. In the process of these reflections leaders are able to recall and understand their experience of leadership more clearly and to discern appropriate next steps. Especially in collaborative settings, including official board and committee meetings, the collective reflections of the group are particularly fruitful. There the disciplines of respectful listening and careful exploration of possibilities in an environment of prayerful discernment prevail.

Leaders in these congregations also study about leadership. They discover and develop abstract concepts that shed light on practices of leadership they are familiar with and on new ways to understand leadership. In this chapter we have reviewed several sets of abstract concepts that provide mental maps for leaders and help to frame their approach to congregational renewal. Terms such as *holding environment, framing issues, orchestrating conflict, mediation, arbitration,* and *authority* serve as orienting devices that help leaders understand the complexities of congregational life and their constructive role in adaptive change. Theological terms such as *ordination, spiritual disciplines, worshipful work, inward journey, outward journey,* and *formation* help congregations orient their work toward spiritual renewal. These terms also serve as reminders that the programmatic and administrative necessities of the organizational life of the church serve the spiritual life of the congregation.

The ongoing life of any congregation is an active experiment in faithfulness. Leaders in these congregations are clear that the life of their congregation is at its heart a spiritual pilgrimage. Like West Raleigh they are attentive to both the inward and outward components of that pilgrimage as they discover opportunities to deepen the spiritual life of the congregation and participate in its ministry and mission.

Conclusion

Marty Lemming, a leader in the children's worship program at West Raleigh, shows me around the children's worship rooms. Her face glows as she describes the children, their worship leaders, and the activities that fill these rooms each Sunday. Marty takes the cover off a beautiful box to reveal exquisitely made wooden figures of people and animals. Her eyes sparkle as she names the characters in the story and describes how it is told. Marty has discovered significant tangible as well as spiritual gifts as a result of her participation in the children's worship program. She was interested in the children's worship program from the beginning but was not sure she wanted to serve as a worship leader for children. So she began by offering to make the simple wooden figures used in the storytelling portion of the program. Patterns were provided, so it seemed like a straightforward task. But as she worked with her saws and sanding equipment, Marty says she became dissatisfied with some of the human and animal forms from the pattern set. Soon she was designing and constructing her own patterns, turning simple figures into pieces of folk-art sculpture. She took careful note of the color, texture, and pattern of the wood grains and used them to give subtle detail to the figures. She took extraordinary care with the shape and feel of the finished figures, sanding and staining them with the children's use in mind. The intention of the children's worship program is that the wooden figures do not call attention to themselves, but serve the child's imagination. Marty's figures are faithful to these intentions, while also incorporating an element of artistic care that is unmistakable.

When I ask Marty about the significance of this careful work, she blushes and looks for a few moments at her own hands. "It is an act of devotion," she says, "a kind of spiritual discipline." While she is making the figures, she is praying for the children and adults in the children's worship program. She envisions them using the figures to enact Bible stories and ponders the "I wonder . . ." questions they might pose as they engage the story. She thinks of how the children might use the figures again to retell the story to themselves during the response time. And she reads the worship journal kept by storytellers and other leaders in the program. There she finds comments and questions posed by children as they encounter God in worship that is suited to their age and development. Throughout the years she has been active in the children's worship program, Marty has taken on many roles, including leadership roles she never thought she would accept. Along with other leaders she has studied Scripture and learned about the worship of the church. With them she has reflected on the ways of God in her own life and in the lives of others. Her spiritual life has been shaped and deepened through participation in the life of this congregation. Marty has learned the Christian life through the experience of congregational life. Her spiritual life and the worship life of the congregation are inextricably linked. The process for Marty and many others at West Raleigh has been gradual, sometimes painful, but always rewarding, as they come to know the Christian spiritual life as intrinsically rewarding.

This book began with two foundational questions: How do we learn the Christian life from the experience of congregational life? How do renewal in worship and spiritual renewal in congregations complement and support each other? Marty's life, embedded in the life of the congregation at West Raleigh, helps us answer these two questions. We learn the Christian life in worship-centered congregations where prayer and spiritual disciplines, study and instruction, mission and ministry, and leadership are part of the congregation's culture. But, as we have seen, participation alone is not enough. Deep learning requires consistent patterns of reflection, where careful attention is given to all dimensions of experience and where hard questions deepen the reflection. Such reflection is grounded in a "holding environment" of faithful relationships where support and challenge are balanced and consistently practiced. A rich vocabulary of faith—a congregational "native language"—supports the life of faith and deepens both curiosity and understanding. And these congregations have long since given up formal politeness, what some have called "the tyranny of nice," in favor of an atmosphere of genuine caring and questioning. Members of these faith communities have general social permission to ask one another about their lives of faith, not because they are nosy but because they genuinely care about one another and want to learn from one another. Pervading this culture of faithful commitment to the Christian spiritual life is the practice of prayer, embodied in a rich variety of spiritual disciplines. Prayer permeates these congregations, both communally and personally, as members gather and scatter.[1]

Above all, these churches center their life together on encounter with God in worship, promised to the church by the risen Lord. Their thirst for the presence of the living God is embodied in all they do, but especially they long for the presence of God within the worshiping assembly. This desire drives them to be uncompromising about the theocentric focus of their worship as well as its coherent integration. They love Scripture because it recounts the stories of God and the people of God. They give careful and abundant attention to the color, sound, light, taste, fragrance, and gracious ambience of worship. The promised presence of God, they know, will be the source and goal of all other dimensions of their congregation's life.

Leaders in congregations often ask me how the reorientation of congregational life is possible. How do congregations center their life together on worship and open themselves to continual formation into the likeness of Christ? Sometimes they are dismayed when I say that, in my opinion, it takes no fewer than ten years. Liturgical reform and programmatic change may come rather quickly, but cultural change in congregations comes slowly, as encounters with God are entered into and reflected on in a variety of ways and the presence of God is discerned in everexpanding circles of divine presence. Congregations need time to learn silence, to develop the skills of full-hearted and full-voiced congregational praise. It takes time to learn the stories of God's way with humankind and to love Scripture. It takes time to learn the relationships among compassion, social change, and spiritual transformation and to reorient decision making toward spiritual discernment and administration toward an act of praise to God. Sometimes when I venture such opinions among congregational leaders, they are dismayed, even downhearted. Many of us have hoped for a "quick fix" for congregational renewal. Other leaders, however, take the prospect of a long process for cultural change in congregations as a gift. They recognize that gradual but deep reorientation in congregations is in harmony with the shape of the Christian spiritual life, as understood by saints throughout the ages. We may recognize the work of the triune God in our lives in a startling, life-changing instant. But it requires a lifetime of attentiveness to the work of the Spirit to appropriate that divine presence.

It is my deepest prayer that this book may contribute in some small way to the reorientation of congregations toward the broadening and deepening of the worship of God—Father, Son, and Holy Spirit.

Notes

Introduction

1. Presbyterian Church (U.S.A.), "Directory for Worship," in *Constitution of the Presbyterian Church (U.S.A.)*, pt. 2, *Book of Order, 2002–2003* (Louisville, Ky.: Office of the General Assembly, Presbyterian Church (U.S.A.), 2002), W-1.1001.
2. Margaret Talbot, "A Mighty Fortress," *New York Times Magazine*, February 27, 2000: 34–41, 66–68, 84–85.
3. Ibid., 36.
4. Miroslav Volf, "Floating Along?" *Christian Century* 117 (April 5, 2000): 398.
5. Stanley Hauerwas, interview by David Heim, in "Ethics in Our Time: Social Witness for the New Century," *Christian Century* 117 (September 27–October 4, 2000): 952.
6. George Gallup, Jr. and D. Michael Lindsay, *Surveying the Religious Landscape: Trends in U.S. Beliefs* (Harrisburg, Penn.: Moorehouse Publishing, 1999), 1–5.
7. Center for Parish Development, *Theological Dimensions of Church Transformation: Readings in Church Transformation* (Chicago: Center for Parish Development, 1994), 42–59.
8. See such works as *Leadership without Easy Answers* (Cambridge, Mass.: Belknap Press of Harvard University Press, 1994) by Ronald A. Heifetz; *The Fifth Discipline: The Art and Practice of the Learning Organization* (New York: Doubleday/Currency, 1990) by Peter M. Senge; *The Reflective Practitioner: How Professionals Think in Action* (New York: Basic Books, 1983) by Donald A. Schön; *Leading With Soul: An Uncommon Journey of Spirit* (San Francisco: Jossey-Bass, 1995) and *Reframing Organizations: Artistry, Choice, and Leadership*, 2d ed. (San Francisco: Jossey-Bass, 1997), both by Lee G. Bolman and Terrence E. Deal.

Chapter 1: Worship at the Center of Congregational Life

1. Presbyterian Church (U.S.A.), "A Brief Statement of Faith," in *Constitution of the Presbyterian Church (U.S.A.)*, pt. 1, *Book of Confessions, 2002–2003* (Louisville, Ky.: Office of the General Assembly, Presbyterian Church (U.S.A.), 2002), 8.0000.
2. Presbyterian Church (U.S.A.), "Directory for Worship," W-1.1000.

3. Marva Dawn, *A Royal Waste of Time: The Splendor of Worshiping God and Being Church for the World* (Grand Rapids: Wm. B. Eerdmans Publishing Co., 1999).
4. Gordon W. Lathrop, *Holy Things: A Liturgical Theology* (Minneapolis: Fortress Press, 1993), 5–6.
5. Thomas H. Groome, *Sharing Faith: A Comprehensive Approach to Religious Education and Pastoral Ministry* (San Francisco: HarperSanFrancisco, 1991), 341.
6. Ibid., 338.
7. Don Harting, "The Hottest Thing in Youth Ministry," *Presbyterians Today* 89 (November 1999): 20–23.
8. James Empereur, *Worship: Exploring the Sacred* (Washington, D.C.: Pastoral Press, 1987), 30. Emphasis added.
9. Frank C. Senn, *New Creation: A Liturgical Worldview* (Minneapolis: Fortress Press, 2000), xi–xiv.
10. There are, of course, many ways to describe the patterns of Christian worship, but for our purposes here the fourfold pattern will serve as a formative model. See Theology and Worship Ministry Unit, Presbyterian Church (U.S.A.) and Cumberland Presbyterian Church, *Book of Common Worship* (Louisville, Ky.: Westminster/John Knox Press, 1993); Episcopal Church, *The Book of Common Prayer and Administration of the Sacraments and Other Rites and Ceremonies of the Church* (New York: Seabury Press, 1979); United Methodist Church (U.S.), *The United Methodist Book of Worship* (Nashville: United Methodist Publishing House, 1992); Church of Scotland, *The Book of Common Order of the Church of Scotland*, 2d ed. (Edinburgh, Scotland: Saint Andrew Press, 1966).
11. Cynthia M. Campbell, "The Promise of Common Prayer," in *Praying in Common*, by Campbell and J. Frederick Holper, Theology and Worship Occasional Paper 6 (Louisville, Ky.: Presbyterian Church (U.S.A.), 1994), 4.
12. L. Gregory Jones, "Geographies of Memory," *Christian Century* 117 (August 30, 2000): 874.
13. Shirley Guthrie, "Evangelism in a Pluralistic Society: A Reformed Perspective," *Covenant Connection* 5 (December 2002): 3.
14. Harold M. Daniels, preface to *Liturgical Year: The Worship of God*, by Ministry Unit on Theology and Worship, Presbyterian Church (U.S.A.) and Cumberland Presbyterian Church, Supplemental Liturgical Resource 7 (Louisville, Ky.: Westminster/John Knox Press, 1992), 7.
15. Lathrop, *Holy Things*, 42.
16. Mary Collins, *Worship: Renewal to Practice* (Washington, D.C.: Pastoral Press, 1987), 73–90. See also Susanne K. Langer, *Philosophy in a New Key: A Study in the Symbolism of Reason, Rite, and Art* (Cambridge, Mass.: Harvard University Press, 1942); Ronald L. Grimes, *Beginnings in Ritual Studies*, rev. ed., Studies in Comparative Religion (Columbia, S.C.: University of South Carolina Press, 1995); Clifford Geertz, *Interpretation of Cultures: Selected Essays* (New York: Basic Books, 1973); Victor Turner, *The Ritual Process: Structure and Anti-Structure*, Lewis Henry Morgan Lectures, 1966 (Chicago: Aldine Publishing, 1969); Gregory Bateson, *Steps to an Ecology of Mind* (New York: Ballantine Books, 1972).
17. Grimes, *Beginnings in Ritual Studies*, 24–39.
18. Philip H. Pfatteicher, *Liturgical Spirituality* (Valley Forge, Penn.: Trinity Press International, 1997), 94.

19. Gwen Kennedy Neville and John H. Westerhoff, III, *Learning through Liturgy* (New York: Seabury Press, 1978), 130.

20. John H. Westerhoff, III, *Living the Faith Community: The Church That Makes a Difference* (Minneapolis: Winston Press, 1985), 57.

21. L. Gregory Jones, "HalloThanksMas," *Christian Century* 116 (December 22, 1999): 1258.

22. Marjorie J. Thompson, *Soul Feast: An Invitation to the Christian Spiritual Life* (Louisville, Ky.: Westminster John Knox Press, 1995), 7.

23. Groome, *Sharing Faith*, 337–38.

24. Presbyterian Church (U.S.A.), "Directory for Worship," W-1.1000.

25. Paul Dietterich and Inagrace Dietterich, *A Systems Model of the Church in Ministry and Mission* (Chicago: Center for Parish Development, 1994), 25–27.

26. Gordon Lathrop, *Holy People: A Liturgical Ecclesiology* (Minneapolis: Fortress Press, 1999), 9.

27. Darrell J. Fasching, *Narrative Theology After Auschwitz: From Alienation to Ethics* (Minneapolis: Fortress Press, 1992), 82–83.

28. Groome, *Sharing Faith*, 337. See also Don E. Saliers, *Worship and Spirituality*, 2d ed. (Akron, Oh.; OSL Publications, 1996), 44.

29. Lathrop, *Holy Things*, 79.

Chapter 2: Experiential Learning in Congregational Life

1. See Margaret Ann Crane and Jack L. Seymour, "Ethnographer as Minister: Ethnographic Research in Ministry," *Religious Education* 91 (Summer 1996): 299–315 and "'Thrashing in the Night': Laity Speak About Religious Knowing," *Religious Education* 92 (Winter 1997): 38–53.

2. David A. Kolb, *Experiential Learning: Experience as the Source of Learning and Development* (Englewood Cliffs, N.J.: Prentice-Hall, 1984), 21.

3. Michael Warren, *At This Time, In This Place: The Spirit Embodied in the Local Assembly* (Harrisburg, Penn.: Trinity Press International, 1999), 25ff.

4. For example, people sometimes refer to a "worship experience" in ways that imply that the concrete experience itself has lost its centrality. Rather than dwelling in the experience itself, they may be distancing themselves from the here-and-now, even while the experience is still in progress.

5. Kolb, *Experiential Learning*, 43.

6. Laurent A. Parks Daloz, et al., *Common Fire: Leading Lives of Commitment in a Complex World* (Boston: Beacon Press, 1996), 25.

7. Craig Dykstra, *Growing in the Life of Faith: Education and Christian Practices* (Louisville, Ky.: Geneva Press, 1999), 40.

8. Robert K. Martin, "Education and the Liturgical Life of the Church," *Religious Education* 98 (Winter 2003): 54.

9. See C. Ellis Nelson, *Where Faith Begins*, James Sprunt Lectures, 1965 (Richmond, Va.: John Knox Press, 1967); Maria Harris, *Fashion Me a People: Curriculum in the Church* (Louisville, Ky.: Westminster/John Knox Press, 1989); Constance J. Tarasar, "Orthodox Theology and Religious Education," in *Theologies of Religious Education*, ed. Randolph Crump Miller (Birmingham, Ala.: Religious Education Press, 1995), 83–120; Nancy L. Ammerman et al., eds., *Studying Congregations: A New Handbook* (Nashville: Abingdon Press, 1998); Denham Grierson, *Transforming a People of God* (Melbourne, Australia: Joint Board of Christian Education, 1984); James F. Hopewell, *Congregations:*

Stories and Structures, ed. Barbara G. Wheeler (Philadelphia: Fortress Press, 1987); Carl S. Dudley, Jackson W. Carroll, and James P. Wind, eds., *Carriers of Faith: Lessons from Congregational Studies* (Louisville, Ky.: Westminster/John Knox Press, 1990); Susanne Johnson, *Spiritual Formation in the Church and Classroom* (Nashville: Abingdon Press, 1989); Dietterich, *Systems Model*.

10. William P. Brown, *Character in Crisis: A Fresh Approach to the Wisdom Literature of the Old Testament* (Grand Rapids: Wm. B. Eerdmans Publishing Co., 1996), 7. Here Brown makes the case that contexts influence particular frameworks for understanding.

11. See John Cowan, *On Becoming an Innovative University Teacher: Reflection in Action* (Buckingham, England: Society for Research into Higher Education and Open University Press, 1998), 44.

12. Kolb, *Experiential Learning*, 32.

13. Peter M. Senge, *Fifth Discipline: The Art and Practice of the Learning Organization* (New York: Doubleday/Currency, 1990).

14. John Dewey, *Experience and Education*, Kappa Delta Pi Lecture Series (New York: Collier Books of Macmillan Publishing, 1938), 35.

15. Kolb, *Experiential Learning*, 31.

16. See Jack Mezirow, *Transformative Dimensions of Adult Learning* (San Francisco: Jossey-Bass, 1991), 37ff.

17. Ibid., 11.

18. See Sharon Peebles Burch, *Collective Absolute Presuppositions: Tectonic Plates for Churches* (New York: Peter Lang, 1999).

19. See John M. Hull, *What Prevents Christian Adults from Learning?* (London: SCM Press, 1985), 89–146.

20. Mezirow, *Transformative Dimensions*, 104–5.

21. Laurent A. Daloz, *Mentor: Guiding the Journey of Adult Learners*, 2d ed. of *Effective Teaching and Mentoring* (San Francisco: Jossey-Bass, 1999), 184–85.

22. Robert Kegan, *Evolving Self: Problem and Process in Human Development* (Cambridge, Mass.: Harvard University Press, 1982), 116.

Chapter 3: How Congregations Worship

1. John XXIII, Bishop of Rome, "Constitution on the Sacred Liturgy," in *Documents of Vatican II*, ed. Walter M. Abbott (New York: Guild Press/America Press/Association Press, 1966), 144.

2. Roy A. Rappaport, *Ritual and Religion in the Making of Humanity*, Cambridge Studies in Social and Cultural Anthropology (Cambridge, England: Cambridge University Press, 1999), 393.

3. Lathrop, *Holy Things*, 5. See also Aidan Kavanagh, *On Liturgical Theology*, Hale Memorial Lectures of Seabury-Western Theological Seminary, 1981 (Collegeville, Minn.: Liturgical Press, 1992), 74–75, 89.

4. J. Frederick Holper, "The Promise of Presbyterian Liturgical Renewal," in Campbell and Holper, *Praying in Common*, 22.

5. Robert N. Bellah, "Liturgy and Experience," in *The Roots of Ritual*, ed. James D. Shaugnessy (Grand Rapids: Wm. B. Eerdmans Publishing Co., 1973), 233.

6. Ronald P. Byars, "Preparing and Leading the Service for the Lord's Day," in *The Companion to the Book of Common Worship*, ed. Peter C. Bower (Louisville, Ky.: Geneva Press, 2003), 72.

7. Don E. Saliers, "Liturgical Musical Formation," in *Liturgy and Music: Lifetime Learning*, ed. Robin A. Leaver and Joyce Ann Zimmerman (Collegeville, Minn.: Liturgical Press, 1998), 387.
8. Harold M. Daniels, "The Sign of the Cross," *Reformed Liturgy and Music* 21 (Winter 1987): 39.
9. Ibid.
10. Ellen T. Charry, "Sacraments for the Christian Life," *Christian Century* 112 (November 15, 1995): 1077.
11. Ibid., 1076.
12. John Calvin, *Calvin: Institutes of the Christian Religion*, ed. John T. McNeill; trans. Ford Lewis Battles, Library of Christian Classics, 20–21 (Philadelphia: Westminster Press, 1960), Book 4, ch. 10, sec. 29, 1207 as cited in Daniels, "Sign of the Cross," 42.
13. Jerry Larsen, *Religious Education and the Brain: Practical Resource for Understanding How We Learn about God* (New York: Paulist Press, 2000), 101.
14. Fred P. Edie, "Liturgy, Emotion, and the Poetics of Being Human," *Religious Education* 96, no. 4 (Fall 2001): 474–88.
15. Ibid.
16. Donald E. Saliers, *The Soul in Paraphrase: Prayer and the Religious Affections* (New York: Seabury Press, 1980), 20.
17. Ibid., 18.
18. Walter Brueggemann, "Newness Mediated by Worship," *Reformed Liturgy and Music* 20 (Spring 1986): 58.
19. Westerhoff, *Living the Faith Community*, 27.
20. Saliers, *Worship and Spirituality*, 6.
21. Thomas H. Groome, *Christian Religious Education: Sharing Our Story and Vision* (San Francisco: Harper & Row, 1980), 192.
22. James F. White, "Rearranging the Furniture," *Reformed Worship* 64 (June 2002): 18.
23. Lucy Chester Jacobs and Clinton J. Chase, *Developing and Using Tests Effectively: A Guide for Faculty*, Jossey-Bass Higher and Adult Education Series (San Francisco: Jossey-Bass, 1992), 17.
24. See Thomas F. Green, *The Activities of Teaching* (New York: McGraw Hill, 1971), 22–23.
25. Lathrop, *Holy Things*, 180.
26. Holper, "Promise of Presbyterian Liturgical Renewal," 22.
27. Leland Ryken, *The Liberated Imagination: Thinking Christianly about the Arts* (Wheaton, Ill.: Harold Shaw Publishers, 1989), 98.
28. Ibid.
29. Stanley R. Hall, *Essential Tenets of Reformed Worship?*, Theological and Worship Occasional Paper 10 (Louisville, Ky.: Presbyterian Church (U.S.A.), 1998), 5–7.
30. *Institutes of the Christian Religion*, ed. John T. McNeill, trans. Ford Lewis Battle (Philadelphia: Westminster , 1960), 1.5.1–2.
31. Brueggemann, "Newness Mediated by Worship," 57.
32. Gilbert Ostdiek, *Catechesis for Liturgy: A Program for Parish Involvement* (Washington, D.C.: Pastoral Press, 1986), 89.
33. Ibid.
34. These categories and the following discussion are drawn from Ostdiek, *Catechesis for Liturgy*, 41–45.
35. Ibid., 44.

36. Ibid., 41–42.
37. Ibid., 42.
38. Ibid., 42–43.
39. Ibid., 44.
40. One could contrast this kind of spiritual leadership with a mechanical "going through the motions" or an ego-driven performance that seems to crave the spotlight.
41. Ostdiek, *Catechesis for Liturgy*, 27.
42. Ibid., 39.
43. Ibid., 25–26.
44. Jo Ann Staebler, "Water of Welcome," *Alive Now* 31 (July/August 2001): 43–44.
45. Resources include Joan Halmo, *Celebrating the Church Year With Young Children* (Collegeville, Minn.: Liturgical Press, 1988); Mary Catherine Berglund, *Gather the Children: Celebrate the Word with Ideas, Activities, Prayers and Projects*, rev. ed. (Washington D.C.: Pastoral Press, 1993); Carolyn C. Brown, *Gateways to Worship: A Year of Worship Experiences for Young Children* (Nashville: Abingdon Press, 1989); Sue Lou, *Get Ready! Get Set! Worship! A Resource for Including Children in Worship: For Pastors, Educators, Parents, Sessions, and Committees* (Louisville, Ky.: Geneva Press, 1999); David Ng and Virginia Thomas, *Children in the Worshiping Community* (Atlanta: John Knox Press, 1981); Elizabeth J. Sandell, *Including Children in Worship: A Planning Guide for Congregations* (Minneapolis: Augsburg, 1991); W. Alan Smith, *Children Belong in Worship: A Guide to the Children's Sermon* (St. Louis: CBP Press, 1984); Ruth L. Boling, Lauren J. Muzzy, and Laurie A. Vance, *A Children's Guide to Worship* (Louisville, Ky.: Geneva Press, 1997); Ruth L. Boling. *Come Worship with Me: A Journey Through the Church Year* (Louisville, Ky.: Geneva Press, 2000); Elizabeth Caldwell, *Come Unto Me: Rethinking the Sacraments for Children* (Cleveland: United Church Press, 1996); Carolyn C. Brown, *You Can Preach to the Kids, Too! Designing Sermons for Adults and Children* (Nashville: Abingdon Press, 1997); Cokesbury Press, *Touch the Water, Taste the Bread: Exploring the Sacraments with Children*, 3 vols. (Nashville: Cokesbury Press, 1998); Robbie Castleman, *Parenting in the Pew: Guiding Your Children into the Joy of Worship*, expanded ed. (Downers Grove, Ill.: InterVarsity Press, 2002).
46. Sonja M. Stewart and Jerome W. Berryman, *Young Children and Worship* (Louisville, Ky.: Westminster/John Knox Press, 1989); Jerome Berryman, *Godly Play: A Way of Religious Education* (San Francisco: Harper, 1991) and *Teaching Godly Play: The Sunday Morning Handbook* (Nashville: Abingdon Press, 1995); Sonja M. Stewart, *Following Jesus: More About Young Children and Worship* (Louisville, Ky.: Geneva Press, 2000); Susan R. Garrett and Amy Platinga Pauw, *Making Time for God: Daily Devotions for Children and Families to Share* (Grand Rapids: Baker Books, 2002).
47. Lathrop, *Holy Things*, 6–7.

Chapter 4: Prayer and Spiritual Disciplines

1. George F. Simons, *Keeping Your Personal Journal* (New York: Paulist Press, 1978), 8.
2. Thompson, *Soul Feast*, 7.
3. Presbyterian Church (U.S.A.), "Directory for Worship," W-1.1001.
4. See Roberta Hestenes, *Turning Committees into Communities* (Colorado Springs, Col.: NavPress, 1991); Philip A. Anderson, *Church Meetings That Matter* (New York: Pilgrim Press, 1987); Charles M. Olsen, *Transforming Church Boards into Communities of Spiritual Leaders* (Washington, D.C.: Alban Institute, 1995).

5. Hestenes, *Turning Committees into Communities*, 13–14. Hestenes offers a chart highlighting the distinctions between committees and communities. While committees have institutional characteristics, relational qualities pervade communities. The same tasks may be accomplished, but the relational aspects of the community alter the character of the tasks and of the participants themselves: "A community is ultimately more productive and more joyful than a traditional committee," 15.

6. Resources for small group ministry include Renovaré Resources for Spiritual Renewal, especially *A Spiritual Formation Workbook: Small Group Resources for Nurturing Christian Growth*, by James Bryan Smith (New York: HarperCollins, 1993); *Guide for Class Leaders: A Model for Christian Formation*, by Grace Bradford (Nashville: Discipleship Resources, 1999); *Women in the Presence: Constructing Community and Seeking Spirituality in Mainline Protestantism*, by Jody Shapiro Davie (Philadelphia: University of Pennsylvania Press, 1995); *Spirit Windows: A Handbook of Spiritual Growth Resources for Leaders*, by Ann Z. Kulp (Louisville, Ky.: Bridge Resources, 1998); *Serendipity Training Manual for Groups*, by Lyman Coleman and Marty Scales (Littleton, Col.: Serendipity House, 1989); *Small Groups in the Church: A Handbook for Creating Community*, by Thomas G. Kirkpatrick (Bethesda, Md.: Alban Institute, 1995); *Teaching for Faith: A Guide for Teachers of Adult Classes*, by Richard Robert Osmer (Louisville, Ky.: Westminster/John Knox Press, 1992); *Starting Small Groups and Keeping Them Going*, by the publisher (Minneapolis: Augsburg Fortress, 1995); *Spiritual Life in the Congregation: A Guide for Retreats*, by Reuben P. Job (Nashville: Upper Room Books, 1997).

7. Stewart and Berryman, *Young Children and Worship*, 16; Stewart, *Following Jesus*, 17.

8. Kenda Creasy Dean and Ron Foster, *The Godbearing Life: The Art of Soul Tending for Youth Ministry* (Nashville: Upper Room Books, 1998), 13.

9. Don Postema, *Space for God: The Study and Practice of Prayer and Spirituality* (Grand Rapids: CRC Publications, 1983), 130.

10. Presbyterian Church (U.S.A.), "Directory for Worship," W-2.1001.

11. Thompson, *Soul Feast*, 32.

12. Dennis J. Hughes and Glaucia Vasconcelos Wilkey, "Encouraging Congregational Spirituality Through Worship," *APCE Advocate* 25 (Winter 2000): 8.

13. Arthur Paul Poers, "Learning the Ancient Rhythms of Prayer," *Christianity Today* 13 (January 8, 2001): 45.

14. Resources for prayer drawn from scripture include denominational resources such as those cited in chapter 1, note 10.

15. Thompson, *Soul Feast*, 33.

16. Ibid.

17. Richard J. Foster and James Bryan Smith, ed., *Devotional Classics: Selected Readings for Individuals and Groups* (San Francisco: HarperSanFrancisco, 1993), 2.

18. Henri J. M. Nouwen, *Reaching Out: The Three Movements of the Spiritual Life* (Garden City, N.Y.: Doubleday, 1975), 96–97.

19. Thelma Hall, *Too Deep for Words: Rediscovering Lectio Divina; with 500 Scripture Texts for Prayer* (New York: Paulist Press, 1988), 28.

20. Thompson, *Soul Feast*, 23.

21. Ibid.

22. Ibid., 24.

23. Ibid.

24. Ibid.

25. This poem of Dom Marmion, a French Benedictine monk, was quoted in Hall, *Too Deep for Words*, 44.
26. Thompson, *Soul Feast*, 90.
27. Dennis Linn et al., *Sleeping with Bread: Holding What Gives you Life* (New York: Paulist Press, 1995), 6.
28. Thompson, *Soul Feast*, 85.
29. Ibid., 87.
30. Ibid., 85.
31. Resources for journal keeping include *Adventure Inward: Christian Growth through Personal Journal Writing*, by Morton T. Kelsey (Minneapolis: Augsburg Publishing, 1980); *Journaling: A Spiritual Journey*, by Anne Broyles (Nashville: Upper Room Books, 1999); *At a Journal Workshop: The Basic Text and Guide for Using the Intensive Journal Process*, by Ira Progoff (New York: Dialogue House Library, 1975); *Keeping Your Personal Journal*, by George F. Simons (New York: Paulist Press, 1978); *Journal Keeper*, by Margaret D. Smith (Grand Rapids: Wm. B. Eerdmans Publishing Co., 1992).
32. Helen Rezatto, "My Diary," *St. Anthony Messenger* (July 1971): 32, as quoted in Simons, *Keeping Your Personal Journal*, 24.
33. Simons, *Keeping Your Personal Journal*, 9.
34. Broyles, *Journaling*, 10–11.
35. Kelsey, *Adventure Inward*, 23–24.
36. See Gerrit Scott Dawson et al., *Companions in Christ Participant's Book: A Small-Group Experience in Spiritual Formation* (Nashville: Upper Room Books, 2001).
37. Kelsey, *Adventure Inward*, 19.
38. Bruce C. Birch, "Memory in Congregational Life," in *Congregations: Their Power to Form and Transform*, ed. C. Ellis Nelson (Atlanta: John Knox Press, 1988), 23.
39. Charles R. Foster, "Communicating: Informal Conversation in the Congregation's Education," in *Congregations: Their Power to Form and Transform*, ed. C. Ellis Nelson (Atlanta: John Knox Press, 1988), 224.
40. The description of spiritual direction offered here is drawn from portions of Marjorie J. Thompson's chapter on spiritual direction in *Soul Feast*, 101–17. Other resources include *Holy Listening: The Art of Spiritual Direction*, by Margaret Guenther (Cambridge, Mass.: Cowley Publications, 1992); *Celebration of Discipline: The Path to Spiritual Growth*, rev. ed. by Richard J. Foster (San Francisco: Harper & Row, 1988), especially chapter 12 ; *Life Together*, by Dietrich Bonhoeffer, ed. by Geffrey B. Kelly (New York: Harper & Brothers, 1954); *Spiritual Friend: Reclaiming the Gift of Spiritual Direction*, by Tilden Edwards (New York: Paulist Press, 1980); *To Pray God's Will: Continuing the Journey*, by Ben Campbell Johnson (Philadelphia: Westminster Press, 1987); *Reformed Spirituality: An Introduction for Believers*, by Howard L. Rice (Louisville, Ky.: Westminster/John Knox Press, 1991); *Companions in Christ Participant's Book*, by Gerrit Scott Dawson et al.
41. Thompson, *Soul Feast*, 104.
42. Ibid., 105.
43. Ibid.
44. Ibid., 104–5.

Chapter Five: Study and Instruction

1. For a discussion of the use of literature as an aid to theological discussion, see Paula J. Carlson and Peter S. Hawkins, *Listening for God: Contemporary Literature and the Life of Faith*, 3 vols. (Minneapolis: Augsburg Fortress, 1994–2000).

2. Jack L. Seymour and Carol A. Wehrheim, "Faith Seeking Understanding: Interpretation as a Task of Christian Education," in *Contemporary Approaches to Christian Education*, edited by Seymour et al. (Nashville: Abingdon Press, 1982), 124.
3. Ibid.
4. Groome, *Christian Religious Education*, 57–66.
5. Ibid., 57–58.
6. Sara P. Little, *To Set One's Heart: Belief and Teaching in the Church* (Atlanta: John Knox Press, 1973), 11.
7. James P. Spradley, *The Ethnographic Interview* (Fort Worth: Harcourt Brace Jovanovich College Publishers, 1979), 17.
8. Brant Copeland, "Responses," *Insights: The Faculty Journal of Austin Seminary* 116 (Spring 2001): 21.
9. Hull, *What Prevents Christian Adults from Learning?*, 112.
10. Shellie Levine, "Children's Cognition as the Foundation of Spirituality," *International Journal of Children's Spirituality* 4 (1999): 121–40.
11. Ibid., 131.
12. Ibid., 128.
13. Sallie McFague, *Metaphorical Theology: Models of God in Religious Language* (Philadelphia: Fortress Press, 1982), 32–42
14. Presbyterian Church (U.S.A.), "Directory for Worship," W-1.2002.
15. Nelson, *Where Faith Begins*, 121–50.
16. Daloz, *Mentor*, 216.
17. Leon Festinger, *A Theory of Cognitive Dissonance* (Stanford, Calif.: Stanford University Press, 1957), quoted in Daloz, *Mentor*, 216.
18. Daloz, *Mentor*, 217.
19. Ibid., 89–124.
20. Mezirow, *Transformative Dimensions*, 150–74; see especially 156–59 on Todd Sloan's research.
21. Dale A. Ziemer, "Creating Readiness: Cultivating Fruitful Conversation," Center for Parish Development, *The Center Letter* 30 (October 2000).
22. Paul Varo Martinson, ed., *Islam: An Introduction for Christians* (Minneapolis: Augsburg, 1994).
23. Carolyn C. Brown, *Developing Christian Education in the Smaller Church* (Nashville: Abingdon Press, 1982); Karen B. Tye, *Basics of Christian Education* (St. Louis: Chalice Press, 2000); Donald L. Griggs, *Planning for Teaching Church School: Identify Main Ideas; Determine Objectives; Design Teaching Activities; Select Resources; Organize Lesson Plan* (Valley Forge, Penn.: Judson Press, 1985); *Basic Skills for Church Teachers* (Nashville: Abingdon Press, 1985); and *Teaching Teachers to Teach: A Basic Manual for Church Teachers* (Nashville: Abingdon Press, 1980); Richard E. Rusbuldt, *Basic Teacher Skills: Handbook for Church School Teachers*, rev. ed. (Valley Forge, Penn.: Judson Press, 1997); Rebecca Grothe, ed., *Lifelong Learning: A Guide to Adult Education in the Church* (Minneapolis: Augsburg Fortress, 1997); Richard Robert Osmer, *Teaching for Faith: A Guide for Teachers of Adult Classes* (Louisville, Ky.: Westminster/John Knox Press, 1992); Christine Eaton Blair, *The Art of Teaching the Bible: A Practical Guide for Adults* (Louisville, Ky.: Geneva Press, 2001); Pat Channer, *Help! We Need to Organize the Education Program: A Handbook for Education Committees and Congregations* (Louisville, Ky.: Witherspoon Press, 1998); Charles R. Foster, *The Ministry of the Volunteer Teacher* (Nashville: Abingdon Press, 1986); Sara Covin Juengst, *Equipping the Saints: Teacher Training in the Church*

(Louisville, Ky.: Westminster John Knox Press, 1998); Melissa Armstrong-Hansche and Neil MacQueen, *Workshop Rotation: A New Model for Sunday School* (Louisville, Ky.: Geneva Press, 2000).

Chapter 6: Ministry and Mission

1. Robert K. Martin, "Education and the Liturgical Life of the Church," *Religious Education* 98, no. 1 (Winter 2003): 43–64.
2. Darrell L. Guder, *The Incarnation and the Church's Witness* (Harrisburg, Penn.: Trinity Press International, 1999), 3.
3. Ibid., 3–4.
4. "The Shorter Catechism," in *Constitution of the Presbyterian Church (U.S.A.)*, pt. 1, *Book of Confessions* (Louisville, Ky.: Office of the General Assembly, Presbyterian Church (U.S.A.), 1983), 7.001.
5. Guder, *Incarnation*, 18.
6. Ibid., 27.
7. Ibid., 52.
8. J. Frederick Holper, "Places at the Table: New Directions in Presbyterian Worship," *Reformed Liturgy and Music* 25 (Spring 1991): 91.
9. Dietterich, *Systems Model*, 6–11.
10. Ibid., 7–8.
11. R. Kevin Seasoltz, "Liturgy and Social Consciousness," in *To Do Justice and Right Upon the Earth: Papers from the Virgil Michel Symposium on Liturgy and Social Justice*, ed. Mary E. Stamps (Collegeville, Minn.: Liturgical Press, 1993), 54.
12. Dietterich, *Systems Model*, 9.
13. Ibid.
14. Guder, *Incarnation*, 25.
15. Dietterich, *Systems Model*, 9–11.
16. See Sara Little, *To Set One's Heart*, 76–85; Allen J. Moore, "Liberation and the Future of Christian Education," in Jack L. Seymour and Donald E. Miller, eds., *Contemporary Approaches to Christian Education* (Nashville: Abingdon Press, 1982), 103–22; Georgeann Wilcoxson, *Doing the Word: A Manual for Christian Education: Shared Approaches* (New York: United Church Press, 1977), 21–22.
17. John Bartlett, *Familiar Quotations: A Collection of Passages, Phrases, and Proverbs Traced to Their Source in Ancient and Modern Literature*, ed. Justin Kaplan, 16th ed. (Boston: Little, Brown & Co., 1992), 74.
18. See Robert A. Evans, "Education for Emancipation: Movement Toward Transformation," in Alice Frazer, Robert A. Evans, and William Bean Kennedy, eds., *Pedagogies for the Non-Poor* (Maryknoll, N.Y.: Orbis Books, 1987), 265.
19. Wilcoxson, *Doing the Word*, 8.
20. Dieter T. Hessel, *Social Ministry*, rev. ed. (Louisville, Ky.: Westminster/John Knox Press, 1992), xvii.
21. Daloz et al., *Common Fire*, 67.
22. Elaine Saum, *How Should Christians Be Involved in the Public Arena? A Study Guide for Presbyterian Congregations* (New York: Presbyterian Peacemaking Program, 1986), 2.
23. Jane F. Ives, *Transforming Ventures: A Spiritual Guide for Volunteers in Mission* (Nashville: Upper Room Books, 2000), 19.

24. See William Bean Kennedy, "The Ideological Captivity of the Non-Poor," in Alice Frazer, Robert A. Evans, and William Bean Kennedy, eds., *Pedagogies for the Non-Poor* (Maryknoll, N.Y.: Orbis Books, 1987), 232–56.
25. Jo Ann Van Engen, "The Cost of Short-term Missions," *The Other Side* 36 (January/February 2000), 20–23.
26. Ibid., 22.
27. Ibid.
28. Ibid., 23.
29. Guder, *Incarnation*, 54.
30. Ibid.
31. Ives, *Transforming Ventures*, 23.
32. David F. White, "Forming a Sustainable Faith in a Consumer Society," *Ministry Matters* 2 (May 2002): 3.
33. Danny E. Morris and Charles M. Olsen, *Discerning God's Will Together: A Spiritual Practice for the Church* (Nashville: Upper Room Books, 1997), 16. See also Suzanne G. Farnham et al., *Listening Hearts: Discerning Call in Community*, rev. ed. (Harrisburg, Penn.: Morehouse Publishing, 1991).
34. Morris and Olsen, *Discerning God's Will*, 67.
35. Ibid.
36. Ibid., 66–67.

Chapter 7: Leadership in Worship-Centered Congregational Life

1. Lathrop, *Holy Things*, 180–203.
2. See Robert K. Martin, "Leading Disciples Inward and Outward: A Practical Educational Framework for Developing Ecclesial Leadership," in *1999 Proceedings of the Annual Meeting of the Association of Professors and Researchers in Religious Education: Educating for Religious Particularism and Pluralism*, Toronto, Canada, October 15–17, 1999, comp. C. F. Melchert, 302–6.
3. Ibid., 304.
4. Ibid., 305–6.
5. Scott Cormode, "Theological Education as Leadership Education" (paper presented at the annual meeting of the Association of Doctor of Ministry Educators Association, 1999).
6. Ibid.
7. Ronald A. Heifetz, *Leadership Without Easy Answers* (Cambridge, Mass.: Bellknap Press of Harvard University Press, 1994), 22.
8. Ibid., 113.
9. Some pastoral care literature refers to pastors as a "non-anxious presence." Because this places an unrealistic expectation on pastors, I prefer the term "less anxious presence."
10. See Heifetz, *Leadership*, 103.
11. Ibid., 117–18. Peter Senge uses the terms *dialogue* and *discussion* in ways that are similar to mediation and arbitration. See his *Fifth Discipline*, 242–43.
12. Heifetz, *Leadership*, 106.
13. Ibid., 118–19.
14. Eugene H. Peterson, *The Contemplative Pastor: Returning to the Art of Spiritual Direction* (Grand Rapids: Wm. B. Eerdmans Publishing Co., 1989), 19.

15. Daloz, *Mentor*, 206.
16. Ibid., 207.
17. Elizabeth Box Price, "Cognitive Complexity and the Learning Congregation," in *1999 Proceedings of the Annual Meeting of the Association of Professors and Researchers in Religious Education: Educating for Religious Particularism and Pluralism*, Toronto, Canada, October 15–17, 1999, comp. C. F. Melchert (photocopy of missing text, 295).
18. Cormode, "Theological Education as Leadership Education."
19. See Robert Kegan, *In Over Our Heads: The Mental Demands of Modern Life* (Cambridge, Mass.: Harvard University Press, 1994), 231. For a description of first-, second-, and third-order thinking, see Kegan's chapters 1–4.
20. See Senge, *The Fifth Discipline*, 185.
21. Price, "Cognitive Complexity," 295.
22. Robert K. Martin, "Encountering God in the Image of Christ: Iconic Leadership as an Incarnational Ministry," in *2000 Proceedings of the Annual Meeting of the Association of Professors and Researchers in Religious Education and the Religious Education Association Biennial Conference: Knowing God: Meeting God in the Peoples of God*, Atlanta, Georgia, November 3–5, 2000, comp. C. F. Melchert, 104.
23. Ibid., 93.
24. Ibid., 102.
25. Ibid., 104.
26. Kenda Creasy Dean and Ron Foster, *The Godbearing Life: The Art of Soul Tending for Youth Ministry* (Nashville: Upper Room Books, 1998), 9.

Conclusion

1. One surprising finding of this study was that congregations who exhibited all of the characteristics just mentioned but neglected practices of deep prayer tended to use worship as motivation, to study only as necessary, and to enter into mission as a necessary chore. Even rich liturgical practice, when unaccompanied by attention to practices of deep communal and personal prayer, did not result in robust spiritual formation. Rather, these churches came to see worship as just one more "program" among many.